GLOBAL CREDIT REVIEW

Volume 3

NUS National University of Singapore | RMI Advancing Risk Management for Singapore and Beyond

World Scientific

Published by

World Scientific Publishing Co. Pte. Ltd.
5 Toh Tuck Link, Singapore 596224
USA office: 27 Warren Street, Suite 401-402, Hackensack, NJ 07601
UK office: 57 Shelton Street, Covent Garden, London WC2H 9HE

and

Risk Management Institute
National University of Singapore
21, Heng Mui Keng Terrace, Level 4
Singapore 119613

Library of Congress Control Number: 2013205296

British Library Cataloguing-in-Publication Data
A catalogue record for this book is available from the British Library.

GLOBAL CREDIT REVIEW
Volume 3

ISBN 978-981-4566-13-1

In-house Editor: Lee Xin Ying

Typeset by Stallion Press
Email: enquiries@stallionpress.com

Printed in Singapore

Message from the Editor

The Risk Management Institute (RMI), a university-level research institute at the National University of Singapore, strives to be a world-class center in risk management where scholars, regulators and industry practitioners gather to advance cutting-edge knowledge that has immediate relevance to the financial system. By advancing the knowledge frontier, we aim to raise the practice of financial risk management.

In line with this objective, this third annual volume of the *Global Credit Review* targets financial practitioners, policy makers and academics with an interest in credit markets. The *Global Credit Review* provides an overview of important developments in the global credit markets and the regulatory landscape. It also covers theoretical and empirical research on credit ratings and credit risk, and reports on recent findings and evolutions of the RMI Credit Research Initiative (RMI-CRI).

The strong performance seen in the US, European and Japanese stock markets in Q1 2013 has brought some much needed optimism to the global economic outlook. But with the tightening of the US budget, the ongoing eurozone crisis and emerging signs of a slowdown in China's economic growth, global GDP growth is likely to be dismal. In the eurozone, poor economic data have increased fears that the sovereign debt crisis will spread to larger economies. While the US economy is growing, it has still not broken free of shackles despite three bouts of quantitative easing. Instead, uncertainties have increased in the credit markets. While hopes rest on China to boost global growth, it has seen a slowing in growth with the new administration's campaign of frugality and the ongoing measures to curb the property market.

To keep abreast with new developments in the credit markets, this volume of the *Global Credit Review* provides some critical analysis, reviews the introduction of new regulations and also offers new insights to address the challenges ahead in the new world.

This third volume of the *Global Credit Review* begins with a very topical article '*Systemic Risk in Europe*' by Professors Eric Jondeau and Michael Rockinger. This is followed by the RMI article '*Changes in the Ratings Game — An Update on Various Developments*'. In the third article, '*Reserve Requirements as Window Guidance in China*', Ms. Violaine Cousin provides insights into the effect of reserve requirements on bank asset quality in China. This is followed by an article by Dr. Markus Bingmer and Dr. Laura Auria on '*The Implementation of the Basel II Default Definition by Credit Risk Assessment Systems: An Analysis of Possible Aggregation Procedures*'. In the fifth article '*Can Credit-Scoring Models Effectively Predict Microloans Default? Statistical Evidence from the Tunisian Microfinance Bank*', Dr. Ibtissem Baklouti and Prof. Abdelfettah Bouri present a credit-scoring framework for microfinance institutions. Next is a joint article by IACPM and KPMG — '*Stepping Up to the Liquidity Challenge: The Changing Role of Credit Portfolio Management*'. We conclude this third volume of the GCR with an updated '*NUS-RMI Credit Research Initiative Technical Report*' which offers technical details on the implementation of the current RMI-CRI corporate default prediction model and its performance. For a more elaborate discussion and update on our default predictions produced thus far, please refer to our *Quarterly Credit Report* for more details.

We hope you enjoy reading this third volume and welcome your feedback on the *Global Credit Review* and our Credit Rating Initiative.

Prof. Jin-Chuan Duan
Director, NUS-RMI
Cycle & Carriage Professor of Finance
NUS Business School

Systemic Risk in Europe

Prof. Eric Jondeau
Institute of Banking and Finance
University of Lausanne and
Swiss Finance Institute
eric.jondeau@unil.ch

Prof. Michael Rockinger*
Institute of Banking and Finance
University of Lausanne and
Swiss Finance Institute
michael.rockinger@unil.ch

* Corresponding author.

Keywords: Systemic risk, marginal expected shortfall, multifactor model, volatility, correlation.

INTRODUCTION

Since the start of the financial crisis in 2007, it became clear that financial institutions (even the biggest ones) might default or at least require some help from the government. In the US, more than 414 institutions have defaulted between 2008 and 2011. Among the largest institutions that have been liquidated, rescued or taken over, are Bear Stearns, Merrill Lynch, AIG and Lehman Brothers. In Europe, several institutions such as Northern Rock, Fortis, and Dexia experienced similar problems. In Iceland, default of the three main banks, Glitnir, Landsbanki, and Kaupthing, and the subsequent transfer of the banks' debt to the central bank, even led to the default of the entire country. The global financial system was on the verge of collapse. Since then, there have been calls for more restrictive regulations regarding too-big-to-fail financial institutions. The G20 countries and supra-national institutions (like the Bank for International Settlements) have created an *ad hoc* commission to propose new regulations such as what the Basel Committee on Banking Supervision (2011, 2012) has suggested.

I. HOW TO MEASURE SYSTEMIC RISK?

Implementing a more restrictive regulation for too-big-to-fail institutions raises the question of how to identify these institutions. What is a systemically risky bank? Is a big bank necessarily systemically risky? What about other financial institutions like insurance companies? To answer these questions, it is necessary to give a precise definition of a systemically risky institution, and therefore of systemic risk itself. As Daniel K. Tarullo, Governor from the Federal Reserve Board of Governors, mentioned in a speech on June 8, 2009, a definition of a systemically risky institution is that its failure to meet its obligations to creditors and customers would have significant adverse consequences for the financial system and the broader economy.

Starting with this relatively general definition, identifying systemically risky institutions requires more precise criteria. In 2010, the Volatility Institute of New York University, headed by Nobel Laureate Robert Engle, has published a set of papers describing both an operational definition and a sound statistical methodology allowing the measurement of the capital requirement of financial institutions in the case of a new financial crisis. According to Acharya *et al.* (2010), systemic risk can be defined as the propensity of a financial institution to be under-capitalized when the financial system as a whole is under-capitalized. This definition can be put into operation from an econometric point of view. One advantage of this research is that it is based on econometric modeling, and thus purely data based. The advantage of such an approach is that it does not rely on qualitative indicators provided by humans that could be either error prone or subject to political pressure. A drawback of this type of approach is that it relies on a model which itself may be incomplete.

The intuition behind those models is that they consider the balance sheet of banks and look at the conditional probability that a bank's capital does not meet the prudential requirements by becoming too small with respect to the bank's assets. This is exactly the notion that a financial institution is under-capitalized when the entire financial system is. Because those models consider the balance sheet explicitly, it implies that parameters such as bank size and leverage come into play. Furthermore, the dynamic aspect gets introduced naturally because one considers the evolution of a firm's asset over time conditional on the evolution of the entire market. More specifically, both levels of certain well-known and easily accessible balance sheet data on the one hand, and the exposure towards aggregate risk on the other hand — measured by stock returns of a market — come into play. Had one considered only the exposure towards market risk, one would have ended up with a measure in the spirit of value at risk. Similarly, only considering balance-sheet ratios would not have given the dynamic nature.

From a technical point of view, the model requires the computation of time-varying parameters and the determination of large extreme events. For the modeling of time-varying parameters, we build on the dynamic conditional correlation model. On the other hand, to correctly describe extreme events, we use the extreme-value theory and copulas to describe the joint behavior of the tails of distributions.

The synthesis of the basic model of Acharya *et al.* (2010) and Brownlees and Engle (2010) is a risk measure called SRISK which stands for systemic risk. SRISK determines the amount of money that would be required for a given institution so that this institution would again satisfy prudential requirements. One advantage of SRISK is that this measure can be added to obtain the risk of various institutions, a very elementary operation. By relating such an aggregate measure to gross domestic product, one gets an idea of how risky a certain financial industry is with respect to an entire country. The measure is therefore not only relatively easy to compute but also easy to interpret.

II. MODELLING SYSTEMIC RISK

In some recent research, Engle and Rockinger (2012) extend those initial models to allow for more risk factors in a European context. The earlier research emerged in a US context for which, given its size and importance, a US-specific factor is sufficient. For European banks, on the other hand, one may expect that they would be not only impacted by the US shocks, but also by European ones or even country-specific shocks. Conversely, it would seem obvious that European country shocks would not have similar impacts on the US economy.

Our model considers a triangular structure where we impose a causal direction on how shocks transmit from one region to another. For instance, we allow for worldwide shocks, which would impact European markets. European shocks in turn would affect specific countries. European shocks come from the fear, sometimes psychological, rather than being based on economic fundamentals that a certain group of countries might jointly face financial difficulties. Furthermore, our model also innovates by allowing for country-specific shocks and firm-specific shocks. Because of this much richer structure of shocks, we are able to describe phenomena that could not be captured by a model with just one worldwide factor. For instance, if one considers the earlier phase of the recent crisis, between 2007 and 2008, European firms were affected by the subprime crisis in the US. Then, from 2008 on, while the subprime crisis started to be effectively treated by US authorities, Europe entered a sovereign debt crisis. If one considers the co-variation between markets, one notices that the European market had less influence on the US market than during the earlier phase when the US market dictated the movements of the European market. Therefore, from a risk management perspective, the explicit modeling of a European risk factor appears to make a lot of sense. This asymmetry in which markets influence

Contents

each other brings about other questions, possibly of a political or economic nature, on how to dampen the reciprocal influences.

Without giving all the methodological details, it is useful to describe the three main characteristics of a financial institution for measuring its systemic risk:

- Its market capitalization, which reflects the size of the firm;
- Its financial leverage (the ratio of the asset value over the equity value), which measures the risk exposure of the institution;
- Lastly, the sensitivity of the stock return of the firm with respect to the evolution of the market as a whole, in case of a severe financial crisis.

In fact, high leverage in itself is not necessarily a problem, because inherently, one of the roles banks have is to take risks by lending to consumers and companies. Leverage becomes a problem if, like Greece, Spain or even the US recently, there is too much lending at an aggregate level. In this case, a bank may be under-capitalized at the worst moment, i.e., when the financial system as a whole is under-capitalized. If a bank then faces a capital shortage, it may be unable to meet its obligations to creditors and customers.

Systemic risk increases when the market cap or the financial leverage of a financial institution increases, or when the share value is more sensitive to the evolution of financial markets in case of a financial crisis.

The first two characteristics — that is, market capitalization and financial leverage — are relatively easy to measure since data is readily available. The third one, however, is not directly observable, in particular because it refers to a hypothetical financial crisis. The approach taken by our research is as follows: using the Monte-Carlo simulation of our complete model, we measure the loss of market cap in case of a deep financial crisis (a 40% decline in six months). This sensitivity is called "long-run marginal expected shortfall" (LRMES). Lastly, we measure SRISK as the capital shortage the bank would suffer to meet its obligations. An institution is said to be in capital shortage if the ratio of equity to assets falls below 8%. The 8% ratio is reminiscent of the regulatory ratio; however, the latter concerns the ratio of capital to risk-weighted assets. Even though the reason for choosing 8% is some what arbitrary, changing it does not affect the ranking of our results in a significant manner. The use of risk-weighted capital brings some worries because of the possibility that financial institutions can manipulate this ratio.

III. THE SITUATION IN EUROPE

The empirical analysis reported here results from collaboration between the Institute of Banking and Finance at the University of Lausanne, and the Volatility Institute at New York University. Our analysis covers the 196 European financial institutions with the largest market caps (at least 1 billion euro as of the end of December 2011). For our research, we worked on data starting before 1990, when available.[1]

Our measures of systemic risk are available online at http://www.crml.ch where they are updated on a weekly basis. On that website, one may also find aggregate measures at the country level. The sample includes 72 banks, 36 insurance companies, 53 financial services and 35 real estate companies. Countries with a large number of firms are the UK (45 institutions), France (22), and Switzerland (21). A first interesting result is that, overall, the aggregate systemic risk measure was about 1,284 billion euro as of the end of September 2012 and is now down to 1,163 billion euro by the end of February 2013. This number indicates the lack of capital the European financial institutions would suffer if there was a new market decline of 40% in six months. The raise of this ratio during the 2007 financial crisis is essentially due to the increase in the leverage ratio and partially due to an increase in the way firms became more dependent to global market movements.

Only banks and insurance companies show significant contributions to systemic risk. Financial services and real estate companies do not. This risk comes not only from a higher financial leverage, but also from a greater sensitivity to the evolution of financial markets. As of the end of August 2012, banks represent about 81% of total systemic risk, insurance companies 17%, and the other financial institutions have a negligible weightage. Although banks clearly rank first, insurance companies display some systemic risk. For example,

Table 1. Aggregate systemic risk measures for various countries.

	SRISK (billion €)	LRMES (%)	Leverage (ratio)	Market Cap (billion €)
France	303.94	42.34	35.11	203.34
United Kingdom	256.90	40.54	18.33	511.25
Germany	154.08	35.38	27.97	160.97
Italy	111.72	41.97	32.12	93.65
Switzerland	74.35	29.90	15.08	214.98
Spain	72.32	48.06	18.88	133.85
Netherlands	70.16	51.09	33.44	46.27
Belgium	35.77	32.01	23.39	35.46
Greece	26.89	30.38	154.72	3.37
Sweden	21.06	35.39	10.92	146.56
Denmark	17.06	30.11	21.61	25.88
Austria	11.06	30.67	16.42	30.54
Norway	7.02	31.06	16.47	25.03
Ireland	6.43	38.87	7.33	51.46
Portugal	6.39	26.32	29.77	7.21
Cyprus	4.16	24.74	37.88	2.84
Luxembourg	3.53	20.90	23.17	4.09

Note: Data as of 22 March 2013. LRMES stands for long-run marginal expected shortfall. This measures by how much the banking sector's returns drop in case of a –40% return of a worldwide index over a six-month period.

ING and AXA are ranked in the top 15 most systemically risky institutions.

It is also interesting to compare the systemic risk across countries (see Table 1). It should be noted that Greece is perceived as highly systemically risky in Europe. However, the main source of risk is the state and not the financial system. Greek banks are relatively small and therefore do not appear as systemically risky at the European level. The most risky countries are the UK, France, and Germany. The first two countries account for 50% of the total risk (27% for the UK, 23% for France), for a shortfall of about 1,000 billion euro of capital in the case of a new financial crisis. The other countries at the top of the rankings are Germany (14% of the total), Italy (8.5%), and Switzerland (7%). This ranking by country clearly reflects the weight of the largest banks in the European financial landscape, even if the sources of risk may be different from one country to the other. For instance, French, German and Italian banks have a much higher average financial leverage than institutions from the other countries. At the same time, British and French banks are more fragile because of their greater sensitivity to the evolution of financial markets.

If one considers Cyprus, a country very much in the headlines recently, one finds that the SRISK measure amounts to about 4 billion euro. This compares with a GDP of about 19 billion euro in 2011. This means that the Cypriot government might have to come up with at least 20% of GDP to get the capitalization back to appropriate levels if a financial crisis hits. It comes as no surprise that currently the country is struggling to get back on the right path. It should also be noticed that in the case of Cyprus, it does not necessarily take an exogenous shock for a country to face systemic risk. Our measure gives some guidance on what can happen if things go bad.

IV. THE SITUATION OF EUROPEAN INSTITUTIONS

The ranking of financial institutions clearly identifies highly systemically risky banks (Table 2): Deutsche Bank (93.9 billion euro), Crédit Agricole (92.4 billion euro), ahead of BNP Paribas, Barclays, Royal Bank of Scotland (RBS) and Société Générale (80, 78, 66, and 57 billion respectively). It should be noted that these six banks do not have the largest market caps in Europe, as they are well below HSBC or Banco Santander. On the other hand, they all have high financial leverage and great sensitivity to the financial markets. For instance, Crédit Agricole has a leverage of over 100, meaning that the assets of the bank are 100 times larger than its equity.

Going down the next five institutions on the list we have the first bank-insurance company, ING, which is also the most systemically risky company in the Netherlands. We also find UBS, the largest Swiss bank. UniCredit is the eighth largest systemically risky bank in Europe as of March 2013.

A last note on the implication of these systemic risk measures for financial institutions: the capital shortage in the case of a new financial crisis can be reduced in different ways. A firm can reduce its size (for instance, by selling too risky units), reduce its financial leverage (by investing less per unit of equity), reduce its risk

Table 2. Ranking of the most systemically risky firms.

	Company	Country	SRISK	LRMES	Leverage	Market Cap
1	Deutsche Bank	Germany	93.9	45.9	66.9	30.2
2	Crédit Agricole	France	92.4	48.2	112.5	16.4
3	BNP Paribas	France	79.6	55.1	37.1	51.1
4	Barclays	United Kingdom	78.1	51.9	41.6	44.0
5	Royal Bank of Scotland	United Kingdom	65.8	46.0	41.4	38.4
6	Société Générale	France	57.4	53.5	57.9	21.4
7	ING Groep	Netherlands	54.6	65.1	51.3	22.4
8	UniCredit	Italy	38.6	51.6	43.2	20.7
9	Banco Santander SA	Spain	38.4	50.0	21.4	58.9
10	Lloyds Banking	United Kingdom	36.0	35.5	28.4	40.2
11	Commerzbank AG	Germany	30.2	42.1	90.6	5.9
12	UBS	Switzerland	29.2	38.4	23.2	45.9
13	AXA	France	25.9	57.0	22.5	33.3
14	Credit Suisse Group	Switzerland	25.7	42.2	27.8	27.7
15	Intesa Sanpaolo	Italy	24.2	43.6	32.8	19.9
16	Natixis	France	22.6	37.7	53.9	9.8
17	Dexia	Belgium	22.6	59.0	4235.3	0.1
18	HSBC Holdings	United Kingdom	17.2	37.9	13.7	151.5
19	Legal & General Group	United Kingdom	16.8	39.9	37.4	11.7
20	Aviva	United Kingdom	16.6	57.6	36.7	10.7
21	Banco Bilbao	Spain	16.4	55.2	16.2	39.7
22	Danske Bank	Denmark	16.0	33.9	32.4	14.5
23	Aegon	Netherlands	14.9	56.5	37.5	9.4
24	CNP Assurances	France	14.2	32.5	47.7	7.3
25	Nordea Bank AB	Sweden	13.7	32.9	19.5	35.6

Note: Data as of 22 March 2013.

(by investing in less risky assets), or by reducing its exposure to market risk (by investing in assets that are less correlated to financial markets).

NOTE

1 The results presented in this study are drawn from "Systemic Risk in Europe", by Robert Engle (Volatility Institute, New York University), Eric Jondeau, and Michael Rockinger (both from the Institute of Banking and Finance, University of Lausanne). See also the following website for the most recent figures: http://www.crml.ch. Both authors wish to thank Elisabeth Van Laere and Oliver Chen for their relevant comments and their help with the editing of the text.

REFERENCES

Acharya, V. V., L. H. Pedersen, T. Philippon and M. P. Richardson (2010), Measuring Systemic Risk, accessed May 2010, from SSRN: http://ssrn.com/abstract=1573171.

Basel Committee on Banking Supervision (2011), Global Systemically Important Banks: Assessment Methodology and the Additional Loss Absorbency Requirement, accessed November 2011, from: http://www.bis.org/publ/bcbs207.htm.

Basel Committee on Banking Supervision (2012), A Framework for Dealing with Domestic Systemically Important Banks, accessed October 2012, from: http://www.bis.org/publ/bcbs224.htm.

Brownlees, C. T. and R. F. Engle (2012), Volatility, Correlation and Tails for Systemic Risk Measurement, accessed October 2012, from SSRN: http://ssrn.com/abstract=1611229.

Engle, R. F., E. Jondeau and M. Rockinger (2012), Dynamic Conditional Beta and Systemic Risk in Europe, accessed December 2012, from SSRN: http://papers.ssrn.com/abstract=2192536.

Changes in the Ratings Game — An Update on Various Developments

RMI staff article

For questions or comments on this article, please contact Dexter Tan at **rmidtkb@nus.edu.sg**

Keywords: Regulations, credit rating alternatives, recommendations, lawsuits, sovereign ratings.

INTRODUCTION

Financial legislations all over the world are trying to clamp down on unreliable credit ratings that have failed investors. Ever since the 2008 financial crisis, regulators worldwide have been trying to reduce the banking system's dependence on biased credit ratings. For years, US-based credit rating agencies (CRAs) have claimed that the ratings they assigned to debt securities are independent opinions and therefore entitled to First Amendment protection as free speech. CRAs had managed to fend off any crackdown from Washington. The US Court fillings, congressional testimonies and SEC documents have illustrated how the CRAs dodged government regulations and court actions. Disputed cases of CRAs' biased ratings were seen in the high profile bankruptcy of energy company, Enron. The company saw its bonds assigned with investment grade ratings by Standard & Poor's (S&P) and Moody's just days before it went bankrupt in 2001. But, a slew of recent high profile lawsuits in the US disproves the independence of CRAs in their works with Wall Street firms on debt deals. The US Senate Permanent Sub-committee on Investigations highlighted a USD 1 billion securities offering backed by subprime loans that Goldman Sachs underwrote in 2007 as an example of questionable industry practices, where the collateralized debt obligations (CDOs) fetched top ratings from S&P's and Moody's. The risky mortgage-related securities were best remembered for leading to the subprime crisis in the US.

Asia too, saw its fair share of credit rating issues with investors succumbed to losses in the minibond saga in the aftermath of Lehman Brothers' insolvency. Asian financial hubs like Hong Kong saw its financial institutions sell some USD 1.8 billion of Lehman arranged minibonds. While in Singapore, the Monetary Authority of Singapore disclosed that investors had bought USD 346 million worth of minibonds from financial institutions, of which over 70% was sold to 8,000 retail investors. Investors were misled when bank dealers made reference to Lehman Brothers as an investment grade company in their marketing materials to clients. The company was listed as the swap guarantor in the minibonds issue, and was then rated A1 by Moody's, A+ by Fitch and by S&P's.[1]

I. A CONSTRUCTIVE RESPONSE TO THE CRA CRITIQUES

Losses incurred by investors have prompted market practitioners to question the CRAs' rating methodologies. In a constructive response to these critiques, several credit rating alternatives have been launched.

Especially in the area of sovereign ratings, a lot of discussion is ongoing as it is clear that the ratings assigned by the Big Three often differ significantly with those of alternative rating professionals and CRAs. Furthermore, market participants also noticed the divergence between sovereign credit default swaps and the ratings assigned to sovereign bonds in Southeast Asia.[2] CDS on bonds issued by Southeast Asian nations and Italian debt averaged 98 bps and 270 bps, respectively. But S&P gave bonds issued by the Indonesian government junk status while Italian bonds have a credit rating three notches higher. The credit ratings are also at odds with the ratio of government debt to GDP which are significantly lower for Indonesia (25%) compared to Italy with a ratio of 126%. Similarly, Moody's assigned an investment grade rating of Baa2 to Italian sovereign bonds but a lower Baa3 rating to bonds issued by Indonesia.

Critics like BlackRock[3], an asset management firm, have launched their own sovereign risk assessment as they noticed that CRAs were too slow in reacting to sovereign bond risks. For example, S&P downgraded Italy's sovereign rating in January 2012 to BBB+, sharing the same rating as Thailand and Kazakhstan. However, for the same period, the IMF's debt to GDP ratios for those countries differs significantly, ranging from 12% for Kazakhstan to 44% for Thailand and 126% for Italy. The unreliability of the credit ratings has prompted BlackRock to set up their own system of assessing the countries' credit profiles.

The BlackRock Sovereign Risk Index was created to help quantify the risk premium in sovereign debt. This is to help investors who are concerned with credit events in sovereign bonds. The index tracks and takes into account important factors and ranks sovereign debt issuers according to their relative likelihood of default. The index is driven by four conceptual categories — fiscal space, external finance positions, financial sector health and willingness to pay. The index places Spain (ranked 41st), Ireland (43rd) and Italy (44th) in the same credit group as Argentina (42nd) and Venezuela (46th). Kazakhstan is however not rated by BlackRock, and Thailand is placed 26th. After S&P's downgrade of Italy in January 2012, the troubled economies of Ireland and Italy, which shared the same BBB+ rating, were ranked some 6 notches above Venezuela, contrasting with BlackRock's classification which put the three countries in the same credit grouping.

One of the initiatives that emerged in the debate on sovereign rating quality is the International Nonprofit Credit Rating Agency (INCRA) that was set up by the Bertelsmann Foundation in April 2012. INCRA is an international nonprofit project by the Bertelsmann Foundation with the objective to break the stranglehold of the existing, commercial CRAs over sovereign ratings. INCRA was seeking USD 400 million. The agency was structured so that management and rating decisions are independent from its financiers. This will reduce concerns about perceived conflicts of interest. In addition, the Foundation claims that INCRA's governance structure and operating procedures provide the needed transparency and legitimacy. More specifically, INCRA has a "Stakeholder Council" who ensures independence of ratings and a "credit policy committee" which functions as a quality control body ensuring that ratings are incorporated according to competent and comprehensive methods. INCRA wants to challenge the current system on two fronts: (1) the way the CRAs conduct sovereign ratings in a for-profit framework and (2) the manner in which CRAs develop methodology and set of indicators on sovereign ratings.[4]

The agency published ratings on six countries so far, including the most recent AA+ rating on the US that was issued on April 14.[5] Although S&P already stripped the US of its gold plated triple A certification 2 years ago in 2011, Moody's and Fitch still give the country its highest rating. INCRA motivates the fact that the US is not assigned an AAA rating due to the political gridlock and increasing inequality in the country. The agency warned that the low voter participation and the partisan division of Congress have made the country less adaptable and socially cohesive than what is seen in a top-rated economy such as Germany. INCRA uses "forward looking indicators" such as its past track record of managing crises, the cabinet's reform capacity, as well as economic and fiscal metrics in its credit assessments. The agency also differs with S&P in its ratings of Brazil, Italy and Japan, where INCRA rated both Brazil and Italy more favorable as compared to S&P and a complete reversal of opinion for Japan.

Box 1 shows a comparison of a list of economies rated by BlackRock, S&P and INCRA.

In 2009, well before INCRA was set up, the Credit Research Intiative undertaken by the Risk Management Institute (RMI) at the National University of Singapore had been launched. As pioneers in providing a non-profit alternative to existing CRAs, the Institute started releasing daily updated probabilities of default

Box 1 — S&P sovereign ratings vs BlackRock sovereign risk index vs INCRA rating.

Economy	BlackRock Sovereign Risk Index Rank (April 2013)	S&P Rating on Ten Year Long-Term Foreign Currency Issue (as of April 2013)	INCRA Rating[6] (April 2013)
Norway	1	AAA	—
Singapore	2	AAA	—
—	—	—	—
Germany	9	AAA	AAA
—	—	—	—
USA	15	AA+	AA+
—	—	—	—
Philippines	24	BB+	—
Poland	25	A–	—
Thailand	26	BBB+	—
—	—	—	—
Brazil	28	BBB	A+
France	29	AA+	AA+
—	—	—	—
Japan	33	AA–	A–
—	—	—	—
Indonesia	36	BB+	—
—	—	—	—
Spain	41	BBB–	—
Argentina	42	—	—
Ireland	43	BBB+	—
Italy	44	BBB+	AA–
Portugal	45	BB	—
Venezuela	46	B+	—
—	—	—	—
Greece	48	B–	—

(PDs) for 17,000 exchange listed companies in the Asia-Pacific region from July 2010. That coverage has since been expanded to 60,400 listed firms across 106 economies in December 2012. Other notable milestones include the increased accessibility of RMI's PD information through common distribution channels. More specifically, in March 2013, Bloomberg and Cbonds — a leading information source on fixed income markets in Russia and emerging markets — started using RMI's Corporate Vulnerability indices (CVI) in their platforms. Bloomberg users are now able to access and download the CVI benchmarks that track the aggregate PDs of companies operating in various countries. More recently in April 2013, the PD forecast model was further enhanced to include default forecast horizons of up to five years.

Further initiatives with goals of bringing more transparency to the rating process are Wikirating and Public Sector Credit Solutions (PSCS), which published an open-source sovereign and municipal rating tool in May 2012. The firms, which employ crowd-sourcing techniques to improve credit ratings, announced on November 26, 2012[7] their plan to work together and share content with each other. PSCS collaborated with Ottawa's Macdonald-Laurier Institute to publish default probabilities for ten Canadian provinces on October 18, 2012. The study concludes that the threshold for a provincial default is an interest to revenue ratio of 25%. Recently on December 5, 2012, the California State Treasurer's Office has commissioned PSCS to develop a default probability model for the city's bonds. The new model was expected to provide the State with an approach to identify troubled cities and update the public and investors about its credit profile.

Funding is vital to the success and survival of non-profit initiatives, as is evident by the failure of the strategy consultancy, Roland Berger's attempt to create a European rating agency (ERA) to challenge the top three major CRAs. ERA's CEO, Markus Krall, said[9] that there were not enough investors to meet the EUR 300 million target for the startup. The firm had envisaged to create an independent non-profit European CRA, whose business model will not have any conflict of interest between credit ratings and clients. Roland Berger, as a partner, had planned to launch the ERA project based on a foundation set up by independent investors. The ERA project would be based on a subscriber-paid model, where investors interested in access to reliable and objective results pay for credit ratings.

1.1. Litigation

Since the onset of the Global Financial Crisis, the number of lawsuits filed against CRAs in the US has increased dramatically. For example, 105 lawsuits had been filed against S&P during the 1-year period after Lehman Brothers filed for bankruptcy on 15 September 2008 versus 68 lawsuits during the previous year. In 2008 alone, S&P was faced with 76 lawsuits and in 2009, S&P was slapped with 120 cases. In contrast, Moody's was hit with 8 cases in 2009 and none in 2008. Moody's indemnification[10] clause in its contracts with clients protects the agency from lawsuits. The clause essentially shifts the liability to issuers, which Moody's said is a common business service agreement. Fitch has also included the indemnification language in its general business agreements. However, more lawsuits against CRAs are expected to gain traction after the European Commission made it easier in January 2013 for regulators to file lawsuits against CRAs for misleading ratings.

II. LANDMARK CASE

On November 5, 2012, S&P, the ratings business unit of McGraw Hill, lost its defense over the rating of risky structured products (constant proportion debt obligation notes, or CPDOs) in Australian courts.[11] The landmark verdict found a rating agency guilty of negligent conduct in assigning a rating. The proceedings were initiated by 12 local councils in New South Wales who lost more than 90% of their AUD 17 million (USD 17.5 million) initial investment capital in securities created by the investment banking arm of ABN AMRO. S&P's Australian unit had assigned a rating of "AAA" to the securities. The prosecution said that the CRA deliberately misled investors when it assigned the highest quality ratings to obligation

notes which lost all its value during the years leading to the financial crisis. The verdict resulted in a second-class action lawsuit against S&P from other investors in April 2013.[12]

Two days after the November Australian court ruling, another lawsuit against S&P was successful. A state court judge in Chicago ruled[13] that Attorney General Lisa Madigan could proceed with her claim that S&P had misled the public when it declared that the ratings on complex structured finance products were objective and independent. S&P sought to dismiss the case on several grounds, with the most convincing defense that their statements were opinions protected under the First Amendment. Two earlier cases set the precedence for proceeding with the lawsuit: (1) in March 2012, a Connecticut state judge refused to dismiss the state Attorney General's case against Moody's; and (2) in 2009[14], a group of investors pressed charges against Moody's in Manhattan, claiming that the agency inaccurately represented the impartiality and fairness of their ratings.

In the most prolific lawsuit involving a CRA as of April 2013, the US Department of Justice (DoJ) has filed a civil suit against S&P (on February 5, 2013) seeking USD 5 billion for the agency's alleged role in misleading investors during the run-up to the financial crisis. The DoJ accused S&P of misrepresenting ratings on mortgage related securities including collateralized debt obligations as independent when the ratings were inflated in order to generate more revenues and increase market share. Court documents also showed that the "agency's desire to maintain and enhance relationship with issuers improperly influenced S&P to downplay and disregard the true extent of the credit risks". If S&P is found guilty and forced to pay such a penalty, it may open the door to further civil action against CRAs by investors who bought presumably safe AAA financial products before the crisis. However, in response to the allegations, S&P's lawyer[15] said that the company's ratings were "identical" to other CRAs.

Further evidence from court documents together with congressional records and interviews of former S&P employees provide a trail of events of how S&P misled regulators and accommodated issuers at the expense of investors. Records at the US Senate committee hearings provided evidence that senior management at the large CRAs were more concerned about the profit making opportunities and the company's market shares rather than the performance of the collaterals when issuing credit ratings on the securities. S&P's credit analysts, for instance, were instructed by one of their managing directors in March 2007[16] to "be cooperative" with issuers as they needed the highest investment grades on repackaged bonds in order to sell them to pension funds and other institutional investors.

S&P issued a formal response to the DoJ complaint in April 2013[17], stating that the government's argument does not hold up, because S&P's independence statement is altogether "too general and vague to constitute the basis for a fraud claim". The ratings firm also cited another recent federal court ruling, upheld by an appeals court that described similar statements as "puffery" on which a fraud case could not be based. The company also said the government cannot prove that the rating agency meant to defraud investors who bought the flawed securities.

III. CRA REGULATIONS

Regulators worldwide are calling for a reduction in the reliance on credit ratings. Members of the G-20 made a similar call in October 2011[18] but progress so far had been slow.[19] The Financial Stability Board has instructed global central bank chiefs to deliver proposals on how to reduce the use of credit ratings and to implement them by January 2016. Individual countries would have to seek ratings of their own by the end of 2015.[20]

3.1. United States

In the US for example, regulators have instructed banks to reduce their reliance on credit ratings. But observers[21] point out that the provision which took effect at the start of this year would be too costly for many US regional banks. According to the Office of the Comptroller of the Currency (OCC) in June 2012, banks should not rely exclusively on external credit ratings. However, the lenders may continue to use such ratings to determine whether a security is investment grade. The OCC also instructed banks to seek credit rating alternatives to judge the quality of their investment securities. They could either engage an expert for the job or perform the task in-house. Critics say that this would increase the compliance costs and decrease investment incomes for small banks. Additionally, banks may be compelled into shifting more of their investments into the safest securities such as the US Treasuries, which do not require much assessment. If this happens, the rule could make it more difficult for municipals and corporate institutions to sell debt to banks. Hardly surprising, bankers are concerned that the rule would divert resources away from core activities like lending. Furthermore, the OCC requirement for banks may conflict with the revised Basel III Liquidity Coverage Ratio standards as the latter relies on credit ratings in a number of instances, including in defining Level 2A and Level 2B Assets and in requiring a bank to calculate the amount of collateral that it would need to post as a result of a three-notch downgrade of the bank's credit rating.

Besides regulating conventional credit ratings, the US is also looking to change the way structured finance products are being rated. On December 18, 2012, the SEC released a report to the Congress on assigned credit ratings, as required by Section 939F of the Dodd-Frank Act. The report assessed the feasibility of establishing a system in which a public or private utility or a self-regulatory organization assigns CRAs to determine credit ratings for structured finance products. Section 939F requires the SEC to implement such a system unless the SEC "determines an alternative system would better serve the public interest and the protection of investors". Among other issues, the report analyzed the potential benefits and concerns of three possible courses of action:

(i) implementation of the Section 15E(W) System (see Box 2),
(ii) implementation of enhancements to the Rule 17g-5 Program (see Box 3), and
(iii) implementation of one or more of several alternative compensation models for CRAs (Box 4).

Box 2 — Potential benefits and concerns of the Section 15E(W) System.

In a December 2012 report to Congress, the SEC presented a study focused on the Section 15E(W) System and listed alternatives to the system, including an existing rule (Rule 17g-5) under the Exchange Act that is designed to reduce the issuer-pay conflict of interest with respect to structured finance products.

In the Section 15E(W) System, an issuer seeking credit ratings for a structured finance product would not be allowed to seek a rating from a CRA but would have to submit a request to the CRA Board. The CRA Board, consisting of a public or private utility or a self-regulatory organization chosen by the SEC, would select a CRA to provide an initial rating to the issuer. The selected CRA may refuse to deliver a credit rating provided it submits an explanation for the refusal. The CRA Board would then select a different CRA to determine an initial credit rating. The CRA Board would evaluate the performance of its members by conducting annual examinations of the CRAs, assessing their methodologies, as well as monitoring the accuracy of their ratings relative to other CRAs.

The advantages and disadvantages of the Section 15E(W) System have been brought up. One benefit is that it helps to solve the issuer-pay conflict of interest, which arises when the CRA is influenced by the issuer to give a favorable rating as compared to the quality of the issue. Issuers do not approach CRAs directly but have to rely on a board of independent members to choose the CRA to rate their debt issue. A second benefit is that it improves CRAs' credibility when accurate ratings are published. The CRA Board is able to evaluate the post-rating performance of structured products and reward the consistently strong performers with more deals. Poor performers would lose their reputation and lose business deals over time. CRAs would therefore be incentivized to compete based on the accuracy of their credit ratings. A third benefit is that smaller CRAs would be given the opportunity to increase their market share and produce quality credit ratings. More emphasis would be placed on the quality of credit ratings of structured products as the CRA Board would represent the investor community.

SEC staff also listed the drawbacks of the system. For example, issuers could still engage in "rating shopping" by seeking a favorable secondary credit rating to

Box 2 (*Continued*)

supplement the rating given by the assigned CRA. Furthermore, CRAs may choose not to participate in the Section 15E(W) System and continue to seek out business deals on their own. The lack of participation from CRAs in the system could undermine the original purpose of the Section 15E(W) System. Less competent CRAs might join the program and delay the issuance of securitized products which would negatively affect the market. The third potential concern is that the cost of setting up the system could be too high and it is not clear how fees for credit ratings can be imposed on some CRAs. Another concern is that it might be too laborious to certify and select the CRAs for rating assignments on a regular basis. The CRA Board runs the risk of assigning a complex rating task to an unqualified CRA, which could compromise the rating of the underlying product. Additionally, associating rating assignments to the past performance of a CRA's credit ratings could result in many conservative initial ratings. In other words, the system encourages CRAs to initiate conservative credit ratings as they would not want to downgrade their initial ratings later so as not to hurt their performance record.

Box 3 — SEC highlights to Congress the benefits and costs of the Rule 17g-5 Program.

The Rule 17g-5 Program requires CRAs that are hired to rate structured finance products to maintain a password-protected website containing a list of each structured finance product, for which it is in the progress of determining an initial credit rating. The hired CRA must provide free and unlimited access to the website with credit ratings assigned to any other CRAs. The hired CRA must also obtain written representation from the issuer of the structured finance product that the CRA can rely on. In addition, the issuer must maintain a password-protected website that other CRAs can access, and provide on this website all information given to the hired CRA for the purpose of determining the initial credit rating.

The advantages of the Rule 17g-5 Program were also mentioned in the same December 2012 report. First, the Rule 17g-5 Program mitigates the conflicts of interest associated with the issuer-pay compensation model. The program mechanism for non-hired CRAs to obtain information from the issuer at the same time as the hired CRA allows non-hired CRAs to monitor and determine an unsolicited credit rating. Thus, the design of the program makes it difficult for issuers of structured finance products to exert influence over the CRAs they hired because any inappropriate rating would be exposed to the market. Thus, the program is intended to mitigate the issuer-pay conflict by encouraging hired CRAs to provide more accurate, unbiased credit ratings because of the possibility that a biased rating could be exposed by a non-hired CRA.

Another benefit of the Rule 17g-5 Program is that it promotes competition amongst CRAs and allows smaller CRAs to compete for market share by developing a good track record through the publication of their ratings. Issuers and investors may choose to hire CRAs with a proven track record after viewing the qualities of their credit assessments. This would lead to a more competitive structured product credit rating industry.

The Rule 17g-5 Program is easy to implement as CRAs and issuers can easily comply with the requirements of the Program as they already have the necessary systems and infrastructures in place.

The biggest concern about the Rule 17g-5 Program is that most CRAs have not been using the information available through this channel to produce unsolicited credit ratings. This was also reported by Fitch[22] when it noted that with the onset of SEC Rule 17g-5 in June 2010, there have been no unsolicited ratings by any of the major CRAs as of October 2011. There were however nine unsolicited commentaries on structured finance transactions between June 2010 and October 2011. Commentaries comply with the regulator's intentions and provide a convenient avenue of communication for CRAs. The timing, information constraints and economics of publishing structured finance ratings are less favorable compared to publishing commentaries. Moving forward, Fitch expects to see more unsolicited commentaries and these will form one of the key channels by which CRAs compete.

Another problem smaller CRAs had about the Rule 17g-5 Program was that the credit ratings they issued would be too costly to produce for free. The agencies argued that it if they issue the ratings for free, there would be little incentive to hire them. Also, investors may not be willing to pay for credit ratings when they are able to receive them for free from the CRA they hired.

Box 3 (*Continued*)

Another disadvantage to the Program cited by CRAs was the concern that issuers may classify all the information on their websites as restricted, which would limit further efforts to produce credit ratings from non-appointed CRAs. As a result, the Rule 17g-5 Program may not always contain the information needed to produce a credible credit rating by non-appointed CRAs without the restricted information from the issuers.

Regulators outside the US also informed the SEC that many foreign firms were not prepared to comply with Rule 17g-5 and were afraid that the local securitization market would be affected. The SEC further extended the deadline till December 2013 from December 2012 for non-users to comply with Rule 17g-5.

Box 4 — Alternative compensation model for the US CRAs.

1. *Issuer-and-investor-pay model*: Payment for ratings comes from fees collected from investors and issuers of new debts. The fees would be collected in a dedicated fund — the US Ratings Fund, which is modeled after the Municipal Securities Rulemaking Board. The fees paid to CRAs, regulated by a board of issuers, investors, rating agencies, intermediaries and directors, would correlate with the CRA's deal volume as well as post-ratings performance.
2. *Alternative user-pay model*: Users of credit ratings would pay CRAs through a system administered by a government agency or independent board where the CRA would bid on the right to issue ratings. The board or agency would judge the bids and determine the best way to rate the bond issue. Users of the system to obtain credit ratings would pay for the expenses and related administrative costs of the system.
3. *Investor owned rating agency model*: The largest fixed income investors would form a board and set up their own CRAs, or investor-owned rating agencies (IORAs). The accuracy and transparency of the credit ratings would be upheld through the IORAs' charters and shareholder agreements. Issuers of bonds would approach the IORAs for ratings as they have sufficient buying power.

The report also explored a number of possible regulatory and statutory changes that could be undertaken. The SEC hosted a roundtable in May 2013 to further discuss the study and its findings with regulators and participants of the industry.

3.2. Europe

Besides the US, regulatory officials in Europe have also stepped up their supervision over CRAs. On January 16, 2013, the European Parliament approved new rules (see Box 5) setting the boundaries on how CRAs may evaluate state bonds and credit profiles of private corporations. The EU has been tightening CRA legislation since the financial crisis. This is the third round of proposals from the EU to regulate the CRAs.

Michel Barnier, European Union Internal Market Commissioner, said[23] that the EU's adoption of the new guidelines for CRAs was a key step towards

Box 5 — New rules for rating services in Europe[24].

1. Sovereign debt ratings can only be published on fixed dates set by the CRA. Unsolicited sovereign ratings would be published twice but not more than three times a year, on dates set by the CRA at the end of the prior year.
2. CRAs will be liable for their credit ratings. Investors relying on credit ratings are able to sue the CRA for rating-related damages if the CRA deliberately breaches the law. Examples of such breaches would be issuing a credit rating outside the pre-determined issuance calendar or having a conflict of interest with the client.
3. Users should not be too influenced by credit ratings. Credit firms and financial corporations are encouraged to develop their own credit assessments and manage risk independently.
4. Shareholders should have limited ownerships of CRAs. CRAs are not allowed to issue ratings to securities in scenarios where a shareholder or member holding 10% of the voting rights in the CRA has an investment stake in the security being rated. Also, no one is permitted to invest more than 5% in more than one CRA, unless both CRAs have the same parent company.

financial stability. He believes the new measures will effectively reduce the risk of a future financial crisis and align with the G-20's commitments to reduce reliance on external ratings and require financial institutions to strengthen their own credit assessment frameworks. The new measures should lessen the impact of sovereign rating changes on bond yields, but the systemic risks from a rapid rise in sovereign bond yields remains.

The European Commission has appointed the Europe Securities and Markets Authority (ESMA) to enforce the new regulations imposed on CRAs. Registered CRAs are supervised on the basis of ensuring rating transparency and minimizing conflicts of interest between CRAs and their clients. For this reason, CRAs are obligated to reveal their rating methodologies, including any assumption, models and rating changes to the authorities. ESMA occasionally consults with the industry on upcoming CRA regulations. Box 6 contains some of the proposals introduced by ESMA in December 2012.

Box 6 — ESMA proposes more rules for European CRAs.

ESMA recently published a consultation paper[25] inviting the public to comment on the scope of future CRA regulations. The paper was briefly mentioned in an interview of the ESMA Chairman, Steven Maijoor, with the Financial Times[26] in July 2012. During the dialogue, the Chairman said that the agency had been studying how the three largest CRAs evaluated the banks with a report released in December 2012. Responses to the paper were collected in February 2013 but ESMA would not be publishing the comments until Q3 2013. The listed proposals consist mainly of clarifications on past EU guidelines and were drafted following feedback from various European jurisdictions. The following points highlight the proposals by ESMA and one of the responses from the European Association of Credit Rating Agencies (EACRA).[27]

1. CRAs should register with ESMA.

CRAs without a physical presence in the EU and fulfilling the prerequisites of Article 5 of *Regulation (EC) No. 1060/2009 of the European Parliament and of the Council of September 16, 2009* on CRAs and amended by *Regulation (EU) No. 513/2011 of the European Parliament of the Council of May 11, 2011* (hereafter CRA Regulation) shall acquire certification from ESMA before assigning credit ratings for regulatory purposes in the EU. CRAs that are carrying out rating activities without registration operate illegally. Agencies, including those providing rating services on behalf of third parties, must not issue ratings until they are registered as CRAs. Moreover, only legal, not natural[28] persons can register with ESMA. Offenders will be fined according to Article 36a and Annex III.54 of the CRA Regulation.

EACRA: The need to register might not apply to all agencies. ESMA should provide clear references to what does and what does not fall under the scope of the CRA Regulation. Not all CRAs exclusively provide credit ratings but also credit scores, market signals information and other business activities. EACRA therefore recommends that CRAs should state which of their activities are classified as "credit ratings" defined under the scope of the CRA Regulation and require registration with ESMA. An institution may be issuing only credit scores and therefore would be exempted from registration. Credit ratings cannot be simply defined as "creditworthiness assessments derived from an established and defined ranking system or rating categories" as this definition can also be used for credit scores.

2. Credit ratings should include the CRA's qualitative analysis.

ESMA expands on the legal definition of credit ratings. The authority is proposing to include the CRA's qualitative analysis as part of their credit ratings. A measure of creditworthiness derived from summarizing and expressing data based only on a pre-set model, without additional substantial rating specific analytical input from a rating analyst, should not be considered a credit rating.

3. ESMA clarifies the definition of private credit ratings.

Existing CRA regulations do not apply to private credit ratings so ESMA is redefining the terms for private ratings. The definition excludes ratings that respond to an individual order placed by a person not within the regulatory purview of Article 2(2)(a) of the CRA Regulation. A rating provided to different persons belonging to a list of subscribers does not fall within the definition of "private credit rating" in Article 2(2)(a) of the CRA Regulation. CRAs have to ensure that the duty

Box 6 (*Continued*)

of confidentiality and limitations on the distribution of private credit ratings are preserved. When issuing private ratings, CRAs have a duty to inquire if the recipient of the private rating has any intention to disclose the rating to the public, in which case the CRA should refrain from issuing the rating.

EACRA: The definition of private ratings can also apply to situations in which an "individual order" may come from a third party other than the client ordering for the rating. EACRA wishes to know specifically if the following scenario translates into a private rating request. A credit assessment provider receives two or more individual orders from different customers not at the same time for a private rating on a same entity delivered individually to each of the customers. Another instance would be when a supplier requests for a private rating on one of its customers or prospects.

4. CRAs shall not establish branches outside the EU to escape supervision.

CRAs shall not establish branches outside the jurisdiction of the EU to perform activities that would prevent ESMA from conducting supervisory tasks set out in Articles 23b to 23d of the CRA Regulation, which includes the ability to carry out on-site inspections and investigations. Therefore, CRAs should cooperate with ESMA when inspections or investigations need to be carried out in non-EU branches. ESMA will assess the need for cooperation agreements with local regulators to ensure adequate supervision of those CRA branches outside the EU. Before setting up branches outside the EU, CRAs have to make sure that the new branches are also subjected to ESMA's regulations, including granting ESMA access to premises, systems and resources.

5. ESMA has the right to penalize CRAs who violate the rules.

ESMA reserves the right to impose periodic payment penalties on unregistered firms issuing credit ratings to the public. CRAs that obstruct ESMA from carrying out their effective supervisory duties will likewise be penalized. If a local authority[29] within the EU receives an application, or a request for information concerning the CRA Regulation, that authority has to immediately refer the request to ESMA.

IV. INTERNATIONAL RECOMMENDATIONS

International regulatory bodies such as the International Organization of Securities Commissions (IOSCO) are helping to guide various countries to adopt effective CRA regulations. The IOSCO Committee 6 (C6) December 2012 report listed certain recommendations[30] regarding the implementation and operation of supervisory colleges for CRAs. IOSCO is seeking the public's comments on the questions posed in the report.

IOSCO's evaluation of CRA regulatory programs across different jurisdictions shows that while the structures, specific provisions, and level of implementation of the programs may differ, the objectives of the four IOSCO CRA principles — quality and integrity of the ratings process, management of conflicts, transparency, and treatment of confidential information — form the building blocks of each of the programs. Ratings issued by the large CRAs are often addressed to worldwide audiences and are meant to be comparable with ratings issued by other CRAs. The work performed in determining the ratings could be done by analysts stationed in various jurisdictions and managed on an IT platform common to many countries. Nonetheless, CRAs are also overseen by multiple supervisors located around the world with varying degrees of supervision methods. This difference in supervision techniques presents a challenge to regulators as each regulator is only concerned with their own CRAs activities confined within their own domestic economy.

According to IOSCO, one way to get around this is to form a "college of regulators" as a forum for governments to exchange information about an international CRA. The college would be independent of IOSCO, but C6, which is responsible for regulating CRAs, would remain the coordinator for the development of CRA policies and guidelines. The roles of the entities are explained in Box 7.

V. IMPROVING CURRENT CRA REGULATIONS

Even as the G-20 prepares to tighten legislations and increase competitiveness in the CRA industry,

Box 7 — IOSCO proposal for CRAs.

IOSCO C6	Role of CRA College of Regulators
Develops principles and standards.	Promotes information sharing among supervisors of an internationally active CRA.
Coordinates discussions between the CRA industry and regulators.	Conducts collective risk assessment with respect to an internationally active CRA.
Interprets IOSCO cross border principles and IOSCO Code of Conduct for CRAs.	Coordinates supervisory activities (subject to agreement with other members).
Revises the IOSCO code of conduct for CRAs.	Provides feedback on application of IOSCO cross-border principles and IOSCO code of conduct for CRAs and makes recommendations to IOSCO C6 for updates or clarification of the IOSCO cross border principles and code.
Attended by policy specialists.	Shares collective risk assessment with IOSCO C6.
	Attended by examiners and/or inspectors of CRAs.

IOSCO believes that establishing CRA colleges would bring about a number of benefits including the following:

1. Improved quality of supervision as a result of the sharing of information and experiences across borders;
2. Improved quality of regulatory analysis for CRAs;
3. Enhanced ability to assess the risks of a particular CRA;
4. Achieve operational efficiencies (i.e., avoiding duplication of work) that would facilitate the more efficient utilization of both supervisors' and CRA's resources; and
5. Fostering the pursuit of common regulatory objectives across various jurisdictions.

regulating CRAs has its fair share of drawbacks. In a report[31] put forth by the C.D. Howe Institute, Professor S. Rousseau listed the disadvantages of current regulations for CRAs. First, regulatory involvement in the credit rating process would hamper rating innovation and might not improve the quality of credit ratings. The SEC might have difficulty keeping up with the pace of new products constantly developed in the financial markets. Secondly, market participants might view registration with the SEC as the authority's official endorsement of ratings. And it may render regulatory authorities accountable to investors for the failures of CRAs. Further actions to enhance existing CRA regulations would be to first eliminate regulatory reliance on ratings (this has been proposed in many countries). Secondly, to make it mandatory for institutional investors to conduct their own due diligence with regard to the creditworthiness of the issuers. The third measure is to require a mandatory disclosure of information of underlying assets by issuers of structured products.

Separately, academics like Professor M. Richardson wrote an article[32] highlighting some of the consequences of the Dodd Frank Act. With regard to the supervision of CRAs under the Dodd Frank Act, the professor argues that the reduced reliance on credit ratings and the push for financial institutions to prove their creditworthiness would lead to more self-regulation. But, self-regulation and misaligned incentives of the financial sector were among the leading causes of the 2008 financial crisis. This is an example of a potential drawback of decreased reliance on third party credit ratings.

5.1. The US State Insurance Regulators

Professor J. P. Hunt[33] mentioned that the Dodd Frank Act omitted the regulation of the use of credit ratings by state insurance regulators. The US insurers often see their assets regulated by state regulators using credit ratings assigned by CRAs. However, the US insurance industry owned nearly 20% of the corporate bonds and 16% of the US municipal bonds in 2011, about twice as much as corporate and municipal bonds held by the US banks. The US Securities Valuation Office (SVO), tasked with the responsibility of assessing the credit risk of insurance company investments, has largely relied on ratings issued by the CRAs to validate the riskiness of invested assets. All state insurance regulators have to follow the National Association of Insurance Commissioners (NAIC) risk based capital guidelines. In 2000, the NAIC temporarily exempted investment grade corporate and municipal securities from the SVO review and allowed insurers to approach either a reputable CRA or the SVO to decide the riskiness of their investment holdings. With this allowance, 80% of the insurers' holdings were assessed by the CRAs.

Insurers and their regulators are heavy users of CRA ratings. Any financial reform that looks at the regulation of CRAs should consider the activities of the NAIC. If the NAIC is creating an inflated demand for CRA ratings among the insurers, then the US Congress's objective of reducing reliance on credit ratings through the Dodd Frank Act is simply not comprehensive enough.

In November 2011, the NAIC studied alternative methods to adopting credit ratings but made no plans to remove ratings from its regulations. After a comprehensive study of the regulatory system and the performance of credit ratings during the recent financial crisis, the NAIC decided that it will not completely replace the CRAs with the expanded functions of the SVO nor will it remove all credit rating references from its regulatory system. This selective approach to credit rating reform is in defiance of the US Congress's broad-based decision to abolish rating reliant regulations.

The US Congress could be waiting for the 2014 implementation of EU Solvency II reforms before deciding on the course of CRA regulations for American insurers. Insurance Europe (IE), representing 34 insurance and reinsurance members operating in Europe, said that the need to refrain from any reference to credit ratings was neither feasible nor desirable in practice. It said that current regulations should also factor in the nature, scale and complexity of insurer's assets. In a letter addressed[34] to the European Parliament and the European Council responsible for CRA regulations, IE said that the Amendment 66 of the proposed CRA regulation which aimed at deleting any references to credit ratings may conflict with provisions of the Solvency II Directive implementing measures such as references to ratings inserted in the capital requirements of Article 109a.

VI. CONCLUDING REMARKS

The relatively long existence of some CRAs shows that they play an important role in financial markets by providing investors with a simple gauge on the credit profile of an obligor, be it a corporation, municipality or country. Investors should presumably be able to make informed decisions by benefiting from the skills of professional risk assessors. However, the recent financial crisis has highlighted that too much dependence of the financial system on CRAs can bring about serious hazards. As a result, regulators are trying to improve the accountability, transparency and competitiveness of the CRAs. CRAs now operate in a tighter legislative environment than before. More specifically, law makers want to hold the CRAs more accountable for their ratings for obvious reasons. The regulatory efforts will in principle improve the functioning of financial markets, but it may in practice become too draconian and end up stifling the normal growth of the world economy.

In addition to the regulatory changes, CRAs are challenged by rating alternatives initiated by commercial entities like BlackRock and non-profit organizations such as Bertelsmann Foundation and the Risk Management Institute at the National University of Singapore. More rating alternatives are likely to emerge and raise the standard of the CRA industry. These new initiatives will provide users with another source of reliable credit ratings. Even with a call to rely less on ratings issued by the CRAs, CRAs will still remain crucial to the running of financial markets, but the changing market environment and the availability of rating alternatives will undoubtedly alter the way CRAs conduct their businesses.

NOTES

[1] SGD 10,000,000,000 Secured Noted Program. Minibond Limited Prospectus. March 30, 2006.

[2] Karunungan, L. and E. Chew. Moody's Misses on Southeast Asia Debt as S&P Errs. *Bloomberg*, March 8, 2013.

[3] Boyd, S. and Y. Xie. Blackrock Sees Distortions in Country Ratings Seeking Revamp. *Bloomberg News*, December 22, 2012.

[4] Blueprint for INCRA — An International Non-profit Credit Rating Agency. Bertelsmann Foundation. April 2012.

[5] Norton, S., W. Siew and A. Hay. Selling Gold Ties Cyprus to Europe, Economist Truglia Says. *Reuters News*, April 19, 2013.

[6] More information can be found at the Bertelsmann Foundation website: http://www.bfna.org/category/publication-type/incra.

[7] N'Diaye, Y. Crowd Sourced Rating Firms Join Forces; Target SEC Registration. *MNI Washington Bureau*, November 26, 2012.

[8] Vieira, P. Study Warns on Provinces' Finances. *The Wall Street Journal*, October 18, 2012.

[9] Webb, A. Roland Berger Is Short on Ratings-Agency Startup Cash, FTD Says. *Bloomberg News*, April 16, 2012.

[10] Wang, M. Moody's Escapes SEC Lawsuit, Now Moves to Shield Itself from Liability. *ProPublica*, September 2, 2010.

[11] Coopes, A. S&P Loses Landmark Australian Derivatives Case. *L'Agence France-Presse*, November 5, 2012.

[12] Australian Investors Launch Second Class Action Lawsuit Against S&P. *Reuter News*, April 17, 2013.

[13] Illinois S&P Suit: Bad Omen for Rating Agencies? *Arab News*, November 10, 2012.

[14] Suit Claims Bank Knew Investments Were Bad. *Reuters*, December 30, 2009.

[15] Forgione, S. S&P Lawyer Says Agency's Ratings Identical to Others. *Reuters*, February 5, 2013.

[16] Smith, E. B. and B. Ivry. S&P Creditability Seen Eroded by Complicity in Soured Deals. *Bloomberg*, March 9, 2013.

[17] Lopez, L. and A.Viswanatha. S&P Asks Federal Judge to Dismiss US Fraud Lawsuit. *Reuters*, April 22, 2013.

[18] Borak, D. International Regulators Approve Reform Package Before G-20 Meeting. *American Banker*, 176(192), October 4, 2011.

[19] Global Regulators Push Ahead With Plans To Curb "Shadow Banks". *Reuters*, November 5, 2012.

[20] In a paper ("Bank Ratings: What Determines Their Quality?") addressing the shortfalls of bank credit ratings, Hau, Langfield and Marques-Ibanez (2012) said that the implementation of the Dodd Frank Act would encourage the emergence of alternative rating agencies such as non-profit and low-cost ones in the US but less likely to happen elsewhere. The authors said that comprehensive data on banking results is kept from the public and regulators in countries outside the US, making it difficult to rate banks.

[21] Rehm, B. A. Small Banks to Get Squeezed by OCC Credit Rating Rule. *American Banker*, 177(217), November 9, 2012.

[22] Linnell, I., M. van der Weijden and K. Duignan. Unsolicited Comments Favoured over Unsolicited Ratings. The "Credit Crisis 4 Years on", Special Report, October 7, 2011.

[23] Commissioner Michel Barnier. Statement by Commissioner Michel Barnier following the vote in the European Parliament on new European rules to regulate credit rating agencies. MEMO/13/14. January 1, 2013.

[24] Tougher Credit Rating Rules Confirmed by Parliament's Vote. Reference: 20130114IPR05310. *Economic and Monetary Affairs*, January 16, 2013.

[25] Consultation Paper. Guidelines and Recommendations on the Scope of the CRA Regulation, December 20, 2012.

[26] Masters, B. Rating Agencies Face Probe. *Financial Times*, July 2, 2012.

[27] Missong, T. and T. Morgenstern. Letter to ESMA on Consultation Paper 2012/841 on Guidelines and Recommendations on the Scope of the CRA Regulation. *European Association of Credit Rating Agencies*, February 20, 2013.

[28] A natural person is any person with a legal capacity commencing from birth. A legal person is an association of people or institution that is recognized by law as having legal personality. It differs from other associations of people in that it possesses legal capacity and can appear before the courts as a plaintiff or defendant.

[29] Authorities defined in the CRA Regulation Articles 3(1)(p) and 3(1)(r), also referred to as National Competent and Sectoral Competent Authorities.

[30] Media release by the International Organization of Securities Commission. IOSCO publishes 2 reports advancing its work on CRAs. December 21, 2012.

[31] Rousseau, S. A Question of Creditability: Enhancing the Accountability and Effectiveness of Credit Rating Agencies. *Institut C.D. Howe Institute. Commentary No. 356*, July, 2012.

[32] Richardson, M. Regulating Wall Street: The Dodd Frank Act. *Economic Perspectives*, 36(3), 85–97, September 22, 2012.

[33] Hunt, J. P. Credit Ratings in Insurance Regulation: The Missing Piece of Financial Reform. *Washington and Lee Law Review*, 68(4), October 1, 2011.

[34] Insurance Europe. Insurance Europe Comments on the Trialoque Discussions on Credit Rating Agencies. *ECO-INV-12-139*, November 16, 2012.

Reserve Requirements as Window Guidance in China

Violaine Cousin
Chinese Banks Analyst and Researcher
cousinviolaine@yahoo.com

Keywords: Non-performing loans, reserve requirements, monetary policy, China, banks, asset quality, central bank, bank regulation, window guidance.

INTRODUCTION

Monetary policy measures such as reserve requirements are often used in emerging markets because they help control more than one issue at a time. In China, reserve requirements regularly make headlines — especially since 2006. Unlike developed markets' central banks, the People's Bank of China (PBOC), the Chinese central bank, is a frequent and avid user of this simple and cheap monetary tool: it was used 38 times between 2006 and mid-2012. This level of usage is clearly unconventional.

The reserve requirement ratio (RRR) sets forth the amount of deposits the banks are required to hold with their central bank compared to the volume of *renminbi* deposits they take from customers.[1] It is a binding and hard constraint on the banks' liquidity. The RRR is a recognized and established monetary policy tool around the world, but its uses as macro-prudential instrument, as defined in IMF (2011) and Lim *et al.* (2011), are much less studied. Nonetheless, it is plausible that a higher RRR makes loans dearer and that commercial banks would then intermediate to those projects and clients which promise a better return — by tilting the balance towards customers with higher creditworthiness and safer revenues for instance.

Such a hypothesis is important to test because asset quality is a central worry in the Chinese banking industry in particular and in all commercial banks around the world in general. If the central bank — which also acts as the lender of last resort — can ensure that banks have good asset quality, these will perform well and will not be in need of emergency funds by the state.

This paper reviews the impact of RRR in China on the asset quality of commercial banks since 2005 — and thus contributes to the research on reserve requirements' impact on the banks' asset quality. By applying the technique of robust regression on a large data set that includes the most important commercial financial institutions in China, this paper shows that setting reserve requirements does indeed have an impact on banks' asset quality. However, the impact is more of a superficial nature, more akin to window guidance (see Appendix E), as the policy appears to inform banks more about the policy stance than to truly induce them into choosing more creditworthy clients in the long term.

The remainder of the paper is organized as follows: Section 1 provides a literature review on the impact of reserve requirements as: (1) a monetary policy tool and (2) a regulatory tool for asset quality concerns. In Section 2, the paper continues with a discussion of the data set and its inherent particularities which call for a robust regression approach. Section 3 discusses the results of the regression and the overall conclusion of the paper.

I. RESERVE REQUIREMENTS — AN OVERVIEW

1.1. Reserve Requirements as Monetary Policy Tool

There is extensive research on the impact of reserve requirements as a tool for monetary policy and it is beyond the scope of this paper to provide an exhaustive overview. Therefore, only the most important issues will be summarized below.

Most authors investigate and discuss the effect of reserve requirements as a monetary policy instrument on: (1) liquidity and money supply; (2) on other policy targets (such as inflation, credit growth or financial stability); as well as on (3) interest rates (e.g., O'Brien, 2007; Glocker and Towbin, 2012b). Others such as Ostry *et al.* (2011) and Reinhart and Reinhart (1999) consider the effect of reserve requirements as one of the instruments in the policy toolbox to control systemic risk and more specifically capital flows.

Glocker and Towbin (2012b) show that raising reserve requirements first affects money supply through requiring a higher ratio that causes the broad money aggregate to decrease and triggers an economic contraction. Overall, the effect of reserve requirements on credit growth is well studied for many economies (see most recently Tovar *et al.*, 2012) and for China in particular (see Ma *et al.*, 2011). A second impact comes from the return on the reserves. If the received interest rate is below the market interest rate (see for example, Figure 1 for China), then an increase in the reserve ratio acts as a tax on banks and the spread between lending and deposit rates widens.

In another paper, Glocker and Towbin (2012a) show that especially in emerging markets which often witness large capital inflows, an additional effect can be observed. More specifically, to act against capital inflows-financed credit booms, emerging market central banks are often reluctant to use interest rates which would appreciate their currency and draw even more inflows. Hence, rather than increasing interest rates, their response often involves an increase of the reserve ratio to tighten conditions. When the spread between lending and deposit rates widens as stated above, lending by foreign investors should become less attractive, reducing the money multiplier and stabilizing inflation. So, setting the reserve ratio is almost a substitute for interest rate setting.

Not only does the reserve requirement helps to smooth the procyclicality of the credit cycle (Tovar *et al.*, 2012; Montoro and Moreno, 2011), it also complements other policy tools for more targeted interventions: for example, it helps fight inflation and restructure the banks' liability structure.

Therefore, it comes as no surprise that RRR is used in China for multiple reasons. He and Wang (2011) suggest four areas where the ratio helps the PBOC to meet its goals — both written and unspoken: (1) inflation, growth and financial stability; (2) money supply (M2), banking system credit and fundraising in capital and money markets; (3) money and bond market interest rates setting; and (4) open market operations, foreign exchange interventions and window guidance (see Appendix E). Moreover, the reserve requirements can be set by PBOC more independently compared to interest rates which need to be approved by the State Council.

Nevertheless, the use of reserve requirements has its drawbacks: (1) because it is often used in combination with other instruments and its effect on a standalone basis is more difficult to gauge for policymakers; (2) it is consequently difficult to calibrate (the requirements also need to be re-calibrated frequently to be more effective); and (3) it can induce disintermediation (see Section 4.3. and Tovar *et al.*, 2012).

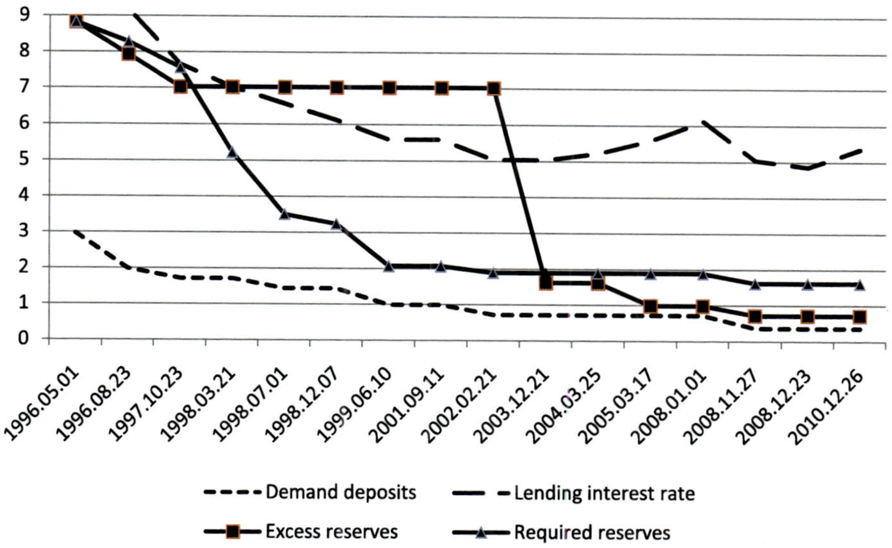

Figure 1. Interest rates on deposits and reserves as set by the PBOC (in %, 1996–2010).

Source: PBOC.

1.2. Reserve Requirements in China

As stated by PBOC in its quarterly monetary report in 2006, RRR is seen as an efficient tool of monetary policy. It progressively changed from being an instrument to ensure sufficient liquidity in times of stress to being an instrument to regulate the liquidity available in the banking system (PBOC, 2006). It can be a "fierce drug" as a small change can have a large effect — albeit only when liquidity in the system is scarce. PBOC prefers using the RRR as a monetary policy tool compared to open market operations and standing facilities as it does not need to rely on the willingness of banks to purchase, nor does it rely on the banks' holdings of low risk assets for rediscounting. In fact, the reserve requirement is used to control demand for liquidity and the excess reserves held by the banks at the central bank (on which there are no constraints) are used for liquidity management by the banks to support their daily payment and settlement obligations.

The RRR is applied strictly on a daily basis (no reserve averaging is possible) based on the level of deposits at the bank within the previous *xun*.[2] The banks have to hold sufficient reserves at closing, otherwise they risk being penalized. As a result, daily liquidity and interest rates are more volatile (Porter and Xu, 2009). The RRR is thus a binding and hard constraint on banks.

The RRR is applied uniformly on all deposits (not on any other type of liability) regardless of the deposit holders or of the deposits' maturity. Some central banks set requirements depending on whether a deposit holder is a government or a private individual and whether the deposit is callable or is a time deposit, for example.

Since 2004, PBOC has introduced a differentiated RRR (see Figure 2) to account for the geographical scope of a bank (rural vs. coastal areas, areas destroyed by the Wenchuan earthquake, etc.), its size and its

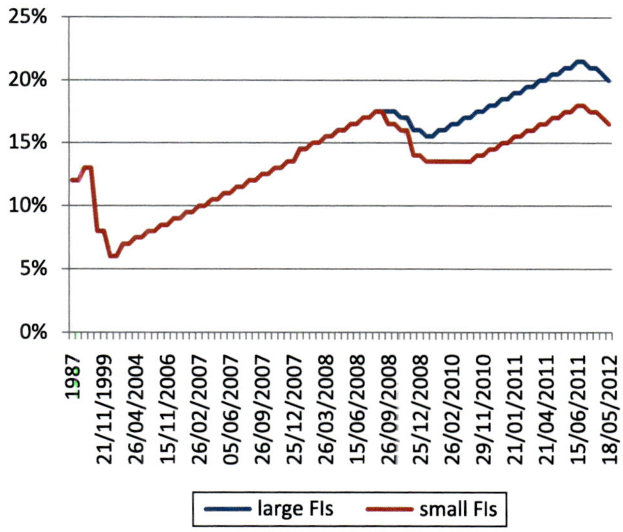

Figure 2. Reserve requirements (ratio in %, 1987–2012).

Source: PBOC, based on the date the ratio becomes effective.

Notes: The graph does not show geographic differentiation as it is much less used than the bank size differentiation; FI = Financial institution.

capital adequacy. A bank located in rural areas or a smaller local bank will face less stringent requirements than one housed in more developed coastal areas or with a larger and more diversified deposit base, for example. Reportedly, the requirements are also based on a bank's asset quality — including the non-performing loan (NPL) ratio, provisioning, loan growth — but the rules remain silent on that aspect (PBOC, 1998, 2004a and 2004b). While the first two aspects (geographical scope and bank size) are publicly known, no information is available[3] on which banks have to hold higher reserves because of lower capital adequacy (in recent years, the banks under the scope of this paper have had capital adequacy ratios well above the stated minimum anyway[4]) or poorer loan quality. Thus the RRR is not solely a tool of monetary policy but now also has a distinct credit policy and macro-prudential flavor.

The PBOC further uses the RRR to signal its policy stance ("signaling hypothesis"). With that signal banks know if they have to tighten lending and loan disbursements or not (in that respect, it is combined with "window guidance" (Wen, 2013), which is less binding but requires from banks an orientation towards certain sectors or borrowers). In fact, banks normally hold sufficient excess reserves to ensure a smooth transition to a higher RRR, but the signaling effect has a deeper impact. Combined with limited liquidity and loan growth, the banks normally tighten their lending criteria or their credit availability. They also do so in expectation of further RRR rises. The signal sent by the higher RRR also prompts banks to adjust the structure of their loan portfolio — for example, by preferring short-term loans to long-term ones in order to react more quickly, or by lending more to safer large enterprises.

Ma *et al.* (2011) have found that in general, reserve money adjusted for RRR changes causes loan growth[5] and a higher ratio leads banks to book less loans. At the same time, to compensate for foregone earnings, the banks have been innovating wealth management products and trust loans (together with trust companies) which can be booked off-balance. The regulatory arbitrage of banks is one of the main current challenges for the China Banking Regulatory Commission (CBRC, the bank regulator) and it also affects the effectiveness of liquidity control of the central bank. On top of the higher riskiness and opacity of the banking system due to regulatory arbitrage, the PBOC policy stance also contributes to a deeper bank disintermediation (i.e., deposits are moving to the gray market or to trust companies where returns are higher).

In China, reserve requirements act as a monetary policy as well as a financial stability instrument — they are of a macro-prudential nature. They help deal with volatile capital inflows, and tackle the challenges arising from the exchange rate and interest rate objectives. As stated by Xia (2009), the PBOC prefers the flexibility of the less costly RRR (compared to open market operations), as it helps sustainable economic growth (depending on liquidity being withdrawn or released), it reduces pressure on inflation, reduces adjustments of the exchange rate and mitigates financial systemic risk.

1.3. Excess Reserves in China

Looking solely at reserves provides a distorted picture since banks also hold large volumes of excess reserves with the central bank, which also yield a return (see Figure 1). While some minimum level of excess reserves is normally to be expected for settlement purposes, it also helps banks respond more smoothly — if at all — to reserve requirements ratio increases (see Figures 3 and 4).

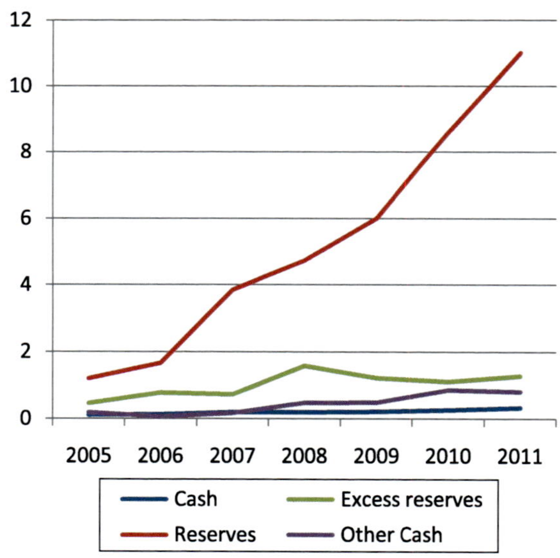

Figure 3. Reserves held by the banks (in trillion CNY, 2005–2011).

Source: Banks' annual reports as stated in the notes, year-end figures.

Note: Sums for all 33 banks are included in this article.

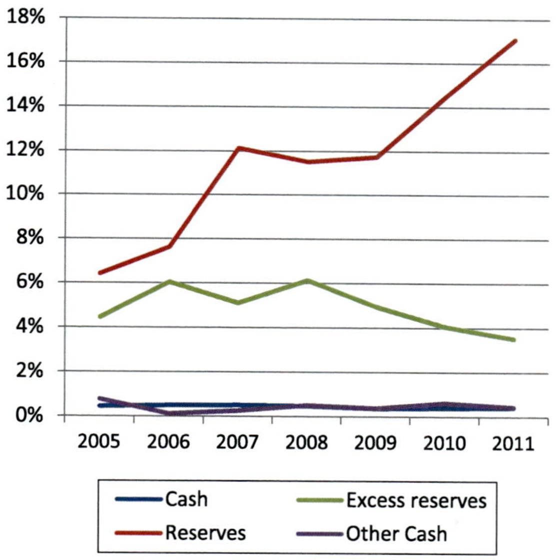

Figure 4. Reserves held by the banks (in % of customer deposits, 2005–2011).

Source: Banks' annual reports as stated in the notes, year-end figures.
Note: Non-weighted averages for all 33 banks are included in this article.

From the above it is clear that excess reserves, while decreasing, remain at around 4% of the customer deposits. Therefore, banks can relatively easily stomach further RRR increases (normally the PBOC increases the ratio in 0.5%-points steps and at most within a month). Nevertheless, the banks have seen a significant decrease in excess reserves (from around 6% to around 4%) since 2008; that is, when PBOC started using the RRR even more frequently.

The effectiveness of the reserve requirement is influenced by the level of excess reserves held at the central bank. But its effectiveness also depends on the availability of deposited funds at banks. Up until 2011, banks could rely without much effort on the fact that Chinese depositors are still captive and investment opportunities are scarce. A combination of foreign investment restrictions, interest rate ceilings, a roller-coaster stock market and an underdeveloped bond market implies that domestic investors have limited choices to earn more than the PBOC rates. It appears that only since the RRR reached a certain level in early 2011 (around 18–19%) liquidity became dearer. At the same time, the banks faced higher capital adequacy ratios, which meant that certain growth levels were then out of reach.

As expected, the levels of excess reserves held by city commercial banks (CCBs) and joint-stock commercial banks (JSCBs) are higher than that for state-owned commercial banks (SOCBs). City commercial banks are mostly limited to the locality where they were established and rely on a small and rather undiversified base for business, with their local governments as the major, but not controlling, owners. In comparison, JSCBs and SOCBs have nationwide reach and the former are generally more commercially minded with the latter being spun off from government offices in the 1980s — thus suffering more from government interference. The fact that CCBs hold more reserves might be explained by the depth of liquidity and capital management in the banks as well as the use of the interbank bond market (in which the smaller banks are deal takers and more active users). With their limited scope and capacity, CCBs need to hold higher liquidity buffers. Larger banks are more likely to establish state-of-the-art risk and capital management frameworks than smaller ones. Smaller banks are further dependent on larger ones to lend on needed liquidity and can rely less on gathering deposits which are more concentrated.

1.4. Impact of RRR Changes on Banks

Although there are some publications in Chinese, the author is not aware of any published article in any other language that analyzes the impact of reserve requirements on bank asset quality in general,[6] or on Chinese banks in particular.

The following summarizes the findings of Chinese researchers with respect to the impact of reserve requirements:

- An RRR increase makes funds dearer so that banks are forced to make more careful choices when lending their funds. They will thus put more effort into choosing more 'worthy' clients (see Guo, 2010). 'Worthy' does not necessarily mean that they are objectively more creditworthy on a stand-alone basis. In fact, it may just mean that the banks will prefer to turn to safer bets, for example, state-owned enterprises (SOEs) which can be expected to be saved in case of need — thus relying solely on government largesse. These also generate more reliable profits than small enterprises. Returns on loans are capped by the central bank, so that risk-adequate returns on riskier loans are not possible. This induces banks towards preferring loans to safer bets, such as SOEs. This can lead to a change in the loan portfolio structure (more lending towards SOEs or in short-term loans, or withdrawing loan funds to use them to buy securities), but it can also influence the non-performing loan (NPL) ratio.

- An RRR increase will decrease the amount of new loans disbursed at the beginning of the year. Normally, banks choose to postpone the disbursement of year-end loans until the new year begins, so as to await signals about acceptable loan growth (in the form of RRR changes or window guidance) (see Guo, 2010).
- An RRR increase will affect overall bank profitability. If the banks cannot lend the same amount as before, they forego interest income, which will negatively affect the bank's profit. The effect will be even greater once the RRR increase also affects the interbank lending rate, thus demanding higher interest on interbank funds. The choice of business to focus on for the banks will be even more important. This is especially true for smaller banks. All other things being equal, they have less scope for product diversification and possibly also less capabilities to do so (Fu *et al.*, 2012).

Yu (2009) analyzes the effectiveness of RRRs on loan portfolios. He finds that RRR has a larger impact on SOCBs than on JSCBs (which rely more on interbank funds than on deposits). SOCBs' loan volumes change as a result of changes in customer deposits and reserve requirements within 6 months, while JSCBs' loan changes depend on deposits changes within one quarter and not on the reserve requirements. Overall, the effectiveness of RRR depends highly on the balance sheet structure of banks.

Table 1. General data on Chinese banks (2011).

	Total SOCBs	Total JSCBs	Total CCBs
Total assets (bln CNY)	51,266	23,701	4,743
Net loan portfolio (LP) (bln CNY), after provisions	25,521	11,966	2,136
LP as % of assets	*49.81%*	*48.01%*	*43.26%*
LP growth yoy	*13.47%*	*19.77%*	*20.20%*
Loan loss reserves (bln CNY), on balance	736	259	50
Non-performing loans (bln CNY) (sum of substandard, doubtful and loss loans; loans overdue for more than 90 days)	295	80	15
Customer deposits (bln CNY)	40,689	16,560	3,321
Capital (bln CNY)	3,180	1,362	274
NPL ratio (total NPLs at year-end/gross loans at year-end)	*1.14%*	*0.60%*	*0.67%*
Basel I ratio (total capital in %, as published)	*13.27*	*11.76*	*12.90*
Net interest income (bln CNY)	1,203	558	107
Net profit (bln CNY), after taxes	620	255	50
Staff (no.)	1,475,649	363,904	49,231
Branches (no.)	65,014	5,895	1,705
Return on equity (% of net profit/total capital)	*19.36%*	*17.72%*	*18.58%*
Return on assets (% of net profit/total assets)	*1.20%*	*1.00%*	*1.07%*
Portfolio quality breakdown (bln CNY)			
— performing	25,026	11,986	1,866
— special mention	937	160	61
— substandard	120	32	7
— doubtful	133	29	4
— loss	41	20	3
NPL amount (sum of the above three categories)	295	80	15

Source: Banks' annual reports for 2011, sums.

Notes: The figures concern only those banks that are subject to the analysis, i.e., all of the existing SOCBs and JSCBs but only a limited number of the CCBs. Unweighted averages are in italics.

II. RESEARCH DESIGN AND METHODOLOGY

2.1. Data Set Development

The data set of this paper is based on publicly available data published by Chinese banks. It covers the published financial statements and their notes for 33 Chinese banks between 2005 and the first half of 2012 (see Table 1). It entails data on the four SOCBs (i.e., historically defined as such by the regulator CBRC and taken as such by scholars: Industrial and Commercial Bank of China, Bank of China, China Construction Bank, Agricultural Bank of China), 13 JSCBs and 17 CCBs (see Appendix A for a complete listing). Due to higher disclosure requirements, the more recent period holds more complete data sets.

The accounting data is published by the banks in their annual and semi-annual reports (semi-annual reports are published only by those banks listed on a stock exchange, see Appendix A). Quarterly reports were not used since they do not contain sufficient information.

Although the data set includes all Chinese SOCBs and JSCBs, it was not possible to collect information on additional CCBs because of the poor disclosure quality. In fact, due to efforts of the bank regulator and the Ministry of Finance who sets the accounting standards, all commercial banks have published their financial statements in a similar way since 2005 (e.g., in terms of Basel I capital ratio or NPL calculation and disclosure), which is also more or less in line with international practices — thus making a comparison and an in-depth analysis possible.

The 33 banks for which data is available account for over 60% of the Chinese banking system's total assets. In fact, the banks encompass all of the SOCBs and JSCBs as well as almost half of the CCBs (in terms of assets). The sample size is sufficiently large to conduct an overall statistical analysis and to differentiate, for example, by bank type.

The data quality is ensured by using a reliable source (published and audited financial statements), based on the same accounting standards. Many doubt the asset quality figures reported by the Chinese banks. While there might be some truth to this as the banks definitely have some leeway in the categorization of loans (see Cousin, 2011), this is true for all banks, not only for Chinese ones. To avoid interpolation interfering with the results, no interpolation was made for missing data.

To ensure data accuracy, the collected data is compared and double checked with data provided by PBOC and CBRC. A caveat of the available data — which is related to the characteristics of the Chinese banking system — is the lack of data covering a full cycle. The current cycle has not yet ended and data before that cycle is either of very poor quality or incomplete.

This paper's analysis looks mainly at two variables: the NPL ratio as the dependent variable and RRR as the independent variable. The non-performing loan ratio is calculated at the end of the reporting period as the sum of the substandard, doubtful and loss loans as published by each individual bank divided by the volume of gross loans for the same period. The reserve requirement ratio is calculated as an average of the current in-force RRR weighted by time (to reflect the changes in the ratio within a reporting period, based on the time it becomes effective) and, whenever needed, by institution type (as the ratio differs for large and small institutions[7]). The basis for that calculation is the ratio published by PBOC (see Table 2).

In addition to the above two main variables, the analysis also covers the relation of other closely related variables to the RRR. More specifically, for the NPL ratio, it is also important to look at special mention

Table 2. Reserve requirement ratio (2005–2012, in %).

On a Yearly Basis		On a Half-Yearly Basis	
Dec-05	7.50%	Jun-05	7.50%
Dec-06	8.53%	Dec-05	7.50%
Dec-07	11.23%	Jun-06	7.50%
Dec-08	16.27%	Dec-06	8.49%
Dec-09	14.98%	Jun-07	10.15%
Dec-10	16.65%	Dec-07	12.30%
Dec-11	20.00%	Jun-08	15.52%
		Dec-08	17.03%
		Jun-09	14.98%
		Dec-09	14.98%
		Jun-10	15.96%
		Dec-10	17.33%
		Jun-11	19.50%
		Dec-11	20.49%
		Jun-12	19.17%

Source: PBOC, with time and institution-weighted calculations made by the author.
Notes: The reserve requirement ratio is defined as the deposits the banks are required to hold with their central bank compared to the volume of *renminbi* deposits they take from customers.

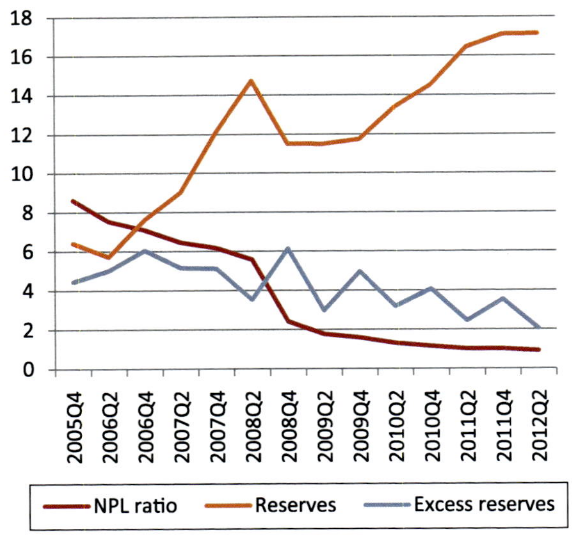

Figure 5. NPL ratios and reserves (in %, 2005–2012).
Source: NPL ratio as stated by CBRC for the SOCBs, JSCBs and CCBs; reserves and excess reserves as stated in the banks' annual reports, as a percentage of customer deposits (calculations by the author).

loans (the intermediary category between performing and non-performing), restructured loans, loans overdue for less than 90 days[8] as well as loan loss provisions raised on balance (as opposed to those expensed in the income statement). In addition, the category of the ten largest borrowers of any bank at year-end requires special attention, since deterioration in creditworthiness of these borrowers can quickly lead to higher NPL ratios.

For the RRR, it is also useful to consider the impact on cash held by banks (in vault and at the central bank), the declared reserve deposits held at the central bank as well as the freely available excess reserves (also held with the central bank). Since the banks hold excess reserves and large volumes of cash, the actual reserve deposits of banks at the central bank might give us a more detailed insight on the influence of reserve requirements on the loan portfolio quality.

2.2. Descriptive Statistics

When plotting the reserves and the NPL ratio for the banks under review, the result appears to show a straightforward and strong link between the two variables (see Figure 5), nevertheless, further analysis suggests otherwise (see below as well as Appendix B).

In general, we expect that as the RRR or the reserves held at the central bank increase, the asset quality of the banks will improve — regardless of whether we look at NPLs or at special mention loans (see Table 3).

2.3. Outliers Analysis

As is clear from Table 4, some of the data is highly skewed. In fact, the data shows that there are a number of outliers in the NPL ratio data. One solution in dealing with outliers would be to delete them (even though

Table 3. Description of variables and expected signs.

	Formula	Source	Expected Sign to RRR
LLP	Loan loss provisions/loan portfolio	Annual report	–
SM	Special mention loans/equity	Annual report	–
Potential bad loans	Sum of special mention, overdue 90 days and restructured loans to equity Referred to as "Badloans" in the statistical analysis	Annual report	–
NPL	Non-performing loans/loan portfolio	Annual report	–
Top10	Volume of loans outstanding to ten largest borrowers in relation to equity capital	Annual report	–
Cash	Cash held at banks or in vault in relation to customer deposits	Annual report	+
Reserves	Required reserves at PBOC in relation to customer deposits Referred to as "Reserv" in the statistical analysis	Annual report	+
Excess reserves	Excess reserves held at PBOC in relation to customer deposits Referred to as "ExReserv" in the statistical analysis	Annual report	+
RRR	Reserve requirements weighted by time, as described above	PBOC	

Table 4. Descriptive statistics.

	Number of Observations	Mean	Standard Deviation	Median	Trimmed Mean	Median Absolute Deviation (MAD)	Minimum	Maximum	Range	Skewness	Kurtosis
LLP	277	0.02	0.01	0.02	0.02	0.01	0	0.22	0.22	9.01	117.43
SM	261	0.02	0.02	0.02	0.02	0.01	0	0.15	0.15	2.79	9.84
Potential bad loans	198	0.39	0.33	0.3	0.34	0.2	−0.48	1.77	2.25	1.77	3.85
NPL	**269**	**0.02**	**0.03**	**0.01**	**0.01**	**0.01**	**0**	**0.25**	**0.25**	**5.41**	**35**
Top10	247	0.35	0.23	0.28	0.31	0.13	0.06	1.97	1.91	3.07	14.09
Cash	235	0	0	0	0	0	0	0.01	0.01	1.09	3.42
Reserves	235	0.13	0.04	0.13	0.13	0.04	0.05	0.21	0.16	−0.15	−0.76
Excess Reserves	234	0.04	0.03	0.04	0.04	0.02	0.01	0.15	0.14	1.1	0.83
RRR	**296**	**0.14**	**0.04**	**0.15**	**0.14**	**0.06**	**0.08**	**0.2**	**0.13**	**−0.34**	**−1.15**

Source: Calculations of the author, rounded figures.

Table 5. Outlier observations.

	Right Outliers	Left Outliers
LLP	ABC 2007, Everbright 2005–2006, GDB 2008, HSB 2005, PAB 2005–2006, BDL 2006	BBB 2011
SM	ABC 2008, CCB 2005, BOC 2005, Bocom 2005, BHZ 2005–2006, BNB 2005, HSB 2005–2006, BDL 2008–2009, BBB 2007–2009, BHK 2008, BXA 2006–2007	—
Potential bad loans	ABC 2008–2010, Bocom 2006, CITIC 2005, SPDB 2006, Minsheng 2006, Huaxia 2005–2008, BSH 2006, HSB 2007, BXA 2009–2010	ABC 2007
NPL	ICBC 2005, ABC 2005–2008, BOC 2005–2006, CITIC 2005, Everbright 2005–2007, GDB 2006–2007, SDB 2005–2007, BBJ 2005, BTJ 2005, HSB 2005, BBB 2007, BGZ 2008, BXA 2006–2008	—
Top10	Everbright 2007, SDB 2005–2006, Bohai 2008–2009, BNJ 2007, BBJ 2005–2006, BHZ 2005, BNB 2005, BTJ 2007, HSB 2006–2007, BBB 2008, BHK 2009, BXA 2010–2011	—
Cash	ABC 2007, ABC 2011, HSB 2006, BHK 2008, BXA 2010–2011	—
Reserves	—	—
Excess Reserves	CITIC 2008, Minsheng 2008, Industrial 2010, Huaxia 2006 & 2008, Hengfeng 2007, BSH 2008, BHZ 2009	—
RRR	—	—

Source: Calculations from the extreme values package in *R* based on Spearman's Rho and the boxplot.stat command.

they are not due to data collection errors). Such a simple and drastic method would however mean that the research is skewed towards normal data (misrepresenting the reality) and that the research does not account fully for the historical state of the banking industry in China.[9] Outliers are also found in the variables related to the asset quality (see Table 5 as well as Appendices C and D). These outliers can be explained by the well-known fact that in the early years of the sample period many banks had deplorable asset quality.

The outliers are the result of either extremely low equity levels (e.g., for SM and potential bad loans) or (extremely) high volumes of bad loans and similarly bad credit decisions. It is in fact noticeable that most outliers are to be found in earlier years — before the last round of bank restructurings took place. This restructuring mainly targeted ABC, SDB, GDB, as well as a number of smaller city commercial banks.

With those outliers, the assumption of normality for the linear regression is not met (while the assumptions of linearity of the relationship between dependent and independent variables and of independence of the error terms may be met, also the assumption of homoscedasticity is violated). Therefore, it is necessary — unless we are prepared to drop valuable and correct observations — to find an alternative to linear regression in order to analyze the relationship between asset quality and reserve requirements. This motivates the use of robust regression methods which are not overly affected by the violation of normality.

2.4. Rationale for Using MM-Estimates Robust Regression

As the number of outliers is high and there is no indication that the data is incorrect or erroneous, it is preferable to use robust methods to continue with the regression analysis. As stated by Andersen (2008), robust[10] regression is a suitable alternative to OLS in those cases. It provides unbiased estimates that are unaffected by outliers or by skewed residual distributions.

In this paper MM-estimation[11] (as proposed by Yohai, 1987) is used as it combines the robustness and resistance of S-estimation (relying on high breakdown points[12] to minimize the dispersion of residuals; otherwise outliers would be treated in the same way as non-outlying data points) with the efficiency of M-estimation (i.e., high asymptotic efficiency: otherwise hypothesis tests would have less power and confidence intervals would be wider). MM-estimation works in three stages: first, a high breakdown estimator is used (a highly robust and resistant S-estimate while minimizing the M-estimate of the scale of the residuals). Then, the latter is computed on the residuals (held constant whilst a close-by M-estimate of the parameters is located) and finally, the solution for the regression equation is found. This method is preferred over other robust regression methods because it combines a high breakdown point with asymptotic efficiency. Moreover, this method works well with different sample sizes. The only drawback is that it handles curvatures poorly, but that is not an issue for this research.

III. ROBUST REGRESSION RESULTS

3.1. Overall Impact on Loan Quality

In almost all cases, RRR has a small but significant and negative influence on NPL ratios — more akin to a side effect (see Table 6). The influence fades away with time, as adding a lag of one or two years flattens the curve. This also is true when comparing results for different bank types. The influence decreases progressively. This is worth noting because normally NPLs take time to unfold.

In fact, a loan is unlikely to be non-performing at the time of disbursement and will become so after a year or two at least, especially because Chinese banks favor bullet loans with a bulk repayment at maturity. Nonetheless, this situation has to be understood under the consideration that Chinese banks tend to prefer disbursing short-term loans which they "evergreen"[13] when and where necessary. Thus, the signal sent by the central bank of a tightening of credit policy could actually directly and swiftly induce the banks into reviewing their disbursements and portfolio quality to ensure that those loans that need evergreening are evergreened, those that do not need further funds are withdrawn and that those in need of review — in terms of loan classification — are dealt with appropriately.

This means that the side effect of the RRR is not to generally improve asset quality in depth but rather to require banks to (superficially) straighten their asset quality and restructure where necessary. As we can see from the further analysis of all loans in Table 7, the reaction is even more pronounced for loans that have a high potential to become non-performing (e.g., special mention loans or other potential bad loans). In fact, it appears that banks interpret a surge in reserve requirements as a tightening of credit conditions as well as a stricter regulatory environment (i.e., a policy signaling effect) and take this opportunity to review

Table 6. Robust regression results (y = NPL, x = RRR).

y = NPL, x = RRR	Intercept Estimate	Std. Error	Sig.	Variable Estimate	Std. Error	Sig.	Robust RSE
All banks, no lag	0.035402	0.003464	***	–0.1443	0.019479	***	0.006031
All banks, one-year lag	0.028688	0.002855	***	–0.1189	0.017640	***	0.005592
All banks, two-year lag	0.023221	0.002214	***	–0.0959	0.014852	***	0.004899
Non-performing loan ratio ≤0.78%[a]	0.004359	0.002125	*	0.0064	0.010827		0.001360
Non-performing loan ratio >0.78%, ≤2.06%	0.035402	0.003464	***	–0.1443	0.019479	***	0.006031
Non-performing loan ratio >2.06%	0.042775	0.004542	***	–0.0986	0.034518	**	0.010640

Notes: [a] denotes all ranges based on first and last quintiles.
Significance (Sig.) codes: 0 '***' 0.001 '**' 0.01 '*' 0.05 '.' 0.1 ' ' 1.
RSE = Residual standard error (std. error).

Table 7. Robust regression results (y = other asset quality ratios, x = RRR).

(x = RRR)	Intercept Estimate	Std. Error	Sig.	Variable Estimate	Std. Error	Sig.	Robust RSE
y = Loan loss provisions, no lag	0.024843	0.002074	***	–0.016159	0.01263		0.007203
y = Special mention loans, no lag	0.041090	0.004520	***	–0.157060	0.02558	***	0.010670
y = Potential bad loans, no lag	0.938400	0.137000	***	–3.782900	0.76920	***	0.169000
y = Concentration to top ten borrowers, no lag	0.494660	0.046890	***	–1.279050	0.26490	***	0.110500

Notes: Sig. codes: 0 '***' 0.001 '**' 0.01 '*' 0.05 '.' 0.1 ' ' 1.

their asset quality — either by putting more effort in choosing creditworthy clients or by restructuring loans and maturities where necessary, thus improving their asset quality and the potential bad loans (see Table 7). This fact also appears to be supported by the results when the NPL ratio is higher: from Table 6 it appears that the effect fades away with increased lag probably because above a certain level, the banks receive warnings from the regulators regardless of the tightening of credit or of the height of the reserve ratio.

3.2. Results Based on Different State Links

Due to the prevalence of the state as a shareholder, it is not meaningful to look at private vs. public banks in China. It is more useful to look at different ownership stake levels and historical ties to different levels of government (i.e., central or local). If the RRR is understood as a signal for a stricter regulatory stance on asset quality ("signaling hypothesis"), then it can be expected that the influence of the reserve requirements is stronger for banks that are closer to the state — large SOCBs as well as smaller local CCBs.

As is clear from Table 8, the impact is indeed highest on SOCBs and lowest on JSCBs, while impact on CCBs is in the middle. SOCBs and to a lesser extent CCBs are known for their closer links to central and local governments. While the link is much less constraining than in earlier years of reform or even prior to reform, the banks still are permeated by the state and the Communist Party (Cousin, 2011, Chapters 2–4). This is true for large banks at a national level and for smaller banks at local levels, and the influence continues to this day. Such a situation is less of a concern for JSCBs which tend to act more freely. Thus, it comes as no surprise that banks

Table 8. Robust regression results based on bank type and ownership (y = NPL, x = RRR).

	Intercept			Variable			
y = NPL, x = RRR	**Estimate**	**Std. Error**	**Sig.**	**Estimate**	**Std. Error**	**Sig.**	**Robust RSE**
SOCBs, no lag	0.058860	0.002255	***	−0.2469	0.014435	***	0.006264
SOCBs, one-year lag	0.047604	0.002507	***	−0.2044	0.016793	***	0.005167
SOCBs, two-year lag	0.038772	0.002281	***	−0.1700	0.016901	***	0.003761
JSCBs, no lag	0.029343	0.002228	***	−0.1202	0.012777	***	0.005004
JSCBs, one-year lag	0.024285	0.001981	***	−0.1025	0.012573	***	0.004394
JSCBs, two-year lag	0.019835	0.001878	***	−0.0852	0.012975	***	0.003455
CCBs, no lag	0.036610	0.007404	***	−0.1522	0.042284	***	0.005269
CCBs, one-year lag	0.028132	0.007226	***	−0.1166	0.045310	*	0.004789
CCBs, two-year lag	0.021677	0.004492	***	−0.0866	0.030065	**	0.004006
Ownership concentration ≤14%	0.028128	0.005874	***	−0.1079	0.033561	**	0.004416
Ownership concentration >14%, ≤40%	0.033972	0.003433	***	−0.1366	0.019191	***	0.005700
Ownership concentration >40%	0.052090	0.005480	***	−0.2257	0.030580	***	0.007958

Notes: Sig. codes: 0 '***' 0.001 '**' 0.01 '*' 0.05 '.' 0.1 ' ' 1.

with closer links to the central and local governments respond more quickly and strongly to reserve requirement hikes. Naturally, this might also be influenced by their liquidity position (but CCBs, as we have seen above, tend to hold the largest percentages of excess reserves as a buffer for constraints on liquidity). In general, large banks have access to ample liquidity and thus under normal situations have no issue to disburse further loans. The RRR is, to a larger extent, a policy signal sent by the central bank and it therefore doubles as another instrument of "window guidance".

The 'signaling hypothesis' is further confirmed by the regression performed under different ownership concentration patterns. More specifically, when looking at the single largest shareholder in each bank for each year (the single shareholder means that the Ministry of Finance will be taken as different from Central Huijin, for example[14]), it becomes clear that the more the first single shareholder holds in the bank's capital, the larger the influence of the reserve requirement changes will be. A shareholder holding a majority in the bank is able to require the bank to review its asset quality quickly and extensively — in line with the requirements of the regulators. The strength of the signal is similar for banks with a large shareholder concentration and those that are SOCBs. They are not necessarily synonymous — many JSCBs have also large ownership concentrations, while this is not the case for CCBs. Some JSCBs are in the hands of large conglomerates while CCBs often have a first shareholder with their local government holding around 20–25%.

We also look at the assumption of the decreasing but still present influence of the state. More specifically, we divide the data set into three time spans — based on the curve of NPLs (see Figure 5): (1) from 2005 to the first half of 2008 (where NPL ratios experience continuous decreases); (2) from end-2008 to 2010 (where NPLs dropped significantly, after ABC restructured its loan portfolio, and remained especially low); and (3) after 2010 (where the NPL ratio remains low and stable).

While the results are less obvious and straightforward for this data set (see Table 9) — maybe due to the number of observations in each period — we still observe that the impact of the RRR has been generally lower in recent years compared to earlier times. Furthermore, the impact on potential asset quality deterioration remains higher than for NPLs, the same as when considering the whole data set. This would confirm the hypothesis that authorities have interfered less in banks' management to induce better loan quality and the RRR has retained a policy signaling effect on banks

Table 9. Robust regression results over different periods (y = asset quality ratios, x = RRR).

	Intercept			Variable			
(x = RRR)	**Estimate**	**Std. Error**	**Sig.**	**Estimate**	**Std. Error**	**Sig.**	**Robust RSE**
y = NPL							
Between 2005 and the first half of 2008	0.040314	0.005405	***	–0.158439	0.041634	***	0.012980
Between 2008 and 2010	0.017180	0.009214	.	–0.038052	0.058008		0.005544
Between 2011 and 2012	0.010160	0.013900		–0.013860	0.070470		0.003024
y = Loan loss provisions							
Between 2005 and the first half of 2008	0.026948	0.003788	***	–0.025398	0.032056		0.009316
Between 2008 and 2010	0.006912	0.010904		0.088656	0.067760		0.007095
Between 2011 and 2012	0.019150	0.021450		0.017040	0.109020		0.004773
y = Special mention loans							
Between 2005 and the first half of 2008	0.0511810	0.007443	***	–0.232495	0.059797	***	0.016610
Between 2008 and 2010	0.0146043	0.016348		0.000364	0.1032388		0.009917
Between 2011 and 2012	–0.0128900	0.033660		0.118930	0.170770		0.006956
y = Potential bad loans							
Between 2005 and the first half of 2008	1.3451000	0.221800	***	–6.781000	1.736300	***	0.319100
Between 2008 and 2010	0.4665000	0.276800	.	–1.015500	1.743000		0.162300
Between 2011 and 2012	0.3738000	0.540700		–0.859600	2.730100		0.107900
y = Concentration to top ten borrowers							
Between 2005 and the first half of 2008	0.5807000	0.075300	***	–2.152200	0.572500	***	0.164500
Between 2008 and 2010	0.8634000	0.185700	***	–3.422600	1.136200	**	0.106000
Between 2011 and 2012	0.0386800	0.293400		0.879000	1.494720		0.056640

Notes: Sig. codes: 0 '***' 0.001 '**' 0.01 '*' 0.05 '.' 0.1 ' ' 1. Ranges based on developments of the NPL ratio as published for the industry by CBRC (see Figure 5).

over the years (i.e., the banks proactively respond to policy messages). Interference through the use of the RRR is less obvious and less common but remains a reality — especially when acting on loans which have a great potential of becoming non-performing. With the RRR, the PBOC can induce a change in behavior in the banks' management of asset quality — but less than before. The fact that it happens less than before could also be due to the fact that asset quality has improved greatly over that time period in the Chinese banking system.

3.3. Impact Under Different Conditions

In a next step, the impact of the RRR is investigated under different conditions: depending on loan growth levels, on disintermediation levels as well as levels of the reserve ratios. As shown in Table 10, the impact of the RRR decreases with higher loan portfolio growth and with higher credit-related off-balance sheet activities. In most cases, the relationship is significant and negative. When portfolio growth is very high, the effect of an RRR increase on asset quality is even

Table 10. Robust regression results based different conditions (y = NPL, x = RRR).

y = NPL, x = RRR	Intercept			Variable			Robust RSE
	Estimate	Std. Error	Sig.	Estimate	Std. Error	Sig.	
Loan portfolio growth ≤60%	0.057494	0.003609	***	–0.2595	0.019858	***	0.005492
Loan portfolio growth >60%, ≤73%	0.034823	0.003753	***	–0.1413	0.021034	***	0.005835
Loan portfolio growth >73%	0.021289	0.008963	*	–0.0779	0.056065		0.005620
Off-balance sheet credit/assets ≤15%	0.050070	0.003919	***	–0.2196	0.024577	***	0.007906
Off-balance sheet credit/assets >15%, ≤28%	0.033494	0.003454	***	–0.1340	0.019327	***	0.005815
Off-balance sheet credit/assets >28%	0.023151	0.003749	***	–0.0912	0.020743	***	0.003136
Reserve requirements ratio ≤10%	0.055900	0.039780		–0.3282	0.489740		0.027770
Reserve requirements ratio >10%, ≤17%	0.035402	0.003464	***	–0.1443	0.019479	***	0.006031
Reserve requirements ratio >17%	0.035850	0.008797	***	–0.1431	0.044820	**	0.003468

Notes: Sig. codes: 0 '***' 0.001 '**' 0.01 '*' 0.05 '.' 0.1 ' ' 1. Loan portfolio growth: yearly growth for each bank; off-balance sheet credit/assets: sum of all credit related off-balance exposures (i.e., off-balance sheet discounted bills, letters of credit, guarantees, credit commitments and credit card limits) divided by unweighted total assets for the same period.

lower. Under those conditions, other things will be at work to impact the NPL ratio: on one side, the growth of gross loan volumes masks changes in NPL ratios and on the other side, regulators will heighten pressure on banks to control asset quality. The same holds for off-balance sheet activities. These activities can be seen as a proxy for the amount of disintermediation that the banks are undertaking. In fact, the larger the disintermediation, the lower the impact of the RRR on asset quality. When banks are lending or acting through other products (such as bills and guarantees), the weight or importance of NPLs and of an appropriate loan quality fades away. With such bills and contingent products, banks shelve exposure off-balance while earning higher interests and fees than on loans. These are not constrained by capital requirements. This is an effective way to reduce undesired exposure. Through the shift to off-balance activities, an increase in NPLs is less likely and asset quality is influenced by the RRR movements to a lesser extent.

3.4. Impact of Excess Reserves

As stated above, banks typically hold large volumes of excess reserves, implying that the effect of the reserve requirement changes will be felt less — at least in terms of liquidity. Therefore, it is also interesting to examine whether the relationship between RRR and NPL holds when considering the reserves of the banks at the central bank instead of RRR (see Table 11). The ratio of actual reserves held by the banks at the central bank to customer deposits is a better variable because they exclude the impact of large excess reserves.

The results are somewhat surprising, since we might have expected that larger actual reserves make loans dearer and thus improve overall asset quality. In terms of significance, the expected sign and residual errors of the results remain similar to when using the RRR; however, the slope differs. In fact, in all cases, the estimates are lower when using reserves than when using the regression with weighted reserve requirements. A plausible hypothesis is that banks consider the RRR movements as a mere signal of policy tightening or loosening — which also infers a different stance of the regulator in terms of macro-prudential policy. Thus, it is not so much the reserves that need to be set aside that impact the availability of credit and thus induces the banks into making better and more careful lending decisions. It seems much more that the RRR creates an expectation in the banks' management regarding which course to take and which measures are appropriate as a result.

Table 11. Robust regression results based on bank type and ownership (y = NPL, x = Reserves ratio).

	Intercept			Variable			
y = NPL, x = Reserves Ratio	Estimate	Std. Error	Sig.	Estimate	Std. Error	Sig.	Robust RSE
All banks, no lag	0.024689	0.003068	***	–0.093311	0.019744	***	0.006625
All banks, one-year lag	0.017322	0.002599	***	–0.053101	0.018597	**	0.005628
All banks, two-year lag	0.013335	0.002898	***	–0.032462	0.022461		0.004491
SOCBs, no lag	0.053248	0.002359	***	–0.224030	0.016425	***	0.006335
SOCBs, one-year lag	0.042360	0.002800	***	–0.179190	0.019620	***	0.006106
SOCBs, two-year lag	0.034520	0.002874	***	–0.148922	0.021666	***	0.004776
JSCBs, no lag	0.024170	0.002253	***	–0.106120	0.015509	***	0.005758
JSCBs, one-year lag	0.019328	0.002185	***	–0.083728	0.016902	***	0.005054
JSCBs, two-year lag	0.015973	0.002556	***	–0.069046	0.022281	**	0.004056
CCBs, no lag	0.024244	0.005029	***	–0.101265	0.032178	**	0.004863
CCBs, one-year lag	0.016748	0.003999	***	–0.058713	0.029951	.	0.004232
CCBs, two-year lag	0.010377	0.003737	**	–0.017149	0.029115		0.003215

Note: Sig. codes: 0 '***' 0.001 '**' 0.01 '*' 0.05 '.' 0.1 ' ' 1.

IV. CONCLUSION

While the setting of the RRR remains a main tool of monetary policy for the PBOC just like other central banks, it is surely also a tool of macro-prudential policy. The RRR is an all-purpose policy tool in China. With one tool, the PBOC can conduct monetary as well as bank regulatory policies.

Chinese banks understand the RRR as a signal for a certain regulatory stance towards asset quality and act accordingly. They do so mainly in the short term by reviewing and restructuring their loan portfolios but are not pressured into improving the quality in depth and over the long term. The further they are from the state, the less interference is felt.

However, the tool has become less useful as a macro-prudential instrument. This points to the possible need for the Chinese regulators to use other more effective ways for banking interventions. In view of the current regulatory arrangement for the financial sector (Cousin, 2011), it is not an option for the Chinese regulators not to intervene. So if the PBOC is to use the RRR for monetary policy anyhow, it can continue to do so as a change in the RRR will not harm the banking sector. Furthermore, using the RRR for directing bank lending into more creditworthy areas is certainly more discrete and elegant than simple window guidance.

Such an approach does not appear very efficient for observers in the developed markets, but it makes perfect sense in the Chinese context. This is true because the Chinese credit market does not price risks correctly and thus does not have a market-based default rate.[15] All Chinese investors and creditors know that the lender of last resort is never far away. Hence, the regulators need more coercive measures to ensure that the lender of last resort is not called upon too often. Regulators need to show that they are efficient and have the proper tools to regulate the banking system in order to gain the confidence of the public and investors, and more tools are better than just one. Therefore, they use all instruments at hand, juggling between administrative (such as the RRR and window guidance) and market measures (such as interest rates setting).

As recently as late January 2013, the PBOC announced that it will add one more arrow to its bow: short-term liquidity operations, which entail (reverse) repurchase agreements between the PBOC and twelve banks (Zhang and Huo, 2013). Thus, it can either pump or restrain liquidity at low costs and swiftly (daily) — even when the RRR remains high. The impact of such a new tool should be followed closely.

Since the relationship between asset quality and RRR is small, and the PBOC uses the RRR purposely for macro-prudential goals, further research should investigate the relationship between the reserves and the capital adequacy of banks — the other pillar of risk management for the bank regulator.

Furthermore, it would also be worth investigating the way that the full set of macro-prudential policies (including ownership levels, loan-to-deposit ratios, etc.) affects the main pillars of bank risk management — asset quality and capital adequacy.

Finally, it has yet to be tested whether the hypothesis of Chinese researchers that bank revenues decrease with higher reserve requirements holds true and how this affects loan portfolio growth.

NOTES

1 A lower (5%) foreign exchange RRR also exists but has much less weight. There is no reserve requirement on other banks' liabilities (i.e., non-deposit ones).

2 A *xun* is a 10-day period. Each month is divided into three *xuns*.

3 Some argue that the effectiveness of the differentiated ratio is rather low since the information on banks is not published and the penalties for not complying are rather low (Wang, 2011). The effect could be larger on banks perceived as systemically important banks.

4 The minimum capital adequacy ratios required by the regulator have increased from 8% to 11%. Over the period considered, the following banks had capital adequacy (Basel I total capital) below the required levels: Agricultural Bank of China (ABC), China Everbright Bank (CEB), Shenzhen Development Bank (SDB, now merging with Ping'An Bank) and Guangdong Development Bank (GDB, now China Guangfa Bank) in 2005, 2006 and 2007 (Evergrowing Bank only in 2007). For ABC and GDB the capital adequacy is assumed to have been below the minimum regulatory levels because the numbers were not published at the time and the banks' asset quality was so poor that the risk weighted capital might have actually been negative. CBRC also requires banks to hold less than 5% of their loan portfolio as non-performing. This was not the case in 2005 and 2006 for ABC, CEB and SDB, in 2007 for ABC and SDB, and in 2008 for BTL and BGZ. No disclosure was made by Evergrowing in 2007 and in 2008 for BCD (All rules according to CBRC, 2004 and 2006).

5 This is in line with the findings of other researchers in other emerging markets (see Terrier *et al.*, 2011; Lim *et al.*, 2011; Vargas *et al.*, 2010; and Montoro and Moreno, 2011). However, these studies concentrate on the quantity of credit available as a result of reserve requirements changes rather than on its quality.

6 A number of articles research the effect of reserve requirements on the quantity of credit (not on the quality), on the macroeconomic and financial stability (e.g., inflation, output gap, nominal exchange rate and house prices) under strains from heavy and sudden capital flows (Agénor *et al.*, 2012; Lim *et al.*, 2011; Terrier *et al.*, 2011).

7 CBRC now defines large institutions as the four SOCBs together with the Bank of Communications. All others are considered small.

8 These are called *yu qi dai kuan* (逾期贷款) in Chinese (for less than 90 days) and also refer to the prior categorization of NPLs previously used in China. Non-performing loans are defined as those overdue for more than 90 days — in line with international reporting practices.

9 For a full and detailed account on the Chinese banking industry, please refer to Cousin (2011) and for more updated information refer to the Economist Intelligence Unit (2012).

10 The word robust refers to two types of robustness: robustness of validity (i.e., resistance of one estimator to unusual observations) and robustness of efficiency (i.e., failure to meet the distributional assumptions of the estimator has little impact on its standard errors) — which is a secondary criterion.

11 For that purpose we have used the lmrob command in the robustbase package in *R*. For further details on the method, we refer the reader to the works stated in the references (e.g., Andersen, 2008; Atkinson and Riani, 2000; Ryan, 2009; and finally, Yohai, 1987) as it would be beyond the scope of the present paper to hold a detailed discussion on robust regression methods and MM-estimation in particular. Further practical details can be found in the packages documentation for the *R* software (e.g., car: http://cran.r-project.org/web/packages/car/index.html, lmtest: http://cran.r-project.org/web/packages/lmtest/index.html, extremevalues: http://cran.r-project.org/web/packages/extremevalues/index.

html and robustbase: http://cran.r-project.org/web/packages/robustbase/index.html).

[12] The breakdown point measures the stability of an estimator. OLS has a breakdown point of $1/n$. Thus, a single outlier can already render the estimates useless. Robust regression estimates can reach 50% breakdown point. Such a high breakdown point is a necessary but not sufficient condition for a good robust estimator.

[13] It is common practice to lend a bullet loan for one year and then extend another follow-up loan without requiring a full repayment of the first loan before disbursing the second.

[14] This makes sense because there have been a number of reports of the Ministry of Finance and Central Huijin acting in different and even opposed ways as shareholders (Hu, 2010). Furthermore, the Ministry of Finance is deemed to have much more clout over banks than Huijin. Generally, the Ministry of Finance is more conservative and more wary of modern banking practices than Central Huijin which has an explicit mandate to reform the banks' management.

[15] The latest developments in the Chinese bond market with the near default of local government bonds which actually regained in pre-eminence and attractiveness are a good example of this situation.

REFERENCES

Agénor, P.-R., K. Alperand and L. Pereira da Silva (2012), Sudden Floods, Macroprudention Regulation and Stability in an Open Economy. Working Paper 267, Banco Central do Brazil.

Andersen, R. (2008), *Modern Methods for Robust Regression*, California: SAGE Publications.

Atkinson, A. and M. Riani (2000), *Robust Diagnostic Regression Analysis*, New York: Springer-Verlag.

CBRC (2004), *Management Rule Regarding Commercial Banks and Transactions with Insiders and Shareholders* [商业银行与内部人和股东关联交易管理办法], Beijing: CBRC.

CBRC (2006), *Core Indicators for the Risk Supervision of Commercial Banks (Trial)*, [商业银行风险监管核心指标 (试行)], Beijing: CBRC.

Cousin, V. (2011), *Banking in China*, Basingstoke: Palgrave Macmillan.

Economist Intelligence Unit (2012), *China Hand — Finance*, March 2012, London: EIU.

Fu, L., H. An and Y. Xu [付亮,安慧琳,徐阳] (2012), Influence of the Reserve Requirements Hikes on the Liquidity of Small and Medium Commercial Banks [存款准备金率上调对中小商业银行流动性的影响]. *Journal of the Economics Institute of Inner Mongolia* [内蒙古财经学院学报], 10(2), pp. 123–125.

Glocker, C. and P. Towbin (2012a), Reserve Requirements for Price and Financial Stability: When Are They Effective? Dir. Gale. des Etudes et des Relations Internationales Documents de Travail — Banque de France.

Glocker, C and P. Towbin (2012b), The Macroeconomic Effects of Reserve Requirements. Dir. Gale. des Etudes et des Relations Internationales, Documents de Travail — Banque de France.

Guo, C. [郭翠荣] (2010), Analysis of the Effect of the Reserve Requirements Policy [存款准备金的政策效应分析]. *Hebei Finance* [河北金融], March, pp. 24–25.

He, D. and H. Wang (2011), Dual-Track Interest Rates and the Conduct of Monetary Policy in China. HKIMR Working Paper No. 21/2011.

Hu, C. [胡采苹] (2010), Huijin Gets Beautiful [汇金换帅], *Caijing Magazine* [《财经》杂志], April 12, 2010.

International Monetary Fund (2011), Macroprudential Policy — An Organizing Framework. Paper prepared by the Monetary and Capital Markets Department (Washington), accessed from: http://www.imf.org/external/np/pp/eng/2011/031411.pdf, November 15, 2012.

Lim, C. F., C. A. Costa, P. Kongsamut, A. Otani, M. Saiyid, T. Wezeland and X. Wu (2011), Macroprudential Policy: What Instruments and How to Use Them? Lessons from Country Experiences. IMF Working Paper 11/238.

Ma, G., X. Yan and X. Liu (2011), China's Evolving Reserve Requirements. BOFIT Discussion Paper 30/2011.

Montoro, C. and R. Moreno (2011), The Use of Reserve Requirements as a Policy Instrument in Latin America. *BIS Quarterly Review*, March.

O'Brien, Y. (2007), Reserve Requirement Systems in OECD Countries, Federal Reserve Papers, accessed from: http://www.federalreserve.gov/pubs/feds/2007/200754/200754pap.pdf, November 15, 2012.

Ostry, J. D., A. R. Ghosh, K. Habermeier, L. Laeven, M. Chamon, M. S. Qureshi and A. Kokenyne (2011), Managing Capital Inflows: What Tools to Use? IMF Staff

Discussion Note 11/06 (2011), accessed from: http://www.imf.org/external/pubs/ft/sdn/2011/sdn1106.pdf, November 15, 2012.

People's Bank of China (PBOC) (1998), Notice on Reforming the Reserve Requirements System [关于改革存款准备金制度的通知]. Rule 118/1998 [银发 [1998]118号].

PBOC (2004a), Notice on the Differentiated Reserve Requirements System [差别存款准备金率制度的通知]. Rule 60/2004 [银发[2004]60号].

PBOC (2004b), Notice of the PBOC on Strengthening the Management of the Reserve Requirements. [中国人民银行关于加强存款准备金管理的通知]. Rule 302/2004 [银发[2004]302号].

PBOC (2006), Quarterly Monetary Report, 2nd Quarter, Beijing: PBOC.

Porter, N. and T. Xu (2009), What Drives China's Interbank Market? IMF Working Paper WP/09/189.

Reinhart, V. and C. Reinhart (1999), On the Use of Reserve Requirements in Dealing with Capital Flow Problems. *International Journal of Finance and Economics*, 4, pp. 27–54.

Ryan, T. P. (2009), *Modern Regression Methods* (2nd ed.), New Jersey: Wiley.

Terrier, G., R. Valdes, C. Tovar, J. Chan-Lau, C. Fernández-Valdovinos, M. García-Escribano, C. Medeiros, M. Tang, M. Vera and C. Walker (2011), Policy Instruments to Lean Against the Wind in Latin America. IMF Working Paper 159, July, accessed from: http://www.imf.org/external/pubs/ft/wp/2011/wp11159.pdf, November 15, 2012.

Tovar, C. E., M. Garcia-Escribano and M. V. Martin (2012), Credit Growth and the Effectiveness of Reserve Requirements and Other Macro-Prudential Instruments in Latin America. International Monetary Fund WP/12/142, June, accessed from: http://www.imf.org/external/pubs/ft/wp/2012/wp12142.pdf, November 15, 2012.

Vargas, H., C. Varela, Y. Betancourt and N. Rodriguez (2010), *Effects of Reserve Requirements in an Inflation Targeting Regime: The Case of Colombia*. Borradores de Economía, No. 587. Banco de la República (Colombia).

Wang, Y. [王勇] (2011), Using the Dynamic Adjustment of the Differentiated Reserve Requirements Well [善用差别存款准备金动态调整]. *Wealth* [《金融博览(财富)》], March, pp. 24–26.

Wen, X. [温秀] (2013), Turning on Loan Growth for 2013 [2013年信贷轻微放水]. *New Century/Caixin* [《新世纪》], accessed 21 January 2013, from: http://magazine.caixin.com/2013-01-18/100484141.html, November 15, 2012.

Xia, C. [夏彩君] (2009), Influence of the Adjustments of the Reserve Requirements on China's Commercial Banks [我国存款准备金的调整对商业银行的影响]. *Though Front* [思想战线], 35, pp. 130–132.

Yohai, V. J. (1987), High Breakdown-Point and High Efficiency Estimates for Regression. *The Annals of Statistics*, 15, pp. 642–656.

Yu, M. [余明] (2009), Analysis of the Impact of the Chinese Reserve Requirements Policy [中国存款准备金政策有效性分析]. *World Economy* [世界经济], 2, pp. 56–65.

Zhang, H. and K. Huo [张环宇, 霍侃] (2013), Like QE but Superior to QE [貌似 QE 胜似 QE]. *New Century/Caixin* [《新世纪》], accessed 28 January 2013, from: http://magazine.caixin.com/2013-01-25/100486299.html, November 15, 2012.

APPENDIX A

Table A.1 List of the banks under this study.

		Listed
State owned commercial banks (SOCBs)		
ICBC	Industrial and Commercial Bank of China	Y
ABC	Agricultural Bank of China	Y
BOC	Bank of China	Y
CCB	China Construction Bank	Y
Joint stock commercial banks (JSCBs)		
BoCom	Bank of Communications	Y
CMB	China Merchants Bank	Y
CITIC	CITIC Bank	Y
SPDB	Shanghai Pudong Development Bank	Y
CMBC	China Minsheng Banking Corporation	Y
Industrial	Industrial Bank	Y
CEB	China Everbright Bank	Y
Huaxia	China Huaxia Bank	Y
SDB	Shenzhen Development Bank (now merging with Ping'An Bank)	Y
Zheshang	China Zheshang Bank	
Bohai	China Bohai Bank	
GDB	Guangdong Development Bank (now China Guangfa Bank)	
Evergrowing	Evergrowing Bank	
City commercial banks (CCBs)		
BSH	Bank of Shanghai	
BCQ	Bank of Chongqing	
BCD	Bank of Chengdu	
BBJ	Bank of Beijing	Y
BHZ	Bank of Hangzhou	
BNJ	Bank of Nanjing	Y
BNB	Bank of Ningbo	
BTJ	Bank of Tianjin	
HSB	Huishang Bank	
PAB	Ping'An Bank (formerly Shenzhen City Commercial Bank)	
BXA	Bank of Xi'an	
BDL	Bank of Dalian	
BGZ	Bank of Guangzhou	
BJS	Bank of Jiangsu	
BBB	Beibu Bay Bank (Guangxi)	
BHK	Bank of Hankou (Wuhan)	

APPENDIX B

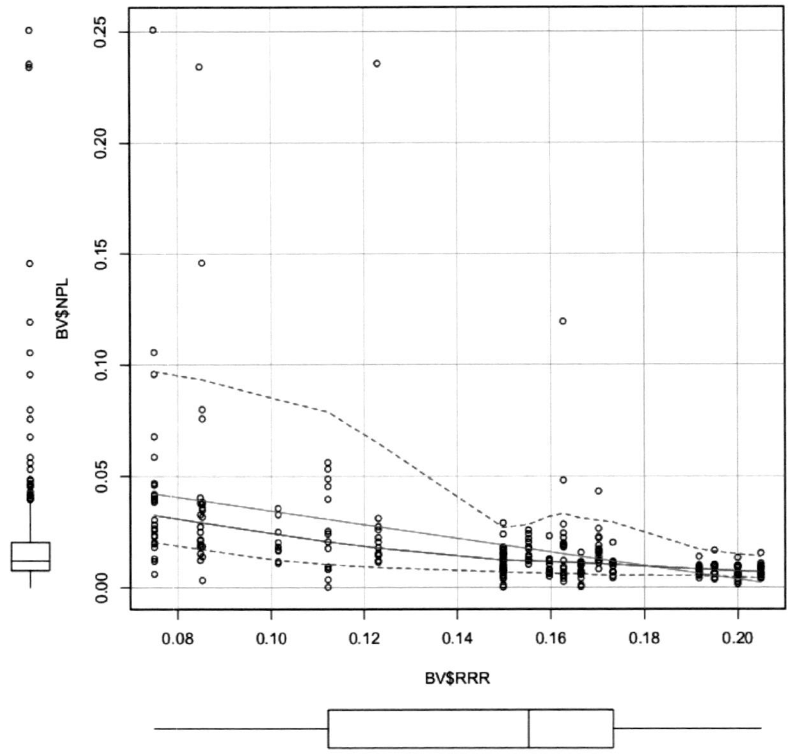

Figure B.1 Scatterplot NPL ratio and RRR.

Notes: Calculations by the author with the *R* package. At the bottom and on the left margins are the box plots and the outlying observations (as points) for each variable. The linear line of best fit and a smoothed (loess) fit line are shown.

APPENDIX C

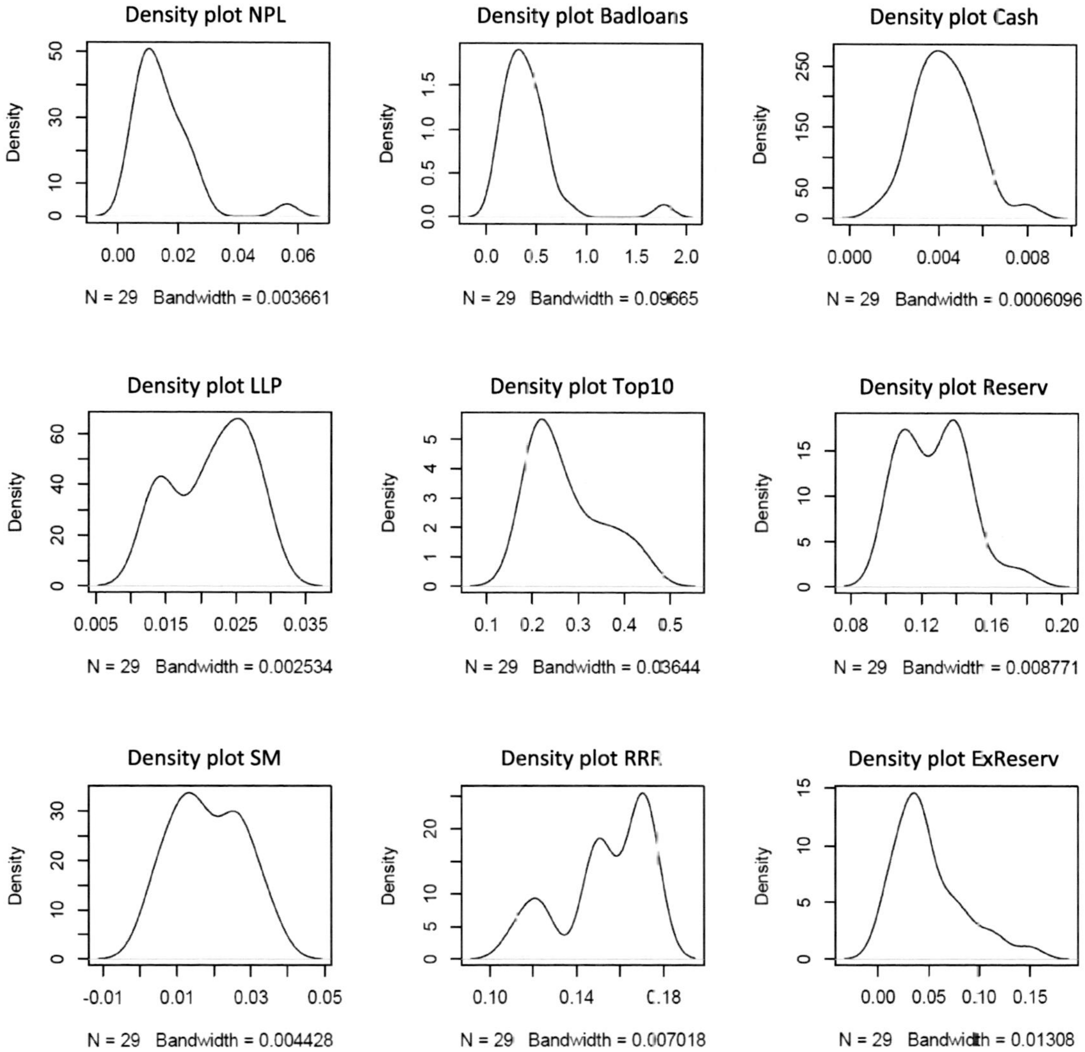

Figure C.1 Density plots.

Notes: Calculations by the author using the *R* package.

APPENDIX D

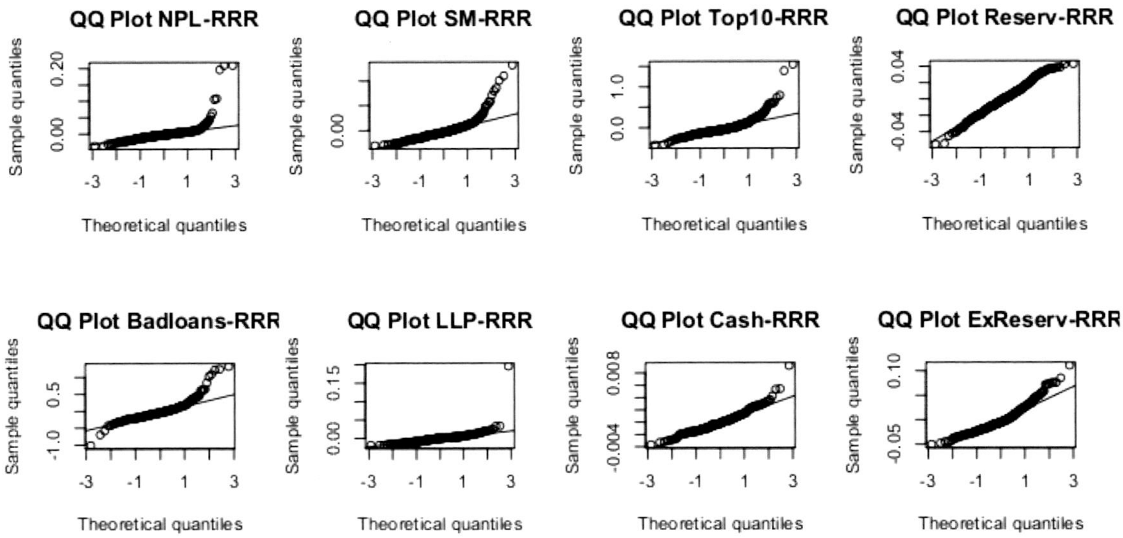

Figure D.1 QQ-plots.

Notes: Calculations by the author using the *R* package.

APPENDIX E

Window Guidance

Geiger states on his website (http://mgeiger.wordpress.com/category/window-guidance/): "The policy of "window guidance" uses benevolent compulsion to persuade banks and other financial institutions to stick to official guidelines. Central banks put moral pressure on financial players to make them operate consistently with national needs."

Before window guidance, credit quotas were defined within the credit plan between 1988 and 1995. The credit plan defined loan volumes to be lent by each bank, and was then broken down at branch level. Enforcement was, however, always an issue and it was thus abolished in 1998. It encouraged credit expansion with no regard to quality. Unfortunately, window guidance works in a similar way, albeit in a more flexible and modern setting, with interference being less thorough.

In fact, the banks define their own lending limits or quotas which they expect to be within bounds acceptable to the central bank and bank regulator; and these are discussed and possibly adjusted where needed. "Window guidance" meetings take place both ways: to increase or to curb loans at large commercial banks in order to either support growth or to keep credit risk in check. In addition, in the case of larger loans, the system works the other way round: banks become simple utilities at the hand of the authorities (such as ministries overseeing a whole industry) which "gently" ask banks to review loans to certain firms or targeted industries or to withdraw their exposure to industries they feel are too risk prone.

Over the years, authorities have chosen not to issue a loan growth target for each year but prefer to intervene in light of monthly disbursement data provided by the banks themselves. In addition, they rely on loan to deposit ratios and capital adequacy requirements to limit growth.

Window guidance is a simple and flexible tool that enables the central bank and other authorities to fine-tune credit growth. Banks that do not comply can be required to buy the PBOC bills or transfer more reserves to the central bank.

The Implementation of the Basel II Default Definition by Credit Risk Assessment Systems: An Analysis of Possible Aggregation Procedures

Dr. Markus Bingmer§
Deutsche Bundesbank,
Frankfurt, Germany
markus.bingmer@bundesbank.de

Dr. Laura Auria*§
Deutsche Bundesbank,
Frankfurt, Germany
laura.auria@bundesbank.de

Keywords: Basel II default definition, materiality, probability of default, aggregation of default information.

*Corresponding author.

§The opinions expressed are those of the authors and do not necessarily reflect those of the Deutsche Bundesbank.

INTRODUCTION

According to Article 18.1 of the Statute of the European System of Central Banks (ESCB), all Eurosystem credit operations must be based on adequate collateral (European Central Bank, 2012, Section 6.1). The Eurosystem Credit Assessment Framework (ECAF) defines the rules, techniques and procedures intended to ensure that the credit quality of collateral for monetary policy operations is adequate. The ECAF considers two kind of collateral as eligible for monetary policy operations: marketable and non-marketable assets. Among non-marketable assets, credit claims play an important role. All eligible collaterals have to fulfill "high credit standards", which means that their expected probability of default (PD) should not be higher than a given benchmark.

The ECAF considers four different rating sources as eligible for assessing the quality of collateral, these are External Credit Assessment Institutions (ECAIs, i.e., rating agencies), Internal Credit Assessment Systems (ICASs) located at national central banks (NCBs), Internal Rating Based systems (IRB systems) from single credit institutes and Rating Tools (European Central Bank, 2012, Section 6.3). Moreover, the ECAF is based on the core principles of consistency, accuracy and comparability which ensure that, independently from the rating source, the credit risk (i.e., the PD of debtors or issuers) of collateral is being accurately evaluated in a comparable and consistent way across the Eurosystem. A unique definition of the default event for all rating sources is of major importance to guaranteeing consistency of output (e.g., the PD). Although this seems obvious, the task of fulfilling this condition is not trivial. Before 2012, the default definition adopted by most of the ICASs in assessing the quality of credit claims was bankruptcy. However, the one adopted by IRB systems was the Basel II definition. According to the ECAF, the reference definition of default to be used within the ECAF from 2012 onwards is the definition used for the IRB systems in the Capital Requirements Directive (CRD, European Parliament, 2006), also known as "Basel II". As can be seen in Box 1, the Basel II default definition is more comprehensive than mere bankruptcy, simply because the event that a company bankrupts, or is unlikely to pay for some reason, or its payment is past due for more than 90 days is more likely to happen than the event that a company becomes insolvent.

Box 1 — Basel II definition of default used within the Eurosystem Credit Assessment Framework, Directive 2006/48/EC.

The CRD — Directive 2006/48/EC — in its Annex VII, Part 4, Chapter 2.1 (European Parliament, 2006), states:

"Point 44:
A default shall be considered to have occurred with regard to a particular obligor when either or both of the two following events has taken place:

(a) The credit institution considers that the obligor is *unlikely to pay* its credit obligations to the credit institution, the parent undertaking or any of its subsidiaries in full, without recourse by the credit institution to actions such as realising security (if held);
(b) The obligor is *past due more than 90 days on any material credit obligation* to the credit institution, the parent undertaking or any of its subsidiaries.

[...] In all cases, the exposure past due shall be above a threshold defined by the competent authorities and which reflects a reasonable level of risk.

Point 45:
Elements to be taken as indications of unlikeliness to pay shall include:

(a) The credit institution puts the credit obligation on non-accrued status;
(b) The credit institution makes a value adjustment resulting from a significant perceived decline in credit quality subsequent to the credit institution taking on the exposure;
(c) The credit institution sells the credit obligation at a material credit-related economic loss,
(d) The credit institution consents to a distressed restructuring of the credit obligation where this is likely to result in a diminished financial obligation caused by the material forgiveness, or postponement, of principal, interest or (where relevant) fees. This includes, in the case of equity exposures assessed under a PD/LGD approach, distressed restructuring of the equity itself;
(e) The credit institution has filed for the obligor's bankruptcy or a similar order in respect of an obligor's credit obligation to the credit institution, the parent undertaking or any of its subsidiaries; and
(f) The obligor has sought or has been placed in bankruptcy or similar protection where this would avoid or delay repayment of a credit obligation to the credit institution, the parent undertaking or any of its subsidiaries."

Although the Basel II default definition for IRB systems is very detailed, the prescription to adopt it within the ECAF implies several practical implementation problems for non IRB systems. While IRB systems directly use information on default events regarding their own credit claims, the other eligible ECAF rating sources have to collect information from different banks or different creditors regarding the same debtor. For example, ICASs mostly collect within a credit register, and thus have to aggregate this information to a unique default/non-default label for every single debtor.

This paper focuses on the aggregation problem of default events, especially from the point of view of national ICASs. As one will see, there are different possibilities to aggregate this information. The aim of this paper is not to give a conclusive position on the optimal aggregation method, but to provide a simplified formal framework to analyze the consequences of different aggregation methods on the basis of previously stated goals and given assumptions. Ideally, for an ICAS, the aggregation method should guarantee output consistency with the other eligible rating sources, especially the IRB systems, and result accuracy.

In the following, Section 1 clarifies the task of aggregating default information and the connected problems. In Section 2, a possible formalization of the aggregation task is introduced and different aggregation procedures are assessed (also on the basis of some hypothetical examples). Section 3 relies on German data and empirically shows the impact of different aggregation methods on the estimated PD by selecting different materiality thresholds. Finally, Section 4 concludes the paper and summarizes the results.

I. THE TASK OF AGGREGATING DIFFERENT DEFAULT REPORTS

Credit risk can be assessed by means of different methodologies. Traditional models like linear discriminant analysis (Fisher, 1936; McLachlan, 2004), logistic regression (Hosmer and Lemeshow, 2000) as well as non-parametric methodologies like support vector machines (SVM, Vapnik, 1995)[1] aim at optimally separating into two groups of defaulted and non-defaulted companies by means of a univariate score function based on available information, such as financial figures of the companies. The score is then mapped by a monotone "link" function to the PD. Raters other than single banks using IRB systems (hence forth IRB banks), however, often get many different dichotomous default reports (e.g., default or non-default) for the same obligor (e.g., in the case of an ICAS, a non-financial company) from different loaners (e.g., credit institutes). Figure 1 is based on data from the German credit register and categorizes obligors by the number *N* of German IRB banks that have reported on each obligor for the period 2010–2011. Here, only eight companies have more than 50 reporting banks. For 4% of the companies, the number of reporting banks is between 3 and 10. Most of the companies (79%) have only one bank reporting to the credit register. This means that for 21% of the companies, more than one bank reports about their default or non-default status.

Non-IRB rating sources thus have the important problem of aggregating the default reports to a single default or non-default statement. But aggregation is only reasonable if all loaners use the same default definition, which is the case for banks using IRB systems.[2] In the following, we assume that all reporting banks use the same default definition (e.g., the Basel II definition of default for IRB systems).[3] Although the definition is the same, it is possible that there are different responses to an obligor by different banks. Thus, the determination of the default label by the NCB is not always clearly defined.

Table 1 shows an example of the aggregation task, using default information of four different banks and ten different obligors. Red cells (with an X) mark default events. The task is only obvious in the case of obligors 4 and 7. Here, all the banks report the same and the NCB can easily classify the obligor. But how should the information be aggregated for the other obligors?

The use of different default aggregation methods results in different default labels for the same

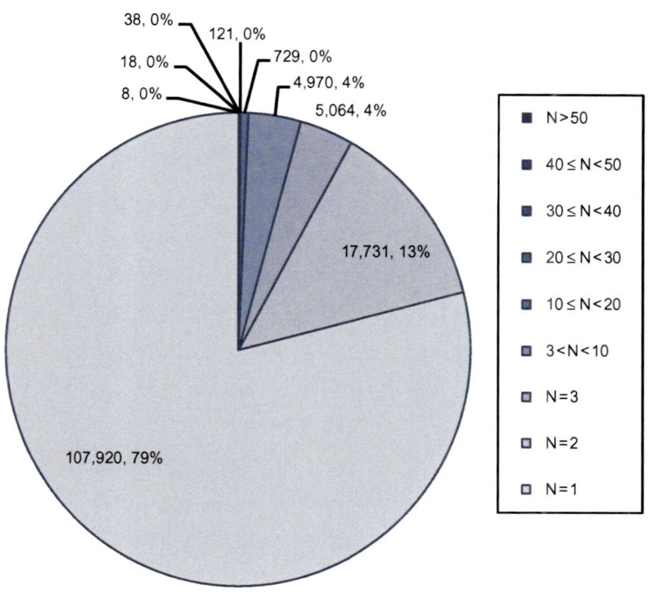

Total number of companies: 136,599.

Figure 1. Structure of data dispersion 2010–2011.
Note: Distribution of companies with reference to the number of reporting IRB banks (*N*).
Source: Data from the German credit register.

Table 1. An example of the aggregation problem of NCBs.

	Bank A	Bank B	Bank C	Bank D	NCB
Obligor 1	X			X	?
Obligor 2	X				?
Obligor 3	X	X	X		?
Obligor 4					
Obligor 5		X			?
Obligor 6		X			?
Obligor 7	X	X	X	X	X
Obligor 8			X		?
Obligor 9			X	X	?
Obligor 10				X	?
Default rate	4/10	4/10	4/10	4/10	?

Notes: Ten obligors belonging to the same risk category have loans at four different banks. If the loan is defaulted, the cell is marked with X. In this scenario, the NCB can only definitely classify obligors 4 and 7. If there are different default indications for an obligor, the aggregation of the default information by the NCB, and as a consequence the default rate, is not clearly defined.

company, which in turn leads to different default rates on a given portfolio and finally different PD estimates. In the next section, a possible formalization of the aggregation task will be introduced and used to assess the consequences of different aggregation methods.

II. A THEORETICAL ANALYSIS OF THE AGGREGATION TASK

In the following, we introduce a formal framework with simplified assumptions to study different aggregation methods. For the first steps, credit amounts and materiality are purposely ignored, but they are considered in Section 2.4.

Let Y_{ij} be the default indicator of bank j for company i and $i \in \{1,\ldots,n\}$. This means that Y_{ij} is a binary random variable (i.e., $Y_{ij} \in \{0,1\}$) with $Y_{ij} = 1$ if the loan of company i defaults at bank j and $Y_{ij} = 0$ if the loan does not default at this bank. Furthermore, $p_{ij} := P\ (Y_{ij} = 1)$ is the (usually) unknown PD, and thus Y_{ij} is Bernoulli distributed with probability p_{ij} for 1 and $1 - p_{ij}$ for 0. Since company i typically has loans at k_i different banks, there is a vector of default indicators $Y_i := (Y_{i1}, Y_{i2},\ldots,Y_{ik_i})'$ for company i (the inverted comma means to take the transpose of the row vector).

In this setting, an aggregation procedure is a mapping g defined as:

$$g\colon\{0,1\}^{k_i} \to \{0,\ 1\}$$
$$Y_i \to Z_i := g(Y_i)$$

which transforms the vector of default indicators Y_i to a single binary indicator Z_i. In fact, a NCB needs a single default statement for each company (whether the company defaults or not). Since Y_i is a random vector and in this case g is a measurable function, Z_i is also a random variable. The choice of g defines the aggregation procedure which implies the event of a default and thus influences the number of defaults for the NCB. This implementation has a direct impact on the PD.

We make the following assumptions:

1. $p_{ij} = p_i\ \forall j \in \{1,\ldots,k_i\}$;
2. $Y_{i1}, Y_{i2},\ldots,Y_{ik_i}$ are independent;
3. $k_i = k\ \forall i$.

The first assumption, that company i has the same (true but unknown) PD at all banks, seems to be reasonable, because the true but unknown PD of an obligor should only depend on the obligor and not on the loan-giving bank (issuer-specific and not issue-specific). Of course, it is possible for a company to have preferences to default on banks with whom they have less favorable terms, and continue their relationship with banks who grant them more favorable terms, but this would mean that we have a contract-specific PD. Assuming that these effects should be negligible, the true unknown PD should be the same for all banks even though the PD estimated by the individual banks may be different. The other assumptions are mainly for ease of computation. In reality, there should be a strong positive correlation among the default indicators of different banks on the same company. Because if the company defaults at one bank, it is likely that it also defaults at others. Another reality is that companies do not have loans at the same banks and the number of loaners is likely to be different across companies (see Figure 1). But for the sake of computational simplicity, all companies are assumed to have loans at the same k banks.

For an appropriate choice of g, the goals of the NCB have to be specified. The most important goal is typically to prevent the banking system from major losses. Thus, an underestimation of the PD should be avoided, because that would imply more defaults than expected. Although a conservative PD estimate is preferred, a too conservative method reduces the amount of eligible collateral. This is obviously due to the fact that a conservative method typically overestimates the PD. So for a company with low credit risk and whose credit claims represent an eligible collateral for the NCB, it may suddenly not be creditworthy any more if the aggregation method becomes more conservative. Thus, the NCB should strive to be consistent with the banks in the market and to estimate the PD in a way consistent with these banks.[4] Therefore, we would like to have:

$$P(Z_i = 1) = p_i \tag{1}$$

which means that company i has the same PD for the NCB as for the individual banks. Later, we will show how this is possible. We begin by introducing different aggregation procedures and discussing to which extent they fulfill these previously mentioned goals.

2.1. Using the Default Information of a Single Bank

A trivial and simple aggregation procedure is given by using only default information of a single bank. This means that:

$$Z_{i1} := g_1(Y_i) := Y_{i1} \quad (2)$$

and we choose Y_{i1} without loss of generality. In fact, given the above-mentioned assumptions, we can take an arbitrary (random) bank j, if we do not want to prefer a particular one. In this case, the distribution of Z_{i1} does not change, because Y_{ij} are identically distributed for all $j \in \{1,\ldots,k\}$. Although procedure g_1 does no real aggregation (instead of aggregating the information, it actually omits information), it has the advantage of being consistent with the PD of the banking system because $P(Z_{i1} = 1) = P(Y_{i1} = 1) = p_i$.

In practical terms, this method does not leverage on the information advantage of a NCB. As can be seen in Table 1, the default rate of the NCB is the same as the one of the chosen bank (in this case, 4/10 for all banks). Under the Law of Large Numbers, the default rate is a consistent ML estimation of the true PD of the given risk category only in the case that the number of debtors within the banking system is sufficiently high ($n \to \infty$). In this case, the NCB will have the same expected default rate as the single banks if the portfolios of these are the same (see assumptions 1–3).

2.2. Considering All Defaults

Another possible aggregation procedure, which is very popular in practice, is to define a company as defaulted, if it defaults for at least one bank. In our setting, this means that:

$$Z_{i2} := g_2(Y_i) := \max\{Y_{i1}, Y_{i2}, \ldots, Y_{ik}\}. \quad (3)$$

The underlying probability that the indicator shows a default is given by:

$$\begin{aligned} P(Z_{i2} = 1) &= P(\max\{Y_{i1}, Y_{i2}, \ldots, Y_{ik}\} = 1) \\ &= 1 - P(\max\{Y_{i1}, Y_{i2}, \ldots, Y_{ik}\} = 0) \\ &= 1 - P(Y_{i1} = 0, \ldots, Y_{ik} = 0) \\ &= 1 - (1 - p_i)^k, \end{aligned}$$

which is the complement probability of having no defaults at all k banks. Thus, this probability is at least as large as p_i ($k = 1$) and in general even larger ($k > 1$).

Furthermore, for increasing k, this probability converges to 1, i.e.,

$$\lim_{k\to\infty} 1 - (1 - p_i)^k = 1,$$

which has the intuitive explanation that as the number of loaners increases, the probability to default at least at one of them does as well. In particular, for small p_i and k, the PD of the NCB increases almost linearly (this means $P(Z_{i2} = 1) \approx kp_i$). So in summary, g_2 represents a conservative procedure, because $P(Z_{i2} = 1) > p_i$ for $k > 1$. Thus, the underlying PD of the default indicator of the NCB is larger than the underlying PD of the IRB banks.

Table 2 shows an application of the aggregation method defined in Equation (3) on the example from

Table 2. A possible aggregation method for the NCB.

	Bank A	Bank B	Bank C	Bank D	NCB
Obligor 1	X			X	X
Obligor 2	X				X
Obligor 3	X	X	X		X
Obligor 4					
Obligor 5		X			X
Obligor 6		X			X
Obligor 7	X	X	X	X	X
Obligor 8			X		X
Obligor 9			X	X	X
Obligor 10				X	X
Default rate	4/10	4/10	4/10	4/10	9/10

Note: The NCB regards the obligor as defaulted, if it is in default for at least one bank. Here, the NCB has a larger default rate than the individual banks.

Table 1. Here, the NCB observes a larger default rate (9/10) than the individual banks (4/10). While a single bank only considers the event that the obligor defaults on its specific loan, the NCB regards the event as a default of the obligor at any reporting bank.

To conclude this section, the procedure of regarding an obligor as defaulted if it is in default for at least one loaner represents a conservative method of aggregation, because it systematically assigns larger PDs than individual banks. For a very high number of reporting banks this probability converges to 1, which is also valid in the presence of dependent default indicators for the same obligor as long as they do not have a correlation of one.

2.3. Building a Default Indicator Based on the Binomial Distribution with the Goal of Consistency

Before introducing a third method, we note that it is irrelevant on which bank an obligor defaults, but it is important on how many banks it defaults. This information can be expressed by the stochastic variable $S_i := \sum_{j=1}^{k} Y_{ij}$ which under assumptions 1–3 is binomially distributed with parameters k and p_i. Since S_i is a binomial variable, its outcome is given by the natural number $s \in \{0,\dots,k\}$. Each of the outcomes of S_i has a probability of occurrence determined by the following binomial function[5]:

$$B(s;k;p_i) = P(S_i = s) = \binom{k}{s} p_i^{\,s}(1-p_i)^{k-s}. \qquad (4)$$

The previous aggregation method in Equation (3) can be equivalently written as:

$$g_2(Y_i) = I_{\{S_i \geq 1\}}$$

where I is an indicator function taking on a value of one if $S_i \geq 1$ and zero otherwise. Our goal is to find an aggregation method g_3 which fulfills:

$$p_i \leq P(g_3(Y_i) = 1) \leq 1 - (1 - p_i)^k \qquad (5)$$

and is thus less conservative than g_2 (in the ideal case it should be close or equal to the lower bound p_i). A possible solution is to choose a threshold $b_i \in N$ (here N represents the set of natural numbers) so that we have a decision criteria:

$$Z_{i3} := g_3(Y_i) = I_{\{S_i \geq b_i\}}. \qquad (6)$$

The value b_i represents the number of default reports of different banks (given a total number of k banks) that a NCB has to count before it defines company i as in default. If we choose:

$$b_i := \max\{s \in \{1,\dots,k\} : P(S_i \geq s) \geq p_i\}, \qquad (7)$$

it fulfills the above requirements defined by the inequality in (5). This threshold b_i always exists because at least $s = 1$ is feasible. In other words, the probability that a company defaults at least at one bank is always larger than or equal to p_i.

Figure 2 shows the resulting b_i for different combinations of k and p_i. b_i is derived from the binomial distribution in Equation (4) as the maximum number of defaults s, which guarantees that the probability of having s or more defaults (for a given k) is not smaller than the true PD, p_i, of a single company. Thus, b_i/k represents the proportion of default reports on a single company that a NCB needs to classify the company as a default without underestimating its true PD.

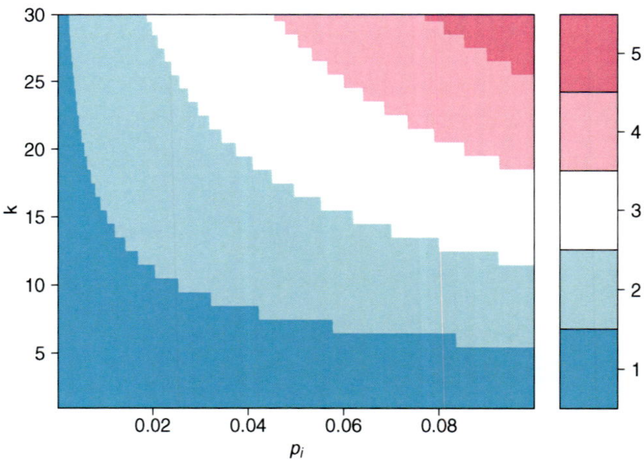

Figure 2. Value b_i derived for different combination of p_i and k.

Notes: If one of them becomes large, b_i will increase. On the other hand, for small values of p_i and k, b_i will be equal to 1.

It is noted that for companies with very small PDs (e.g., $p_i < 0.004$), the value of b_i equals one unless the number of loans a company has at different banks k is extremely large. Thus, there is no improvement as compared to the aggregation method g_2. But for larger PDs, the value of b_i increases. This result has interesting implications. It means that for a given number of reporting banks, k, in the case of better rating classes with a low expected PD, a low number of defaults will be sufficient to put the debtor in a default status at the NCB, if the NCB does not want to underestimate the PD of the company with respect to its true p_i. If the number of reporting banks is high, which is the case for bigger companies, or if the true PD is high, a consistent PD estimation from the viewpoint of the NCB will need an aggregation process which requires a higher number of defaults.

Table 3 shows a trivial application of the above-mentioned aggregation method (for $k=4$ and $p=0.4$ for all obligors). According to the binomial distribution, the required b should equal 2. Therefore, all companies which defaulted at two or more banks are also regarded as in default by the NCB. In this example, the NCB observes a default rate equal to anyone of the banks. In contrast, method g_2 can only guarantee the fulfillment of the inequality in (5).

The most interesting result of this analysis is that the percent of companies which should default before a NCB classifies a company as in default depends on the risk category of the company when the goal of aggregation is consistency with the PD of the reporting banks. Although one may want to adopt different b's for different PDs, the PD of a company is unknown in advance. Thus, a NCB should first rely on the previous estimation of PD in order to adjust the required b.

Moreover, the aggregation methodology described above does not consider the actual loan amount in default. If $b > 1$ and only one bank reports a default, the event will not be counted as a default by the NCB. But if the loan amount in default is large relative to the total loans of the company, this default will be very relevant to the NCB and the banking system. On the other hand, classifying a company as in default if a very small proportion of its total credit amount has defaulted at one bank could also lead to undesirable consequences. In the following section, more information such as the defaulted credit amount will be added to the discussion.

Table 3. An example of the aggregation problem of NCBs.

	Bank A	Bank B	Bank C	Bank D	NCB
Obligor 1	X			X	X
Obligor 2	X				
Obligor 3	X	X	X		X
Obligor 4					
Obligor 5		X			
Obligor 6		X			
Obligor 7	X	X	X	X	X
Obligor 8			X		
Obligor 9			X	X	X
Obligor 10				X	
Default rate	4/10	4/10	4/10	4/10	4/10

Notes: In this scenario, the NCB regards the obligor as defaulted, if it is in default for at least half of the reporting banks ($k/2=2$). Here, the NCB has the same default rate as the individual banks. Indeed if $k=4$ and $p=4/10$, then according to the binomial distribution and the third aggregation method $b=2$.

2.4. Considering Materiality of Defaults

For a credit institution, it is not only relevant to determine whether a debtor defaults or not, but also important to see whether a default is "material". As shown in Box 1, the CRD states a Basel II default as "the obligor is past due more than 90 days on any *material* credit obligation to the credit institution". German law has implemented the IRB-default definition of the CRD in the Solvency Regulation § 125 (Solvabilitätsverordnung, SolvV); here, materiality is required both for "90 days past due" as well as for "unlikeliness to pay" (German Federal Ministry of Finance, 2006). For 90 days past due, it is made concrete by the condition that "the current overall obligation of that obligor exceeds the current advised limit by more than 2.5 percent [...]".

Analogous to the rules for the IRBs, a NCB should not only rely on binary default information (1 = default or 0 = non-default), but also consider the effective amount in default when aggregating default reports. For a NCB, it is less relevant as to how many banks reported a default on a company than how much of its total credit volume is in default. Tables 4 and 5 show examples with more information on the value of the loans. Here, defaults are marked in red. In Table 4, the amount in default (100) is large in comparison to the total loan amount (102) of the companies. Thus, the NCB should regard the obligors as in default.

In Table 5, we observe the opposite situation where only a very small proportion of the total loans is in default (1/201). Thus, there is no need for the NCB to regard the obligor as in default.

These examples show the difficulty in comparing the default rates of NCBs and individual credit institutions. In both tables, the default rate of the individual banks equals one-third. Although the default pattern does not change between the two examples, there are totally different results for the

Table 4. An example of the aggregation problem of NCBs.

	Bank A	Bank B	Bank C	NCB
Obligor 1	100	1	1	100/102
Obligor 2	1	100	1	100/102
Obligor 3	1	1	100	100/102
Default rate	1/3	1/3	1/3	3/3

Notes: The numbers represent the loan volume of the obligors at specific banks. In the case of a default (red cells), the credit volume should be regarded as a total loss. The NCB collects all information and can determine the amount in default in relation to the total loans. Because of a large proportion, the NCB counts 3 defaults.

Table 5. An example of the aggregation problem of NCBs which is similar to Table 4.

	Bank A	Bank B	Bank C	NCB
Obligor 1	1	100	100	1/201
Obligor 2	100	1	100	1/201
Obligor 3	100	100	1	1/201
Default rate	1/3	1/3	1/3	0/3

Note: In this case, the NCB does not count any default, because only a small amount of the loans of each obligor is in default.

NCB. In the first case, the NCB has a default rate of 100% which is larger than any one of the individual banks and agrees with the result of the second aggregation method (see Section 2.2). In the second case, no defaults are counted and the default rate of the NCB is smaller than any one of the individual banks. In the following, 'small' and 'large' default proportions shall be translated into a mathematical form analogous to the SolvV definition of materiality.

Still in the theoretical setting of the previous sections (1. A company has the same PD at all banks; 2. The default events are independent between banks; and 3. All companies have loans at the same banks), we introduce some additional formal structure. We suppose that behind each default indicator Y_{ij}, there is a random variable X_{ij} which influences the outcome of Y_{ij}. Let v_{ij} denote the total credit amount company i has at bank j and D_{ij} be a random variable which represents the amount that has defaulted (thus $D_{ij} \in [0, v_{ij}]$). Then, we define $X_{ij} := \frac{D_{ij}}{v_{ij}}$, representing the random proportion of the loan which has defaulted. Thus, X_{ij} is also a random variable with $X_{ij} \in [0,1]$. As stated before, a German bank regards an obligor as in default, if at least 2.5% of the loan volume is in default. Thus, we can write $Y_{ij} = I_{\{X_{ij} \geq 0.025\}}$ where I is an indicator function with the value of one if $X_{ij} \geq 0.025$ and zero otherwise. Since Y_{ij} depends on X_{ij}, it can be expressed as $Y_{ij}(X_{ij})$.

Although we have not made any assumptions regarding the distribution of D_{ij} or X_{ij}, we know that:

$$P(X_{ij} \geq 0.025) = P(I_{\{X_{ij} \geq 0.025\}} = 1) = P(Y_{ij} = 1) = p_i \tag{8}$$

and thus $P(X_{ij} < 0.025) = 1 - p_i$. Furthermore, we assume that the expectation and the variance of X_{ij} exist and are given by μ_{ij} and σ_{ij}^2 respectively. Although we can assume an almost arbitrary distribution for X_{ij}, there are already some limitations for its expectation μ_{ij}. The expectation is large if the mass of the distribution of X_{ij} is concentrated on the right side of the unit interval [0,1], and small if it is concentrated on the left. Thus, it is maximal if $X_{ij} = 1$ in the case of default with probability of occurrence

p_i, and if X_{ij} is close to 0.025 in the case of non-default with probability of occurrence $(1 - p_i)$. For the expectation being minimal, the weight of $(1 - p_i)$ has to be on 0 and the weight p_i on 0.025. It follows that:

$$0.025p_i \leq \mu_{ij} < 0.025(1 - p_i) + p_i.$$

With this additional structure new aggregation methods can be formalized and already used methods further specified.[6] For this purpose we define the proportion in default (PID) for obligor i as:

$$PID_i := \frac{\sum_{j=1}^{k} D_{ij}}{\sum_{j=1}^{k} v_{ij}} = \frac{\sum_{j=1}^{k} X_{ij} v_{ij}}{\sum_{j=1}^{k} v_{ij}}. \tag{9}$$

A possible aggregation method is given by:

$$Z_{i4} := g_4((X_{i1},...,X_{ik})) = I_{\{PID_i \geq m\}} \tag{10}$$

whereas $m \in (0,1]$ is called the materiality threshold. If $PID_i \geq m$, then the default is said to be "material". Defaults which are not material are not regarded as a default by the NCB. Thus, the materiality threshold plays an important role, because it has a direct impact on the number of default events and the estimated PD. For example, assuming that $m_1 < m_2$, then the PD is larger using a threshold of m_1 in contrast to a threshold of m_2, because a default with a materiality threshold of m_1 happens more easily than a default with a threshold of m_2. So which threshold should be chosen? If a NCB should not be more or less conservative than the banks in the market, it would be natural to use the same material threshold which is used by banks, that is 2.5% (i.e. $m = 0.025$).[7] Does the choice of the same threshold guarantee consistency of PDs?

For ease of investigation of g_4 we make some additional assumptions for our theoretical setting:

4. $D_{i1}, D_{i2},\ldots,D_{ik}$ are independent identically distributed (i.i.d.);
5. $v_{ij} = v_i \; \forall j \in \{1,\ldots,k\}$, that is, the credit volume at each bank is equal;
6. X_{ij} or D_{ij} is reported for all i and j by the banks.

Thus, $X_{i1}, X_{i2},\ldots,X_{ik}$ are also independent and identically distributed. Of course, companies typically have different credit volumes at different banks, the defaulted amount will not be independent and banks do not report a default if $X_{ij} < 0.025$. But with these assumptions PID_i can be rewritten as:

$$PID_i = \frac{\sum_{j=1}^{k} X_{ij} v_i}{\sum_{j=1}^{k} v_i} = \frac{1}{k}\sum_{j=1}^{k} X_{ij} =: \bar{X}_i,$$

which is the average defaulted credit proportion of the banks. Finally, we can summarize the aggregation rule (10) as:

$$Z_{i4} = g_4((X_{i1},...,X_{ik})) = I_{\{\bar{X}_i \geq 0.025\}}. \tag{11}$$

Since we would like to consider the materiality of defaults, we cannot only rely on the binomial distribution. Without making any further assumptions on the distribution of X_{ij}, what can we say about $P(Z_{i4} = 1)$? If all X_{ij} are at least as large as m (which happens with probability p_i^k), then that is also the case for $\bar{X}_i$. But because there are also other possibilities for $\bar{X}_i$ being larger than m, it follows that $P(Z_{i4} = 1) \geq p_i^k$. On the other hand, we get an upper bound by the same argument. If all X_{ij} are smaller than m, then $\bar{X}_i < m$ (which happens with probability $(1 - p_i)^k$). Since there may be combinations where only some X_{ij} have to be smaller than m, for $\bar{X}_i$ being smaller than the materiality threshold, then $P(Z_{i4} = 0) \geq (1 - p_i)^k$. Thus, the complementary relation is $P(Z_{i4} = 1) \leq (1 - p_i)^k$. Finally, we obtain the inequalities:

$$p_i^k \leq P(Z_{i4} = 1) \leq 1 - (1 - p_i)^k.$$

Since we also have $p_i^k \leq p_i \leq 1 - (1 - p_i)^k$, then $P(Z_{i4} = 1)$ can be larger or smaller than p_i.

Now, we have the tools to derive some conclusion on the relation between p_i and the $P(Z_{i4} = 1)$; that is, the consistency of the underlying PD of the NCB with the p_i of the banking system. We write $\bar{X}_i^{(k)} := \frac{1}{k}\sum_{j=1}^{k} X_{ij}$ and know that the expectation of $\bar{X}_i^{(k)}$ is given by μ_i (still assuming that $X_{i1}, X_{i2},\ldots,X_{ik}$ are i.i.d.) and the variance by σ_i^2 / k. Thus, the variance is decreasing for increasing k, and the distribution of $\bar{X}_i^{(k)}$ becomes more and more concentrated on μ_i (due to the Law of

Large Numbers). We can distinguish the two following cases:

i) If $m < \mu_i$, then there exists a $k_0 \in N$ with

$$P\left(\overline{X}_i^{(k)} \geq m\right) \geq p_i, \quad \forall k \geq k_0.$$

ii) If $m > \mu_i$, then there exists a $k_0 \in N$ with

$$P\left(\overline{X}_i^{(k)} \geq m\right) \leq p_i, \quad \forall k \geq k_0.$$

Table 6. An example of the aggregation problem of NCBs considering the credit volume.

	Bank A	Bank B	Bank C	Bank D	NCB
Obligor 1	25/1000	0/1000	0/1000	25/1000	50/4000
Obligor 2	25/1000	0/1000	2/1000	15/1000	25/4000
Obligor 3	25/1000	3/100	3/100	20/1000	31/2200
Obligor 4	1/100	1/100	1/100	1/100	0/400
Obligor 5	0/100	3/100	3/1000	50/1000	3/2200
Obligor 6	0/1	250/10000	3/1000	50/1000	250/12001
Obligor 7	2.5/100	2.5/100	2.5/100	2.5/100	10/400
Obligor 8	2/100	2/100	40/1000	2/100	40/1300
Obligor 9	1/1000	2/1000	500/1000	500/1000	1000/4000
Obligor 10	0/1000	23/1000	24/1000	1000/1000	1000/4000
Default rate	4/10	4/10	4/10	4/10	4/10

Notes: Numbers in the numerator indicate the defaulted amount and numbers in the denominator the total credit volume at each single bank as well as at an aggregated level at the NCB. The NCB collects all information and can determine the amount in default in relation to the total loans. It only counts the defaulted amount if the reporting banks set the debtor into a material default. Here, default labels and default rates may vary quite clearly from the ones of the previous aggregation methods, according to the distribution of the credit volume among the reporting banks.

Furthermore, in both case we have:

$$\lim_{k\to\infty} P\left(\overline{X}_i^{(k)} \geq m\right) = y, \quad \text{with } y \in \{0,1\},$$

with y = 1 in the first case and y = 0 in the second. So for small p_i, we would also expect μ_i to be small. If it is smaller than m and k is large, then the PD of the NCB is smaller than the PD of the IRB banks. On the other hand, for large p_i, we would also expect μ_i to be large. If it is larger than m, then the PD parameter of the NCB is larger than the PD of the IRB banks.

Table 6 shows the same example as in the previous sections but factoring in the credit volume information. There are two numbers in every cell where the numerator represents the defaulted amount and the denominator represents the total credit amount. If all banks report the same default or non-default (obligors 4 and 7), and all of them have the same materiality, then the NCB has the same materiality result as the single banks. However, this will mostly not be the case in reality.

In summary, although aggregation method g_4 considers materiality of defaults, it is less conservative than g_2 and may overestimate or underestimate the true PD. This heavily depends on the distribution of X_{ij}, involving the relation between the materiality threshold m, the expectation for the average defaulted credit proportion of the banks μ_i, the number of reporting banks k and the true p_i. To conclude this section, Table 7 shows the advantages and disadvantages of the different aggregation methods.

Table 7. Summary of the advantages and disadvantages of the different aggregation methods.

Aggregation Method	Advantages	Disadvantages
g_1: Take a random single bank	– Consistent with PD of banking system	– Not considering all information – Not considering all material defaults
g_2: Count any default with a single bank	– Risks are minimized – Considers all defaults	– Larger PDs than individual banks – Reduces availability of collateral
g_3: Minimum number of defaults derived from the binomial distribution	– Less conservative than counting all defaults	– Needs the unknown PD – Does not consider the defaulted credit volume
g_4: Consider materiality of defaults	– Considers the defaulted credit volume – Considers material defaults	– Probability of the default event for the NCB can be larger or smaller than the PD of the single banks, depending on the materiality threshold, the true PD of the company, as well as the distribution of the defaulted credit amount

III. AN EMPIRICAL ANALYSIS OF AGGREGATION WITH THE MATERIALITY THRESHOLD

In this section, the impact of different materiality thresholds m on the estimated PD for German data is empirically investigated. The data set contains financial figures for year 2010 on 16,203 German non-financial companies. For each company i, a score value s_i is available, which is a function of r different financial ratios, i.e.,

$$s_i = f(ratio_{i,1},\ldots,ratio_{i,r}),$$

summarizing relevant information in the financial statements. The score used is the result of the credit risk analysis at the ICAS of the Deutsche Bundesbank consisting of several modules. First, a discriminant analysis is performed, and then an expert system modifies the resulting score. Finally, an optional support vector machine module is applied (for additional details see Auria and Paul, 2012).

The default events are split into two categories:

- "hard defaults" (which represent bankruptcy of the company); and
- "soft defaults" (which represent all other kinds of defaults according to Basel II).

During the year 2010, 47 out of 16,203 companies became bankrupt and 169 additional soft defaults were reported. Information collected from the credit register also includes the credit volume, which is used by the NCB to calculate the "materiality".

As mentioned in the previous section, company i is only regarded as in default if $PID_i > m$. So the number of deemed soft defaults depends on the materiality threshold m. A large threshold means fewer events deemed as default. For the ease of exposition, we will refer to soft defaults only if the NCB classifies a company in default not due to bankruptcy.

Figure 3 shows an example of this situation based on the German data set. In the case of $m = 0.025$ (which represents the Basel II threshold for IRB banks) there are about 160 soft defaults whereas for $m = 0.5$, only 70 remain to be soft defaults which is a reduction of about 56%.[8] Furthermore, a difference of 90 defaults in relation to the total number of companies in the sample may seem small, but this can have a large impact on the PDs of all companies.

This is demonstrated by using a logistic regression model. For this purpose the PD is modeled by means of the link function to the given score as:

$$P(Z_{i4} = 1 \mid s_i) = \frac{\exp(\beta_0 + \beta_1 s_i)}{1 + \exp(\beta_0 + \beta_1 s_i)}.$$

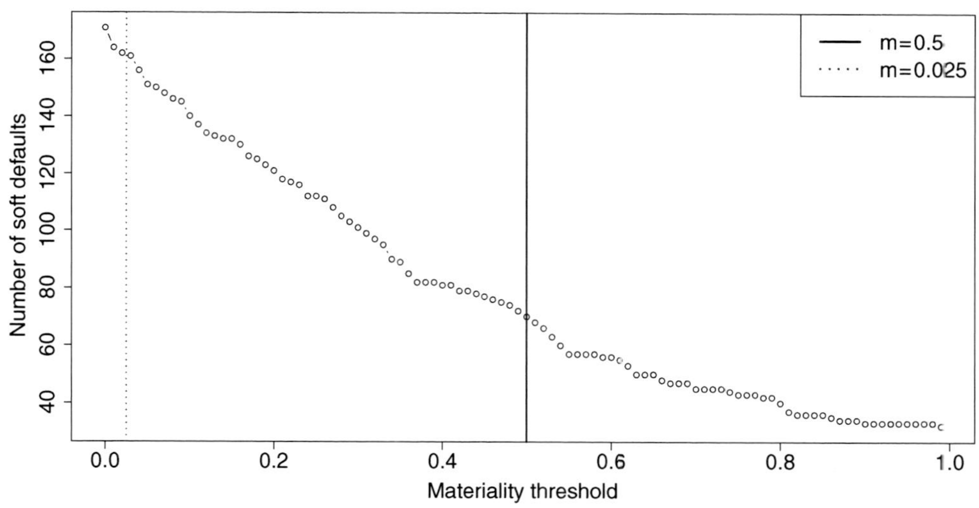

Figure 3. Number of soft defaults and the materiality threshold m.

Notes: The number of soft defaults (all kind of defaults without bankruptcy) depends on the materiality threshold m. An increase of the threshold results in a decrease of the number of defaults, because not all default events are counted.

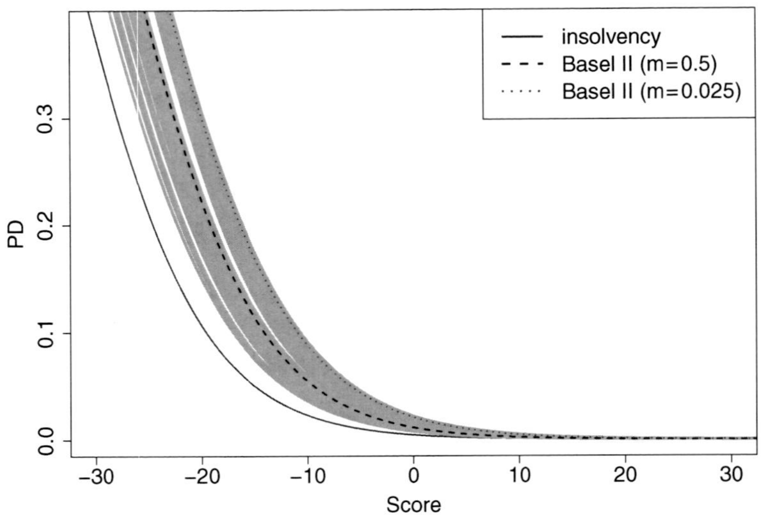

Figure 4. Logit–PD curves using the score variable in combination with different default definitions and materiality thresholds *m*.

Figure 4 shows the consequences on the estimated PDs by using different materiality thresholds. The solid line represents the PD curve resulting from the default definition using only insolvencies and the dotted line represents the PD curve resulting from the Basel II default definition with a materiality threshold of $m = 0.025$. As expected, the dotted lines are above the solid one, because it is more likely to have a Basel II default than bankruptcy. Furthermore, the grey area represents possible PD curves when taking $m \in (0,1]$ and the dashed line is based on the materiality threshold of $m = 0.5$. Although an increase of m from 0.025 to 0.5 affects 'only' the default status of 90 out of 16,203 companies, it affects the estimated PD of all companies.

As seen in the previous section, under the goal of a consistent PD estimate with the banking system, the choice of the proper materiality threshold should depend on the true p_i for the companies of a portfolio and the distribution of the defaulted credit amount. By pursuing consistency with the banking system, the materiality threshold should be lower for higher credit qualities than for worse rating categories.

IV. CONCLUSION

This paper analyzes the issues and consequences related to applying the Basel II default definition for IRB banks to other rating sources like national ICAS. For this purpose, four different aggregation methods are introduced in a mathematical framework that includes the method of counting all defaults as well as the procedure of considering materiality of defaults. All methods are explained by examples (Tables 1–6), and the pros and cons are discussed (Table 7).

As demonstrated, the observed default rates for a NCB are highly affected by the way observed defaults for individual credit institutions are aggregated at the level of the NCB. Although the definition of a Basel II default for IRB banks is very detailed, there are no rules determining how a NCB should aggregate this information. But the aggregation method critically influences the default rate of a given portfolio and thus typically affects the estimated PDs.

The goals of (1) consistent output among the different Eurosystem rating sources, (2) preventing the banking system's losses, and (3) ensuring accuracy of results, are a valuable reference for the choice of the aggregation method. There is no "right" or "best" aggregation method, because all of them have advantages and disadvantages with respect to these goals (see Table 7). The method of counting all defaults or the procedure of considering materiality of defaults will prevent the banking system's losses. However, the underlying probabilities of the default event using these methods will typically not be the same as the PDs of the reporting IRB banks. This paper demonstrates that the adoption of "materiality" helps in defining meaningful results, but consistency between the PD by the NCB and the PD of the reporting IRB banks depends on the credit quality of the analyzed collateral and the distribution of the defaulted credit amount.

Further research is needed on this topic by relaxing some of the assumptions used in this article, such as the independence of default events for the same company at different loaners or the assumption of having the same credit volume at every bank. Research along this line should refine our understanding, but the general qualitative conclusions reached in this paper should stand.

NOTES

1 For an overview on the SVM methodology and a comparison of the three above-mentioned methodologies, see, for example, Fassbender and Auria (2010).

2 Non-IRB systems, however, use a different default definition according to the CRD, which does not contain all elements stated in Box 1.

3 For this reason, the following empirical analysis will be only based on the reports of IRB banks.

4 Of course, by estimating the PD the NCB should be accurate, but accuracy relies on the comparison between the default rates and the PD, the default rates being dependent on the default aggregation process. So the first step is to choose an appropriate aggregation method and then estimate the credit risk assessment model accurately.

5 Whereas in the classical binomial case default events are being counted for different companies, here default events are being counted for the same company at different banks. Assumption 2 is in our case more restrictive.

6 For example, using the second aggregation method, Z_{i2} equals one if at least one X_{ij} is larger than 0.025.

7 In the ideal case, the NCB has full information and knows for every obligor and for every bank the defaulted amount of the loan and the total loan value. Unfortunately, full information is not usual and sometimes the NCB only knows the total loan amount of each bank and if there has been a default or not. This means, if an amount of 4 out of 50 has defaulted, the NCB gets the message that there is a loan with a total value of 50 and a default has happened.

8 Although $m = 0.5$ seems quite large, there are concrete examples (mostly still internal statements within the banking supervision or other national central banks) using this materiality threshold.

REFERENCES

Auria, L. and N. Paul (2012), Die Bonitätsanalyse der Deutschen Bundesbank (BBk) im Rahmen des Europäischen Sicherheiten-Rahmenwerks für geldpolitische Operationen, in O. Everling, J. Leker and S. Bielmeier (eds.), *Credit Analyst*, München: Oldenburger Verlag. pp. 125–150.

European Parliament, 2006/48/EC, Capital Requirements Directive (CRD).

European Central Bank, Eurosystem (2012), The Implementation of Monetary Policy in the Euro Area, General Documentation on Eurosystem Monetary Policy Instruments and Procedures.

Fassbender, M. and L. Auria (2010), Support Vector Machine as a Multivariate Statistical Technique for the Assessment of Credit Risk — A Comparison with Classical Techniques as Linear Discriminant Analysis and Logit Based on Deutsche Bundesbank Data, in R. Böhmler (ed.), *30 Jahre Fachhochschule der Deutschen Bundesbank, Festschrift*, Frankfurt am Main: Deutsche Bundesbank. pp. 375–396.

Fisher, R. (1936), The Use of Multiple Measurements in Taxonic Problems. *Annals of Eugenics*, 7, pp.179–188.

German Federal Ministry of Finance, 2006, *Regulation Governing the Capital Adequacy of Institutions, Groups of Institutions and Financial Holding Groups (Solvency Regulation (Solvabilitätsverordnung, SolvV))*, as last amended by Article 1 of the Regulation Amending the Solvency Regulation (Verordnung zur Änderung der Solvabilitätsverordnung) of 23 December 2009 (Federal Law Gazette I, p.3971), 14 December 2006.

Hosmer, D. and S. Lemeshow (2000), Applied Logistic Regression, 2nd edition. New York: John Wiley & Sons.

McLachlan, G. J. (2004), *Discriminant Analysis and Statistical Pattern Recognition*, Wiley Interscience.

Vapnik, V. (1995), *The Nature of Statistical Learning Theory*, New York: Springer.

Can Credit-Scoring Models Effectively Predict Microloans Default? Statistical Evidence from the Tunisian Microfinance Bank

Dr. Ibtissem Baklouti
Faculty of Economics and Management
University of Sfax, Tunisia
bakloutiibtissem@yahoo.fr

Prof. Abdelfettah Bouri
Faculty of Economics and Management
University of Sfax, Tunisia
abdelfettah.bouri@fsegs.rnu.tn

Keywords: Credit scoring, micro-credit default risk, logistic regression, Tunisian microfinance bank.

INTRODUCTION

Two major objectives targeted by microfinance institutions (MFIs) are: (1) serving economically disadvantaged clients with relatively small loans; and (2) maintaining self-sustainability or profitability (Robinson, 2001).

In so far as micro-entrepreneurship credit granting is concerned, conventional tools such as analysing financial statements or payment histories are unsuitable because they are typically not available. On serving the poor, MFIs are most often forced to determine the potential credit risk incurred by lending based on the loan officers' impressions and subjective value judgment regarding the customer's likelihood to have financial problems. Under the pressure of high demand for micro-credits, many MFIs conclude that it is neither practical nor cost-effective to train and maintain an adequate staff of experienced credit evaluators. Achieving self-sustainability without external subsidies will thus be difficult as costs are high and margins are small (Bumacov and Ashta, 2011; Dellien, 2003; Kuhn and Olsen, 2008; Schreiner, 2003; Viganò, 1993). In addition, MFIs cannot apply high interest rates as this would compromise the targeted social objectives and prevent the poor from getting the much needed credit assistance, particularly for those living in rural areas (Morduch, 1999). To overcome such dilemmas, extensive efforts to lower the operating costs (i.e., time and manual credit-processing costs) are seen as appropriate solutions. It is obviously vital for MFIs to improve the efficiency of their portfolio risk management as well as to apply accurate pricing policy, because those will help them achieve a better equilibrium between self-sustainability and expansion of outreach. In this respect, some MFIs have responded by developing certain credit-scoring models, which provide an objective risk-assessment tool and represent an alternative to other ways of increasing operational efficiency and decreasing operating costs. According to Schreiner (2004), credit scoring consists of using what is known from the past to forecast what might take place in the future. It compares known characteristics or facts about the borrowers and loans with similar past cases in order to estimate the credit risk posed by potential borrowers. Although this method is not at all new for the conventional banking sector, it constitutes an innovation for MFIs. Since the late 1990s, credit scoring began to gradually find its way to the microfinance field (Simbaqueba *et al.*, 2011).

Many descriptive or non-quantitative studies have highlighted the applicability of credit scoring to MFIs. For instance, Simbaqueba *et al.* (2011) concluded that the credit-scoring system may be a technology meant for improving micro-lending significantly. In particular, they advanced two arguments in favor of applying credit scoring as a credit risk management tool for MFIs. First, they argued that the credit-scoring model is the perfect solution to maintain self-sustainability, which would, consequently, facilitate the expansion of outreach with few additional resources. Second, they noted that credit-scoring models reduce the effects of discrimination and prejudice by individual loan officers, which will increase the outreach and regain the lost profit margins that would occur when good-credit applicants were rejected. However, Simbaqueba *et al.* (2011) contended that the scoring technique can be more efficient only if all borrowers form a homogeneous population and the environment is stable to ensure that similar credit behavior will prevail on future borrowers.

In practice, credit-scoring models have been used by a number of microfinance organizations: ACCION (in Bolivia, Ecuador, and Peru); Women's World Banking (in Colombia and the Dominican Republic); two World Savings Bank Institute (WSBI) members — Banco BCSC (in Colombia) and Banco Estado (in Chile); Crediamigo (in Brazil); Credit Indemnity (in South Africa), etc. With respect to scientific studies, evidence regarding the credit-scoring models for MFIs is still at an embryonic stage and opinions on its applicability diverge. Although some researchers highlight the necessity of implementing a credit-scoring model in MFIs (e.g., Viganò, 1993), other specialists think that it is difficult to adapt such an approach and incorporate it as an integral part of credit risk assessment in the context of microfinance (Schreiner, 2004; Van Gool *et al.*, 2011). While credit-scoring models have been successfully applied in retail banking, whether MFIs can benefit from credit-scoring models remains an open question.

Using a database of 156 microcredits granted by two Tunisian MFIs, Ben Soltane and Trigui (2008) examined the factors that affect default among borrowers. They find that the age of the borrower, the nature of business, the borrower's business experience, the length of repayment period, the degree of credit rationing, and the wealth of the borrower are negatively related to default rates; whereas the legal status of the business, the guarantor, the rate of indebtedness of the borrower, the loan size, and the presence of other lending institutions are positively related to default rates. In this article, we go beyond Ben Soltane and Trigui (2008) by checking whether using a scoring model amounts to an effective approach. We test the applicability and merits of credit scoring with regard to the Tunisian microfinance sector. The second aspect distinguishing the present work from Ben Soltane and Trigui (2008) lies in using a larger sample of Tunisian microcredits to reach more accurate parameter estimates. Our results show that a credit-scoring model can reduce loan defaults in MFIs but it is not yet able to entirely replace the human-intensive microfinance credit process. Actually, credit-granting decisions in microfinance must be jointly based on the credit-scoring result in collaboration with MFIs' credit officers.

The remainder of this paper is structured as follows. Section 1 presents a literature review on credit scoring in MFIs and presents a thorough analysis of the reported strengths and weaknesses related to credit scoring for microfinance. Section 2 defines the relevant data and describes the methodology. The results are presented in Section 3, followed by a discussion on the applicability of a credit-scoring model to the MFIs. Finally, Section 4 gives concluding remarks and paves the way for potential further studies.

I. CREDIT SCORING IN MICROFINANCE INSTITUTIONS: THE LITERATURE

Viganò (1993) has pioneered the application of a credit-scoring model to a rural development bank in Burkina

Faso, in a bid to predict the creditworthiness of entrepreneurs that are the most difficult to evaluate. She suggested that a suitable creditworthiness analytical tool is crucial to bank management in a development setting and it will help manage the principal-agent problem. Viganò (1993) proposed a quantitative model of creditworthiness based on a multivariate discriminant analysis to identify the determinants which can be weighted in the loan evaluation process. She used a database of 100 observations collected through questionnaires and direct interviews with loan officers. The input comprises 53 variables, including the borrower's personal characteristics, borrower's relationship with the bank and data on the enterprise. The result shows that the scoring model has accurately classified 77% of the 100 applications. In particular, the model has managed to correctly classify 91.84% of the 49 applications in the category of bad credit applications and 62.75% of the 51 applications in the category of good credit applications. Hence, she concludes that applying relatively simple credit-scoring techniques to the development bank proves to have quite good performance, particularly with regard to the reduction of Type I errors.

The study conducted by Viganò (1993) has opened a way for further research on the credit-scoring applicability in the microfinance sector. Schreiner (2004) investigates whether micro-lenders in poor countries could take advantage of scoring systems. He proposed a credit-scoring model based on a logistic regression to predict the probability that micro-lender loans issued in Bolivia would go 15 days or more overdue. The data consists of 39,956 loans provided to urban individuals engaged in trade and manufacturing. His result shows that factors such as the business sector, loan size and past repayment behavior are significant in the probability of overdue loans faced by a Bolivian micro-lender. In addition, he concludes that the credit-scoring model proves to have enough predictive power to significantly enhance the evaluation performance of the microcredit applicants' credit risks, though it is less powerful than most scorecards used for the issuance of credit cards. He concludes that credit scoring is a marked improvement in the microfinance area, but it complements — rather than substitutes — loan officers and their subjective evaluations.

In the same context, Vogelgesang (2003) analyzed repayment determinants for loans issued by Caja Los Andes, a microfinance Bank in Bolivia. He focused on the period 1996–2000 which is characterized by an increasingly strong competition and supply of microcredits, high levels of indebtedness, and the onset of an economic crisis. Vogelgesang (2003) hypothesized that credit-scoring models allow for a cautious selection of clients and thus permit MFIs to retain high repayment levels in a more competitive environment. She developed a credit-scoring model based on a bivariate probit estimation using information relevant to 8,002 customer loans. The independent variables are divided into four categories: personal characteristics, information about the clients' businesses, the loans' terms and conditions, and information about the market environment. In her study, two regression models were developed; in the first, she used as dependent variable loans with few late payments (one day overdue) and in the second model, loans with more late payments was used (at least ten days overdue). She found that clients with loans simultaneously obtained from multiple sources are more likely to default than others and customers in areas with intense competition and microloan supplies (*ceteris parisbus*) have an overall better repayment behavior. She also discovered that the credit-scoring model's discriminatory power appears to be relatively low. For instance, when using a threshold value of 15%, the model has just been able to correctly classify 59.7% of all observations.

Van Gool *et al.* (2011) have further extended microfinance credit-scoring applications by developing and evaluating two logistic regression models, using data retrieved from a Bosnia–Herzegovinian microlender. For the sake of a proper comparison, Van Gool *et al.* (2011) assessed the credit-scoring models' performance for microfinance in terms of stability, readability and discriminatory power.[1] The discriminatory power is measured by means of the area under the receiver operating characteristic curve (AUC), while most other papers have used percentage correctly classified (PCC) or (pseudo-) R^2. Van Gool *et al.* (2011) have noted that the AUC measure has not been reported before by the credit-scoring studies for microfinance. In their paper, the authors used information pertaining to 6,722 individual loans, divided into a 70% training set (4,705 entries) and a 30% test set (2,017 entries). The dependent variable is devised on the basis of expert advice obtained from the

Bosnian micro-lender, which defines a bad customer as having an average of a two-day delay in paying back the installments. In total, 16 explanatory variables have been considered in this study, classified into three major categories: borrower, loan, and lender characteristics.[2] To analyze the applicability of credit scoring for micro-lenders, Van Gool *et al.* (2011) considered two binary logistic models, one based on dummy-coded variables and the other based on the weight-of-evidence coded variables.[3] In terms of prediction accuracy, the result indicates that the out-of-sample AUC falls at the lower end of previous credit-scoring studies on credit cards, consumer loans, etc. Therefore, they concluded that the discriminatory power of a fully automated credit-scoring system for microfinance is too weak to fully replace the human-intensive microfinance credit process.

More recently, using a database of 5,500 borrowers from a Peruvian MFI, Blanco *et al.* (2013) have developed a credit-scoring model by using a multilayer perceptron neural network (MLP) specially designed for the microfinance industry. The independent variables are divided into 4 categories: personal characteristics (marital status, gender, etc.), the microenterprise economic and financial ratios, characteristics of the current financial operation (type, interest, amount, etc.), and variables related to the macroeconomic condition. In addition, they compared the performance of the MLP model against linear discriminant analysis (LDA), quadratic discriminant analysis (QDA), and logistic regression (LR). They found that the multilayer-perceptron credit-scoring model offers the better fit for MFIs, achieves higher accuracy and lowers misclassification costs as compared to the classic LDA, QDA and LR models. They concluded that MFIs can benefit from credit-scoring models to attain an increase in efficiency, a reduction in costs, and an improvement in professional image.

Several authors have discussed the benefits of credit scoring by MFIs. First, the credit-scoring model helps expedite credit approval decisions. Allen (1995) showed that the time taken in the loan approval process with credit scoring has decreased from two weeks to 12 hours per small-business loan. Furthermore, it helps reduce arrears and thus less effort is needed for collecting overdue payments from delinquent borrowers.[4] This greater efficiency improves both the MFI's outreach and its sustainability. In this regard, Schreiner (2003) advances that loan officers can use this time-saving device to search for more eligible borrowers, improving both depth and breadth of outreach. In his Bolivian-related study, Schreiner (2001) suggests that rejecting the riskiest 12% of loans disbursed in the year 2000 would have reduced the number of loans overdue for 30 days by 28%.

Second, a credit-scoring model allows the adjustment of interest rates and fees to reflect the credit risk (risk-based pricing) (Dennis, 1995; Kulkosky, 1996; Kuhn and Olsen, 2008; Schreiner, 2003). The scoring model serves to objectively identify the most important risk factors. This allows the development of more effective advanced risk-management systems, leading to a quantitative risk culture (Freytag, 2008; Schreiner, 2005; Van Gool *et al.*, 2011). Furthermore, by making the criteria more explicit, credit scoring is likely to help reduce loan officers' misjudgement in matters of evaluation, thus minimizing human bias in the credit decision process (Dennis, 1995; Kuhn and Olsen, 2008; Schreiner, 2005). Finally, the advantage of scoring lies in its "trialability", as it can be tried out in a low-cost manner via "back-testing" (Schreiner, 2005).

While several authors have evaluated the advantages of credit scoring, some others have argued that credit scoring is subject to several limits. First, the credit-scoring technique cannot model risks such as unwillingness to repay and inability to repay due to natural catastrophes (Freytag, 2008; Schreiner, 2003; Van Gool *et al.*, 2011). Ignoring qualitative factors and blindly applying a credit-scoring framework in the microfinance context can lead to inaccurate evaluations and hence to high arrears and more defaults. Second, credit scoring for microfinance requires a large amount of high-quality data on many loans, which many lenders cannot provide (Dellien, 2003; Freytag, 2008; Schreiner, 2004). Besides, installing the credit-scoring model will incur a large fixed cost. Success in credit scoring requires periodic updating and persistent training for people using it (Schreiner, 2003). Indeed, credit-scoring models need constant updating because as time goes by, populations will undergo certain changes which get reflected in the distribution of credit applications. A credit-scoring model's predictive power might be lost if such changes are not incorporated into the model. Finally, according to Simbaqueba *et al.* (2011) and Cornée (2009), the credit-scoring technique cannot give an adequate ruling on a borrower's creditworthiness if the project to be funded is too innovative, in which case it becomes an uncertainty rather than a risk.

II. DATA AND MODEL

2.1. Sample Selection and Variables Identification

A dataset of 5,022 credit applications granted between 2004 and 2009 is provided by the Tunisian Microfinance Bank (39.7% turned out to default and 60.3% performed well). Having such a large sample is necessary to build our credit scoring model. 3,348 observations (two-thirds of the total sample) have been randomly selected as the training sample, while the remaining 1,675 applications (one-third of the total sample) are retained for validation. The dependent variable is created on the basis of the institution's expert advice, which defines "bad" borrowers (defaulters) as those who have not repaid their loans by the due date (legal follow-up). The dependent variable represents the customer's credit status, taking a value of 1 if a borrower has defaulted and 0 otherwise. The choice of the explanatory variables depends largely on data availability. In this study, ten independent variables are divided into three groups: socio-demographic, loan-characteristic and credit-behavioral. Table 1 below describes all the independent variables used in this study, together with their reference symbols, classification and description.

In developed financial markets, lenders are prohibited from discriminating against borrowers on the basis of gender, amongst other factors. Microfinance

Table 1. Variables overview.

Variable	Variable Description
Borrower-Demographic Variables	
X_1 = Borrower's age	≤23 (X_{11}), 24–25 (X_{12}), 26–34 (X_{13}), 35–40 (X_{14}), 41–45 (X_{15}), >45 (X_{16})
X_2 = Borrower's gender	Male (X_{21}), female (X_{22})
X_3 = Marital status	Single (X_{31}), married (X_{32})
X_4 = Educational level	Low educational level (X_{41}), graduate and higher educational level (X_{42})
X_5 = Job experience (in years)	<2 (X_{51}), 2–4 (X_{52}), 4–7 (X_{53}), > 7 (X_{54})
Loan-Characteristic Variables	
X_6 = Credit amount	≤1935 (X_{61}), [1936, 2399] (X_{62}), [2400, 3598] (X_{63}), [3599, 4349] (X_{64}), [4350, 4998] (X_{65}), [4999, 5918] (X_{66}), [5919, 8832], (X_{67}), >8832 (X_{68})
X_7 = Credit purpose	Business creation (X_{71}), business extension (X_{72})
X_8 = Business sector	Agriculture (X_{81}), services(X_{82}), artisanal (X_{83}), small trades (X_{84})
Credit-Behavioral Variables	
X_9 = Number of previous loans	Two loans (X_{91}), one loan (X_{92}), new customer (X_{93})
X_{10} = Previous loans default	New customer (X_{101}), all credits paid back duly (X_{102}), delay in paying off in the past (X_{103})

Notice that our continuous variables have been discretized by converting them into categorical ones, with dummy variables assigned to each category. If we use linear models like logistic regression, the discretization of continuous variables can help capture the non-linear relationship between the attributes and the dependent variable, and allow the model to capture non-monotonic patterns in particular. Discretization also helps to eliminate the problem of extreme values. In addition, as noted by Tufféry (2011), discretization improves the logistic model robustness by grouping individuals together, because coefficients can be uncertain if the number of individuals is small. The discretization process of continuous variables can be based on expert knowledge existing among the financial institution staff. However, the common approach of discretization of continuous variables into categorical ones is statistically based. The categorization of a continuous variable can be chosen so that the default risk in the created categories is as homogeneous as possible within certain categories but quite different within other categories. Tufféry (2011) noted that there is no universal way to discretize continuous variables. The CHAID decision tree is used to determine the categories (Thomas, 2000). In our dataset, we have two continuous variables: "age of the borrower" and "credit amount". To capture the non-linear and even non-monotonic behavior of these variables, we have converted the continuous variables into categorical ones by using the CHAID decision tree.

seems to be far from such rules. In micro-lending, the borrower's profile greatly affects the credit-scoring profile. As a matter of fact, qualitative information is much more relevant than quantitative data, given the absence or unreliability of book-keeping practices (Viganò, 1993).

2.2. Model Description

Several methods can be used to develop the credit-scoring system. Historically, statistical techniques have been widely used, including discriminant analysis (DA), logit and probit models. Many authors have concluded that the logistic regression yields a superior classification accuracy compared to DA (Blanco *et al.*, 2013; Lee *et al.*, 2002; Ohlson, 1980; Wiginton, 1980).

Both logit and probit techniques model probabilities, which are easier to interpret than the output of a DA model. Although they often yield similar results, the logit model assumes that the default probability is a logistic function of a linear combination of the explanatory variables, while the probit model assumes that the probability of default is determined by a normal distribution function where any linear combination of the explanatory variables is assumed to be normally distributed. Owning to the fact that many categorical variables in this study cannot be normally distributed, the logit model is more suitable for our purpose (Abdou *et al.*, 2008).

As the acceptance of a credit-scoring method highly depends on its accuracy, transparency and economic interpretability, the logistic regression method also seems most natural. Thus, we have adopted a binary logit model:

$$\log\left(\frac{P_i}{1-P_i}\right) = \beta_0 + \beta_1 X_1 + \beta_2 X_2 + \cdots + \beta_n X_n \quad (1)$$

where the dependent variable is the logarithm of the odds, $\log\left(\frac{P_i}{1-P_i}\right)$; P_i is the default probability; β_0 is the intercept and β_i, $i=1, 2,\ldots,n$, are the regression coefficients; and X_i, $i=1, 2,\ldots,n$, are the explanatory variables.

The purpose of applying a logistic regression model in credit scoring lies in determining the conditional probability of a specific observation belonging to a default class, given the values of the independent variables defining a credit application. This probability can be written as:

$$P_i = \frac{e^{\beta_0+\beta_1 X_1+\beta_2 X_2+\cdots+X_n}}{1+e^{\beta_0+\beta_1 X_1+\beta_2 X_2+\cdots+X_n}}. \quad (2)$$

III. EMPIRICAL RESULTS

3.1. Univariate Analysis

An overview of the variables, their distributions and the default frequencies is provided in Table 2. As can be seen in this table, most of the loans are granted to borrowers aged between 26 and 34. The default frequency increases in the early stage of life and then declines in the later stage. Concerning the borrower's gender, the result shows that men make up the largest share of this Tunisian MFI's clients. This confirms results of other studies showing that women face more difficulties than men in terms of accessing credit (Buvinic and Berger, 1990; Godquin, 2004). It is also worth noting that the default frequency is slightly higher for the unmarried borrowers than for the married ones. A large portion of this MFI's clients do not hold any graduate or higher-educational degree: about 88% of the borrowers have reached a low educational level and only 12% of them are graduates. Interestingly, borrowers who do not have a high-educational level are more likely to pay back their loans; that is to say, default frequency rises with the increase of education level. Regarding the borrower's job experience, one can conclude that the majority of loans are granted to the most experienced borrowers (48.2%). Default frequency drops with an increase in this variable, i.e., with more knowledgeable customers. With respect to credit amount, the results indicate that the default rate varies with the loan amount, ranging from 16.2% for the highest loan amount (7th class) to 62.9% for the lowest loan amount. Moreover, most of the loans are provided to the business-creation undertakings (80.90%), though no difference in the default payment rates between the business-creation and business-extension projects can be noticed. Table 2 also highlights that credits granted to finance agricultural projects have the lowest default rate (1.2%). With

Table 2. Descriptive statistics.

Variable	Value	Percentages (%)	Default Frequency (%)
Borrower's age	≤23	11.8	33.2
	24–25	8.2	40.4
	26–34	40.5	46.0
	35–40	20	41.5
	41–45	9.8	32.2
	>45	9.7	24.3
Borrower's gender	Male	75.1	38.8
	Female	24.9	42.5
Marital status	Single	51.8	44.1
	Married	48.2	34.9
Educational level	Lower educational level	87.9	35.2
	Graduate and higher educational level	12.1	72.0
Professional experience	<2 year	5.2	55.7
	2–4 years	25.9	44.3
	4–7 years	20.7	39.6
	>7 years	48.2	35.5
Credit amount	≤1935	10	62.9
	[1936,2399]	9.2	48.3
	[2400,3598]	20.8	48.4
	[3599,4349]	10.1	37.0
	[4350,4998]	10	28.0
	[4999,5918]	10	44.0
	[5919,8832]	19.9	16.2
	>8832	10.1	47.2
Credit purpose	Business Creation	80.9	39.7
	Business Extension	19.1	39.6
Business sector	Agriculture	16.6	1.2
	Services	33.2	46.4
	Artisanal	3.3	41.5
	Small Trades	46.9	48.4
Number of previous loans	One loan	91.7	38.9
	Two loans	7.3	48.9
	New customer	1	46.2
Previous loan defaults	New customer	94.7	39.0
	All credits paid back duly	4.6	50.2
	Payment delay in paying off in the past	0.7	63.9

respect to the number of previously-accorded loans, Table 2 illustrates that default happens more frequently for repeated borrowers. Finally, borrowers who had past payment delays are more risky than those who never had a past payment delay.

3.2. Model Estimation

Table 3 shows the estimation output of the credit-scoring model. Only seven among the ten included variables are statistically significant. More specifically,

Table 3. Estimated coefficients, standard errors and significance levels relevant to the final logistic regression model.

Variable		Coeff. (β)	S.E.	*p*-value	Exp (β)
Intercept X_0		1.438	0.454	0.002*	4.211
Borrower: Demographic Variables					
Age of the borrower X_1	≤23 (X_{11})	−0.256	0.221	0.088***	0.774
	24–25 (X_{12})	−0.028	0.307	0.897	0.973
	26–34 (X_{13})	0.382	0.186	0.040**	1.465
	35–40 (X_{14})	0.513	0.190	0.007*	1.671
	41–45 (X_{15})	0.148	0.218	0.049***	1.159
	>45 (X_{16})	0.0000	N/A	N/A	N/A
Gender of the borrower X_2	Male (X_{21})	0.226	0.099	0.022*	1.253
	Female (X_{22})	0.0000	N/A	N/A	N/A
Marital Status X_3	Single (X_{31})	0.386	0.108	0.000*	1.471
	Married (X_{32})	0.0000	N/A	N/A	N/A
Educational level X_4	Lower educational level (X_{41})	−2.366	0.171	0.000*	0.094
	Graduate and higher educational level (X_{42})	0.0000	N/A	N/A	N/A
Loan-Characteristic Variables					
Credit amount X_6	≤1935 (X_{61})	3.214	0.244	0.000*	24.886
	[1936,2399] (X_{62})	2.462	0.236	0.000*	11.731
	[2400,3598] (X_{63})	1.777	0.202	0.000*	5.912
	[3599,4349] (X_{64})	1.273	0.223	0.000*	3.573
	[4350,4998] (X_{65})	1.309	0.231	0.000*	3.704
	[4999,5918] (X_{66})	1.492	0.216	0.000*	4.445
	[5919,8832] (X_{67})	0.467	0.190	0.064***	1.595
	>8832 (X_{68})	0.0000	N/A	N/A	N/A
Business sector X_8	Agriculture (X_{81})	−5.610	0.588	0.000*	0.004
	Services (X_{82})	0.160	0.092	0.084***	1.173
	Artisanal (X_{83})	0.030	0.233	0.896	1.031
	Small Trades (X_{84})	0.0000	N/A	N/A	N/A
Credit-Behavioral Variables					
Number of previous loans X_9	One loan (X_{91})	1.171	0.173	0.000*	3.253
	Two loans (X_{92})	0.246	0.106	0.020**	1.279
	New customer (X_{93})	0.0000	N/A	N/A	N/A

Notes: Coeff. (β) is the coefficient. S.E. is the standard error. *p*-value refers to the significance of the predictor. Exp (β) shows the odds ratios (OR) for each predictor.

***denotes that the variable is significant at 10%, ** at 5%, and * at 1%.

age, gender, marital status, educational level, credit amount, business sector, and number of previous loans have significant effects on the loan applicant's repayment capacity.

The model is estimated by using the logistic regression via maximum likelihood estimation. A positive (negative) sign suggests an increasing (decreasing) default probability with an increase of the explanatory variable, *ceteris paribus*. The magnitude of the coefficient reflects the sensitivity of default probability to the explanatory variable.

Based on the results in Table 3, one can conclude that age has a non-monotonic effect on default rates. The youngest and oldest borrowers appear to have the lowest default risk, while the middle-age group seems to have the highest bankruptcy rate. This result is inconsistent with the findings obtained by Arminger *et al.* (1997) that the default probability decreases with an increase in borrower's age. The borrower's gender is a significant variable showing that female customers are more likely to repay than males. The odds ratio indicates that men are 1.253 times more likely to default than females do. This finding proves to be consistent with the studies conducted by Bhatt and Tang (2002); Dinh and Kleimeier (2007); Schreiner (2004); and Viganò (1993). Unmarried borrowers are more likely to default than married ones. Single borrowers are 1.471 times more likely to default than married borrowers. This finding is consistent with the result attained by Agarwal *et al.* (2009). Educational level (X_4) is also found to be a significant predictor. In fact, customers with a higher level of education seem to be more risky borrowers than those with a lower educational level. This result contradicts the widespread assumption and empirical finding by Bhatt and Tang (2002) that borrowers with graduate and higher educational level may have the greatest financial success and the highest repayment rate.

The credit amount variable gives a reliable indication of default. Customers who have requested the lowest credit amount tend to default more. This result is contradictory to the findings of Van Gool *et al.* (2011), but is consistent with the study conducted by Ben Soltane and Trigui (2008). Also, certain business sectors (X_8) are significant. Borrowers engaged in agriculture are more likely to repay than those engaged in small-trade activities. Besides, borrowers engaged in services are 1.173 times more likely to default than the entrepreneurs engaged in small-trade projects. This finding is consistent with the study conducted by Van Gool *et al.* (2011). Also, the number of previous loans (X_9) appears to be a significant predictor, showing that customers who received a loan from the bank before (one or two loans) have a higher probability to default compared to the new customers. Default is more frequent for the repeated borrowers and hence the lender-borrower relationship does not seem to reduce the probability of default. This finding is at odds with the conclusion reached by Dinh and Kleimeier (2007).

3.3. Calibration

Despite the widespread agreement on the importance of model validation, opinions diverge as to the definition of appropriate criteria necessary for devising a successful classification model. As mentioned by BCBS (2005) and Medema *et al.* (2009), no universally accepted validation method exists. Van Gestel *et al.* (2005) and Van Gool *et al.* (2011) argued that the validation methodologies should be closely related to the three main model requirements: stability, readability, and discriminatory power. To be well-defined, the model needs to satisfy certain conditions, i.e., it must offer stability. Stability is defined as a model in which performance measures score similarly when tested in- and out-of-sample; furthermore, *p*-values need to be below 5% for all coefficients included in the model. The model must also be readable in the sense that its coefficients can be interpreted easily. Finally and more importantly, the model must have good discriminatory power. The discrimination power is defined by the BCBS (2005) as the ability to correctly rank observations on the basis of default probabilities.

Academic researchers dealing with the subject of credit-scoring models generally agree that the percentage of correctly classified total loans (PCC_{total}) would serve as a reliable accuracy measure of a model's ability to separate risk. PCC_{total} is defined as the number of correctly classified loans relative to the total number of loans. Owing to its simplicity, this performance criterion is one of the most widely applied norms in the credit-scoring literature (Desai *et al.*, 1997; Dinh and Kleimeier, 2007). Nevertheless, this measure assumes that misclassification costs of bad and good loans are equal. For lending institutions, misclassification costs are obviously unequal. Specifically, the misclassification costs associated with Type I error, which occurs when a bad credit applicant is classified as a good credit applicant and lending is made, are much higher than those associated with Type II error, which occurs when a good credit applicant is classified as a bad credit applicant and credit request is rejected.

To address this limitation and take into account misclassification costs, various studies have relied on two additional accuracy measures: sensitivity (SENS) and specificity (SPEC). SENS is defined as the number of classified good loans relative to the total number of predicted good loans. SPEC is defined as the proportion of correctly classified bad loans to the total number of predicted bad loans. In the literature, more advanced methods that take these two costs explicitly into account are used for model validation. These include the Kolmogorov–Smirnov (KS) statistic, receiver operating characteristic (ROC) curve and AUC measure. The ROC Curve and its summary index (AUC) have been widely used in assessing credit-scoring models (Blöchlinger and Leippold, 2006; Van Gool *et al.*, 2011). The ROC curve gives a graphic representation of a scoring model's discriminatory power. Indeed, for each possible cut-off level, it represents the "hit rate" (SENS) and "false alarm rate" (1–SPEC). If the model is perfect, the ROC curve will pass through the point (0,1) and the AUC will be equal to 1. The higher the model accuracy, the more the ROC curve lies close to the top left corner. Therefore, the AUC provides a convenient measure of the general accuracy that is independent of the cut-off value applied. The greater the AUC, the better the model will be. Van Gool *et al.* (2011) argued that the AUC measure is the most comprehensive measure for assessing a credit-scoring model's accuracy.

3.3.1. *Quality of the logistic regression model*

The results in Table 3 indicate that the regression coefficients (β) are statistically significant except for (X_{12}) and (X_{83}), which indicates that the model has some predictive power.

Regarding the accuracy displayed by our credit-scoring model, the R^2 statistic cannot be computed for logistic regression models. The pseudo R^2 statistics, namely the Cox-Snell R^2 and Nagelkerke R^2 statistics, are designed to have properties similar to the true R^2 statistic. The Nagelkerke R^2, for example, equals 0.437, indicating that a decent amount of variation can be explained by a credit-scoring model.

3.3.2. *Validation of the credit-scoring model*

Table 4 reports predictive accuracy with a cut-off of 0.50. As reported in Table 4, the model correctly predicts 74.6% of the observations in the validation sample.

A separate examination of the loans as Bad versus Good reveals that the correctly classified percentage is mainly driven by the Good loans, as the PCC_{good} (80.2%) proves to be much higher than the PCC_{bad} (66%). The SPEC measure indicates that among the rejected loans, 68.35% would have defaulted whereas 31.65% would have been repaid. 31.65% of the loans that have been incorrectly rejected should be interpreted as the cost of foregone business opportunities (Type II error). Note that SPEC is an abstract measure because a bank cannot check whether its rejected loan applicants would have defaulted; 21.58% of the loans are incorrectly accepted which leads to losses due to missed interest and principle payments (Type I error).

Both sensitivity and specificity rely on a single cut-off point to perform classification. A more complete description of classification accuracy is captured by the AUC. The AUC value is equal to 0.832. This confirms the statement that the model exhibits good discerning power to separate default and non-default borrowers.

We compare our model's performance with the results reported in previous credit-scoring studies for MFIs. In Burkina Faso, Viganò (1993) indicated that

Table 4. Predictive accuracy with a cut-off of 0.50.

	Prediction		
Observation	**Non-default**	**Default**	**PCC**
Non-default	814	201	PCC_{good} = 80.2%
Default	224	434	PCC_{bad} = 66%
			PCC_{total} = 74.6%
SENS	78.42%		
SPEC		68.35%	

the credit-scoring model has a $PCC_{total} = 77\%$, which is similar to our result. For the Bolivian case, Schreiner's (2004) different calibrations are able to achieve a maximum PCC_{total} accuracy of 91%, higher than that reported in our study. When comparing our model's discriminatory power to that of Van Gool *et al.* (2011) in the Bosnian context, one should notice that the results are very similar in terms of PCC_{total}. Our model performs slightly better in terms of the AUC. Indeed, the AUC of Van Gool *et al.* (2011) is around 0.7, lower than our model's AUC of 0.832. The model of Blanco *et al.* (2013) in the Spanish context has the highest AUC values ranging from 0.9079 to 0.9543. This leads to the conclusion that in terms of predictive accuracy, the credit-scoring models for microfinance prove to have higher discriminatory power for developed countries and developing ones.

More importantly, we compare our model's performance with the results reported in previous credit-scoring studies that are relevant to financial institutions beyond MFIs. In line with Schreiner (2004), our scoring model appears to have less predictive accuracy than most of the credit-scoring models related to credit cards, consumer loans, etc. (Dinh and Kleimeier, 2007): $PCC_{total} = 97.98\%$; Desai *et al.* (1996): $PCC_{total} = 86.90\%$). This comparison suggests that the lack of certified financial statements regarding microenterprises in MFIs greatly affects a model's prediction success rate, and that risk in these institutions needs to be assessed via specifically designed models.

Based on these results, one might conclude that a credit-scoring model can reduce loan defaults. In fact, by substituting its traditional credit approval method with a credit-scoring model alternative, our microfinance bank may expect a decrease in its default ratio from 39.7% to 21.58%. However, regarding the applicability of credit scoring for microfinance, the discriminatory power reached by our model is too weak to justify a complete reversal of the micro-lender's standard loan-granting process towards a fully automated credit scoring. Credit scoring is not yet able to entirely replace the human-intensive microfinance credit process, mainly in the developing countries. Consequently, it is worth underlining that credit scoring in microfinance can flag high-risk cases and act as a cross-check on the loan officer's judgment but will by no means substitute loan officers. However, it is worth noting that in order to back our conclusion, other factors need to be studied, e.g., the cost of a slower approval process. These factors can be taken into account in future studies. As a matter of fact, credit-granting decisions in microfinance must be jointly based on the credit-scoring result in collaboration with MFIs' credit officers. Actually, this finding is consistent with the results of Van Gool *et al.* (2011) as well as Schreiner (2004).

IV. CONCLUSION

This paper presents a literature review on a credit-scoring framework for MFIs and provides a thorough analysis of the reported strengths and weaknesses. Evidence regarding the credit-scoring models for MFIs is still at an embryonic stage (Blanco *et al.*, 2013; Schreiner, 2004; Van Gool *et al.*, 2011; Viganò, 1993). In addition, we present an empirical study with a special credit-scoring model and analyze its workability and feasibility for MFIs and the extent to which MFIs can benefit in the same way as it has been successfully adopted in the retail banking area. A logistic regression model has been developed using a data set of 5,022 credit applicants from the Tunisian Microfinance Bank.

It is noteworthy that the high-quality results are obtained using a stable and readable logistic regression model, which will likely enable the Tunisian Microfinance Bank to better identify the determinants of microcredit defaults. Our results indicate that the model can actually help reduce loan defaults. Substituting the traditional credit approval method by a more reliable credit-scoring model could enable the Tunisian Microfinance Bank to witness a decrease in its default ratio from 39.7% to 21.58%. However, the discriminatory power of our model is still too weak to support a complete reversal of the micro-lender's standard loan granting process. Actually, credit scoring is not reliable enough to replace loan officers. Therefore, it is recommended to introduce a credit-scoring system as a refinement tool in the lending process, through which we can combine statistical and human best practices.

NOTES

1 The model must be stable in the sense that *p*-values for all well-determined coefficients included in the final model need to be below 5%. The model must also be readable in the sense that its coefficients can be interpreted easily (model must not be a black box).

2 Van Gool *et al.* (2011) define two variables that belong to the lender characteristic: (1) a dummy variable that indicates the branch in which the loan application was filed (there are 28 branches over Bosnia–Herzegovina); and (2) a proxy for the loan officer's experience.

3 In the weight-of-evidence approach, categories of an explanatory variable are grouped together in n groups based on similarity of WoE measured by: $g_i/(g_i+b_i)$, where g_i is defined as the number of non-defaulted loans that belong to the ith group and b_i is defined similarly for the defaulted loans. Then, each of the newly created n groups receives a coding based on its distribution of defaulted and non-defaulted loans. Every weight of evidence variable is composed of n values, one for each of the groups. Hence, this approach works with one variable for all categories of an explanatory variable.

4 According to Dellien (2003), loan officers in large MFIs in Colombia and the Dominican Republic that specialize in individual lending spend on average 40% to 50% of their time collecting overdue payments from delinquent borrowers.

REFERENCES

Abdou, H., J. Pointon and A. E. Masry (2008), Neural Nets Versus Conventional Techniques in Credit Scoring in Egyptian Banking. *Expert Systems with Applications*, 35(3), pp. 1275–1292.

Agarwal, S., J. Driscoll, X. Gabaix and D. Laibson (2009), The Age of Reason: Financial Decisions Over the Lifecycle with Implications for Regulation, *Brookings Papers on Economic Activity*, pp. 51–117.

Allen, J. C. (1995), A Promise of Approvals in Minutes, Not Hours. *American Banker*, 160(39), p. 23.

Arminger, G., D. Enache and T. Bonne (1997), Analyzing Credit Risk Data: A Comparison of Logistic Discrimination, Classification Tree Analysis, and Feed-Forward Network. *Computational Statistics*, 12(2), pp. 293–310.

Basel Committee on Banking Supervision (2005), Studies on the Validation of Internal Ratings Systems, Working Paper No. 14, May 2005.

Ben Soltane, B. and B. Trigui (2008), Determinants of Repayment Performance of Individual Borrowers from Microfinance Institutions: Evidence from Tunisia. *African Journal of Business and Economic Research*, 3(1), pp. 66–87.

Bhatt, N. and S. Y., Tang (2002), Determinants of Repayment in Microcredit: Evidence from Programs in the United States. *International Journal of Urban and Regional Research*, 26(6), pp. 360–376.

Blanco, A., R. Pino-Meijas, L. Juan and R. Salvador (2013), Credit Scoring Models for Microfinance Industry Using Neural Networks: Evidence from Peru. *Expert Systems with Applications*, 40, pp. 356–364.

Blöchlinger, A. and M. Leippold (2006), Economic Benefit of Powerful Credit Scoring. *Journal of Banking and Finance*, 30, pp. 851–873.

Bumacov, V. and A. Ashta (2011), The Conceptual Framework of Credit Scoring from its Origins to Microfinance, Second European Research Conference on Microfinance, Groningen, The Netherlands, June 2011.

Buvinic, M. and M. Berger (1990), Sex Differences in Access to a Small Enterprise Development Fund in Peru. *World Development*, 18(5), pp. 695–705.

Cornée, S. (2009), Internal Credit Rating in Social Banking: The Role of Subjective and Experiential Factors, CREM-IGR (University of Rennes 1), accessed from: http://cermat.iae.univ-tours.fr/IMG/pdf/CORNEE.pdf, June 4, 2009.

Dellien, H. (2003), Credit Scoring in Microfinance: Guidelines Based on Experience with WWB Affiliates in Colombia and the Dominican Republic. *Women's World Banking*, 1(2), pp. 1–15.

Dennis, W. (1995), Fair Lending and Credit Scoring. *Mortgage Banking*, 56(2), pp. 55–59.

Desai, V. S., D. Conway, J. N. Crook and G. Overstreet (1997), Credit-Scoring Models in the Credit-Union Environment Using Neural Networks and Genetic Algorithms. *Computer Journal of Mathematics Applied in Business and Industry*, 8(4), pp. 324–346.

Desai, V. S., J. N. Crook and G. A. Overstreet (1996), A Comparison of Neural Networks and Linear Scoring Models in the Credit Union Environment. *European Journal of Operational Research*, 95(1), pp. 24–37.

Dinh, T. H. T. and S. Kleimeier (2007), A Credit Scoring Model for Vietnam's Retail Banking Market. *International Review of Financial Analysis*, 16(5), pp. 471–495.

Freytag, C. (2008), Credit Scoring: Why Scepticism Is Justified, in I. Matthaus-Maier and J. Von Pischke (eds.), *New Partnerships for Innovation in Microfinance*, Berlin, Heidelberg: Springer.

Godquin, M (2004), Microfinance Repayment Performance in Bangladesh: How to Improve the Allocation of Loans by MFIs. *World Development*, 32(11), pp. 1909–1926.

Kuhn, M. and A. B. Olsen (2008), Credit Scoring in Microfinance. *Opportunity International*, 9, pp. 1–14.

Kulkosky, E. (1996), Credit Scoring Could Have a Downside, Experts Say. *American Banker*, 161(208), p. 8.

Lee, T., C. Chiu, C. Lu and I. Chen (2002), Credit Scoring Using the Hybrid Neural Discriminant Technique. *Expert Systems with Applications*, 23(3), pp. 245–254.

Medema, L., R. Koning and R. Lensink (2009), A Practical Approach to Validating a PD Model. *Journal of Banking and Finance*, 33, pp. 701–708.

Morduch, J. (1999), The Microfinance Promise. *Journal of Economic Literature*, 37, pp. 1569–1614.

Ohlson, J. A. (1980), Financial Ratios and the Probabilistic Prediction of Bankruptcy. *Journal of Accounting Research*, 18(1), pp. 109–131.

Robinson, M. (2001), *The Microfinance Revolution*. Washington, DC: World Bank.

Schreiner, M. (2001), Informal Finance and the Design of Microfinance. *Development in Practice*, 11(5), pp. 637–640.

Schreiner, M. (2003), Scoring: The Next Breakthrough in Microfinance. Consultative Group to Assist the Poorest (CGAP), Occasional Paper, No. 7, Washington DC.

Schreiner, M. (2004), Scoring Arrears at a Microlender in Bolivia. *Journal of Microfinance*, 6(2), pp. 65–88.

Schreiner, M. (2005), Scoring for Microfinance. Conference on SME Financing: Issues and Strategies, State Bank of Pakistan, Lahore, May 10.

Simbaqueba, L., G. Salamanca and V. Bumacov (2011), The Role of Credit Scoring in Micro Lending Advanced Technologies in Microfinance: Solutions and Challenges, in A. Ashta (ed.), *Advanced Technologies for Microfinance: Solutions and Challenges*, Hershey, PA: IGI-Global.

Thomas, L. C. (2000), A Survey of Credit and Behavioral Scoring: Forecasting Financial Risk of Lending to Consumers, *International Journal of Forecasting*, 16, pp. 149–172.

Tufféry, S. (2011), *Data Mining and Statistics for Decision Making*, Chichester: John Wiley & Sons, Ltd.

Van Gestel, T., B. Baesens, P. Van Dijcke, J. Suykens, J. Garcia and T. Alderweireld (2005), Linear and Non-Linear Credit Scoring by Combining Logistic Regression and Support Vector Machines. *Journal of Credit Risk*, 1(4), pp. 31–60.

Van Gool, J., W. Verbeke, P. Sercu and B. Baesens (2011), Credit Scoring for Microfinance: Is It Worth It? *International Journal of Finance and Economics*, 17(2), pp. 103–123.

Viganò, L. (1993), A Credit-Scoring Model for Development Banks: An African Case Study. *Savings and Development*, 17(4), pp. 441–482.

Vogelgesang, U. (2003), Microfinance in Times of Crisis: The Effects of Competition, Rising Indebtness, and Economic Crisis on Repayment Behavior. *World Development*, 31(12), pp. 2085–2114.

Wiginton, J. C. (1980), A Note of the Comparison of Logit and Discriminant Models of Consumer Credit Behavior. *The Journal of Financial and Quantitative Analysis*, 15(3), pp. 757–770.

Stepping Up to the Liquidity Challenge: The Changing Role of Credit Portfolio Management

IACPM and KPMG

Results Analysis of IACPM and KPMG's Benchmarking Survey (2012)

For questions or comments on this article, please contact:

Som-lok Leung
Executive Director, IACPM
somlok@iacpm.org

Marcia Banks
Associate Director, IACPM
Marcia@iacpm.org

Rob Kiernan
Principal Advisor, KPMG
rob.kiernan@kpmg.co.uk

Keywords: Credit portfolio management, funding liquidity management, asset and liability management, capital, liquidity, Liquidity Coverage Ratio, asset liability management.

INTRODUCTION

In 2011–2012 the International Association of Credit Portfolio Managers (IACPM), in collaboration with KPMG, undertook a comprehensive benchmarking survey on funding liquidity management and credit portfolio management (see Box 1 for a summary of key themes). The goal of the survey was to assess the growing linkages between credit portfolio management and asset and liability management related to funding costs, portfolio analytics and stress testing, and to benchmark how firms are changing organizational structures and mandates to integrate credit portfolio and liquidity risk management. Thirty-four IACPM member firms, located globally, participated in the study.

I. STEPPING UP TO THE LIQUIDITY CHALLENGE: THE CHANGING ROLE OF CPM

As the regulatory change agenda becomes even more all encompassing, the challenge of how to optimize and manage both capital and liquidity is key for Boards and Senior Management. Optimization of liquidity is now vital — and creates a significant opportunity to utilize the analysis, business and operational skills from across the business to manage the cash, risks and change required. Credit Portfolio Managers have already established a pivotal role in financial institutions, using their skills in key areas such as origination and distribution, profitability enhancement, capital optimization, and balance sheet management.

Historically, credit portfolio management (CPM) focused on the measurement, modeling, pricing, and active management of credit risk. Triggered by the financial crisis in 2008 and the changes in the regulatory, industry and business landscape that followed, financial institutions face ongoing higher funding costs and liquidity risk. CPM teams' responsibilities have therefore been redefined, and widened to include increased involvement in addressing

Box 1 — Summary of the key themes

- Credit Portfolio Management (CPM) roles and responsibilities are expanding to include significantly greater linkages with Liquidity, Treasury and Asset and Liability Management (ALM) for their organizations as a result of credit market, funding conditions and the Basel III regulations regarding liquidity.
- In many institutions, CPM plays a central — and growing — role in integrating credit and liquidity cost factors into origination strategies with the line of business via transfer pricing methodologies.
- CPM is playing an expanded role in modeling specific aspects of liquidity at many banks, providing ALM with analytical information about the portfolio and funding projections by portfolio, product and, to a lesser extent, obligor.
- Systems, modeling and associated reporting are ongoing challenges as firms work to implement integrated credit, market and liquidity risk management, and planning across organizations amid tight budgets.
- Organizational changes continue to be made to align CPM, risk and liquidity functions across the firm and facilitate integrated risk management. Most CPM units see continued expansion of their roles in the future and envisage closer linkages, formal and/or informal, with the Treasury.

regulatory requirements — as well as funding liquidity risk management in their organizations, with further expansions envisaged in the next year. CPM units are still going through the process of embedding these changes, with many expecting further changes to their roles and responsibilities in the near future. Organisational structures are changing, breaking down the traditional divisions in functional responsibilities (e.g., between Treasury and Credit) and in the way that different risk types are addressed.

IACPM engaged with KPMG in the UK to conduct a survey of its members' developing practices in funding liquidity risk management. Thirty-four IACPM member firms, representing almost half of the eligible IACPM membership, participated in the survey. 35% of the participating IACPM members are domiciled in North America, 23% in Asia-Pacific and 22% in Europe, representing banks of different balance sheet

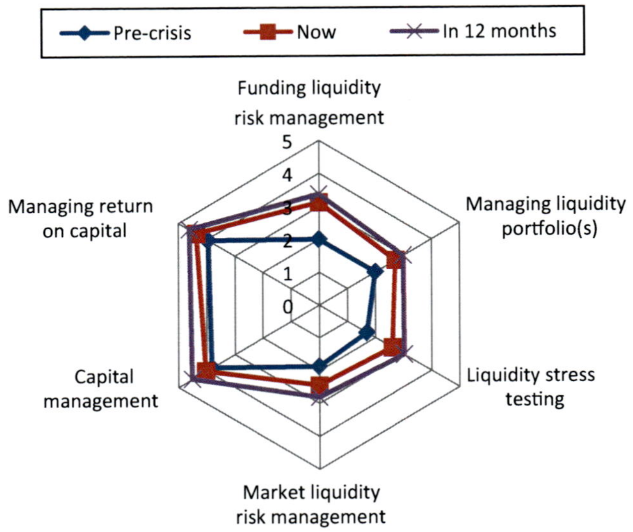

Figure 1. CPM activities in order of importance — pre- and post-crisis (ranked 1 to 5).

sizes, from greater than $500 million to less than $50 billion. The survey aimed to understand and benchmark how IACPM member firms adapted to the new environment and ever-evolving financial landscape, and specifically the role of CPM units in this process.

The importance of liquidity risk management for businesses in the post-crisis marketplace and the critical input of the CPM in delivering this effectively become apparent from the current and future objectives cited by those surveyed (see Figure 1 for more details).

II. REGULATORY CHALLENGES

The global financial crisis has led to wide-ranging and ongoing regulatory changes, which are influencing CPM's established roles in institutions.

Regulatory change — particularly the Basel Committee's focus on the Liquidity Coverage Ratio and Net Stable Funding Ratio — has forced the industry to focus on liquidity. The changes in managing funding liquidity risk result in evolving roles for CPM and open up new opportunities for CPM teams to add value to their firms. The liquidity requirements set by the Basel Committee are likely to prove an even bigger challenge than those on capital. For many banks, these requirements are 'the iceberg below the water'. Pre-crisis, liquidity was a clear second to capital — until recently, the primary focus had been on the challenges posed by the substantial capital requirements. Now, the additional liquidity standards will necessitate operational, financial and structural change, and a significant move away from short-term wholesale funding towards a longer-term funding strategy. Effective liquidity management is now a big boardroom issue.

The scarcity and cost of funding, combined with the need to hold high quality liquid assets, is affecting decisions around asset origination and the management of credit portfolios. The impending implementation of the Basel III regulation is changing the way institutions manage funding liquidity risk. As a result, liquidity considerations are demanding significant time and attention from financial institutions — and from more and more credit portfolio managers. New regulations in funding liquidity risk have been a significant driver for change in the business — and preparing for the implementation of new rules and for further change is a key focus for banks and an essential part of their plans for the future. In this new operating environment, CPM units have gained a strong involvement in the internal assessment of regulatory change and in determining the options to manage the new requirements (Figure 2).

CPM units are addressing the practical aspects of managing changes required by regulators, providing insights into the impact of these changes and acting as internal sources of expertise.

The new regulatory rules continue to drive additional liquidity, capital, stress testing and reporting requirements, to which CPM provides an increased amount of insights, experience and operational input related to implementing change and addressing operational aspects of managing risk. In improving the integration of the management of risk types, CPM is engaging with the challenges of systems and modeling enhancements, associated analytical reporting and a closer interaction with key stakeholders — notably the Treasury — and these remain the key areas of focus.

CPM is playing an increasingly central and growing role in integrating credit and liquidity cost factors into origination strategies via transfer pricing methodologies, serving as a central conduit for providing integrated market, cost and liquidity information to the line of business. As regulatory requirements related to liquidity are being implemented, the role of CPM in providing credit and liquidity costs and related portfolio acquisition/distribution strategies is growing. In most firms, Treasury/ALM determines fund transfer pricing and funding strategies for the institution and provides them to CPM and the line of business. CPM units now serve as focal point for coordination between Treasury and the line of business to integrate relevant costs for credit/loan origination, to assist in framing forward-looking risk management strategies for credit origination, and to execute risk distribution where appropriate.

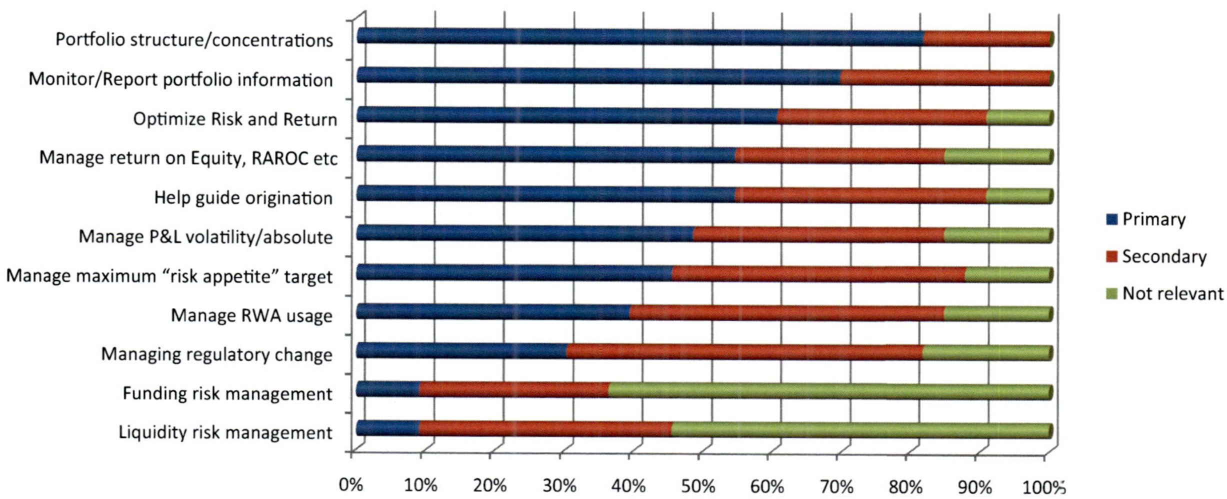

Figure 2. Key objectives for CPM.

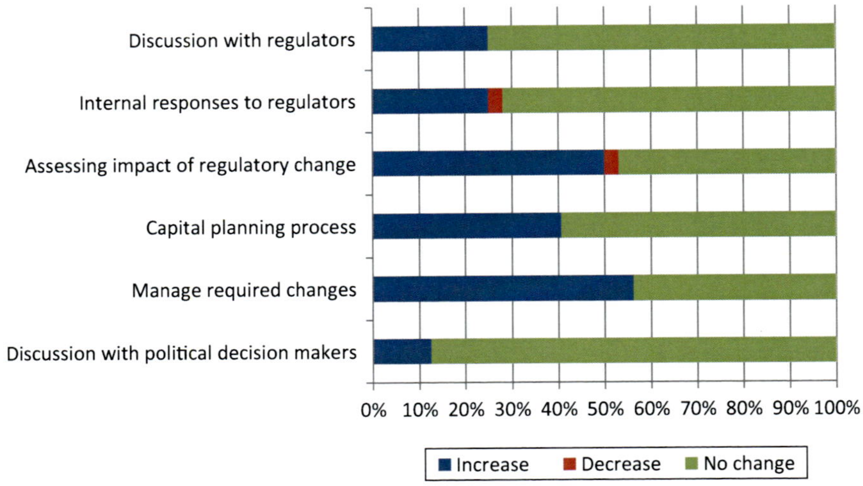

Figure 3. CPM units' changing involvement in addressing regulatory liquidity requirements.

III. SIGNIFICANT CHALLENGES

These significant changes come with multiple challenges. Some of the key challenges include a lack of the right system requirements and the anticipated budget and resource constraints.

The changing regulatory environment and the move towards implementation of established rules continue to challenge the industry. Regulation is a significant cause of these changing systems and reporting requirements, forming one of the biggest challenges faced by CPM teams (Figures 3 and 4). Regulatory change is also driving other business challenges, such as the cost impact on business planning and deal assessment — especially in pricing. The differing regulatory approaches and stages of implementation (e.g., local regulators versus Basel III) are an area where CPM teams are having an effect on business planning and operational change — meaning that the CPM is now working even more closely with the business, especially Treasury, as a key function.

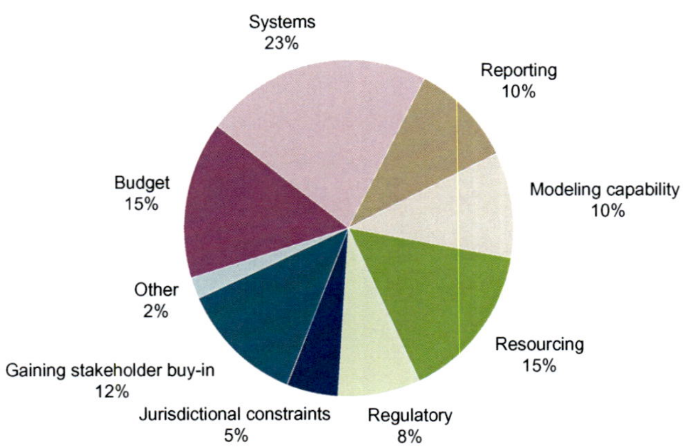

Figure 4. The biggest challenges.

IV. MANAGING LIQUIDITY RISK

The survey identified that CPM now has a strong coordination role between other business units and with the Treasury itself. A few firms are already fully integrated and around 20 percent are merging some functionality. This is part of an ongoing process of embedding these new roles and the new mandate for CPM units within the firm. CPM and Treasury units are working together to implement and enhance systems that incorporate liquidity costs in new deal pricing and profitability assessment. There is also evidence that firms are enhancing their transfer pricing approaches.

CPM units have expanded their functional responsibilities beyond traditional areas of credit portfolio management and risk/return into the area of funding liquidity risk management, increasingly working alongside treasury colleagues and providing expertise, insights and a link to the operational side of their businesses (Figures 5 and 6). They are leveraging their usual coordination role by liaising among the various business units, leading to better risk management for the firm. Almost three quarters of CPM respondents

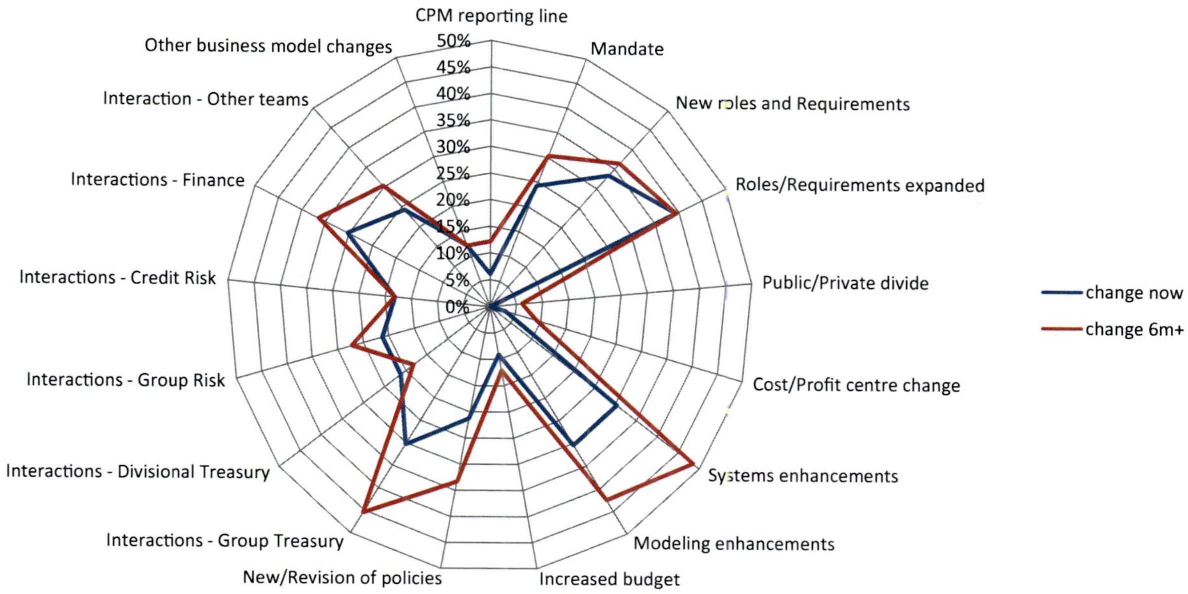

Figure 5. Evolving CPM activities in response to enhanced liquidity risk management requirements.

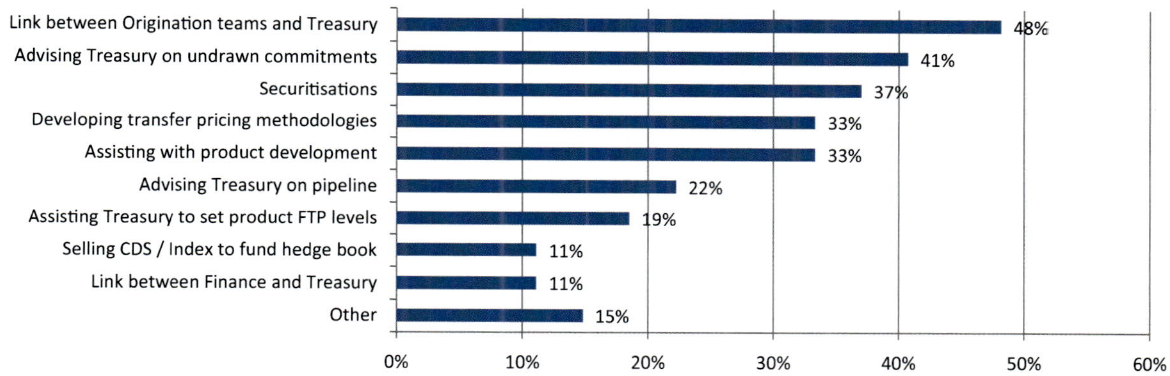

Figure 6. Current areas of CPM involvement in managing funding liquidity risk.

report having an increasing role in liquidity risk management, mostly in an operational and internal advisory capacity.

V. MODELING LIQUIDITY RISK

Improving and developing the different aspects of modeling liquidity risk is an area of focus for most senior management — and an area where firms want to become more sophisticated. CPM teams are now involved in modeling liquidity risk due to their role as providers of analytical outlook and portfolio information and their

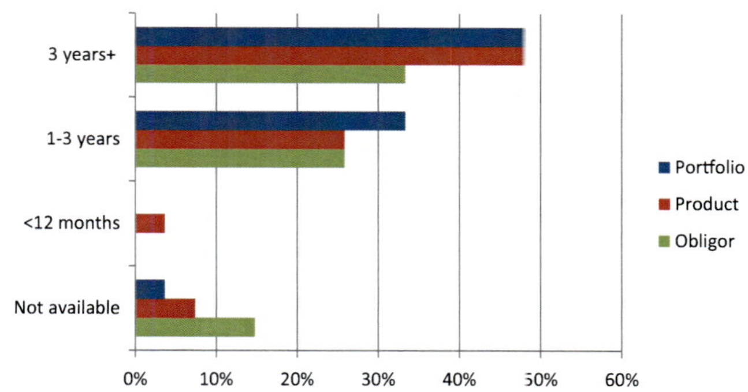

Figure 7. Time horizon of available historical drawing behavior data.

ability to draw on historical information on a portfolio, product and, to a lesser extent, specific obligor level (Figure 7). Treasury and ALM have traditionally determined the scenarios for liquidity stress testing.

CPM is actively working to develop modeling and systems in liquidity risk management. There is a wide range of approaches and degrees of sophistication. For example, the reference curves for fund transfer pricing are diverse across institutions. Infrastructure and systems are seen as one of the major hurdles in developing models and systems to meet the new requirements of liquidity risk management.

VI. A CONTINUING JOURNEY

New regulations in funding liquidity risk have been a significant driver for change in the business — and preparing for the implementation of the regulations and for further change is a major part of the plans for the future. CPM units have gained a strong involvement in the internal assessment of regulatory change and in determining the options to manage the new requirements, playing an important part in helping businesses address the many challenges in the current marketplace and helping their organization to manage funding liquidity risk effectively.

CPM now plays a central role in integrating credit and liquidity cost factors into origination and distribution strategies via transfer pricing methodologies, serving as a focal point between Treasury and the line of business. These new roles and organizational models are still being addressed, as well as tactical issues relating to systems, data and models. Challenges remain — including budget constraints — as banks work to integrate the different risk types and systems.

Successful firms will continue to leverage the position of CPM to address the wider cost and profitability considerations associated with liquidity — in addition to managing credit portfolio risks. The overall benefits will see improved risk management across the firm and the optimization of risk/return within institutions that are fully exploiting their CPM advantage.

This new journey has only just begun, and there is still more change to come.

NUS-RMI Credit Research Initiative Technical Report

Version: 2013 Update 2b

RMI staff article

For any questions or comments on this article, please contact Oliver Chen at ochen@nus.edu.sg

Keywords: Non-profit credit research initiative, credit risk, probability of default, forward intensity.

This document describes the implementation of the system which the Credit Research Initiative (CRI) at the Risk Management Institute (RMI) of the National University of Singapore (NUS) uses to produce probabilities of default (PDs). As of this version of the Technical Report, RMI covers around 60,400 listed firms (including delisted ones) in 106 economies around the world (see Table A.1). Of the over 39,000 active firms under the CRI coverage, around 34,000 firms have sufficient data to release daily updated PDs. The PD for all firms is freely available to users who can provide evidence of their professional qualifications to ensure that they will not misuse the data. General users who do not request global access are restricted to a list of 3,000 firms. The individual company PD data, along with aggregate PDs at the economy and sector level, can be accessed at http://rmicri.org.

The primary goal of this initiative is to drive research and development in the critical area of credit rating systems. As such, a transparent methodology is essential to this initiative. Having the details of the methodology available to everybody means that there is a base from which suggestions and improvements can be made. The objective of this Technical Report is to provide a full exposition of the CRI system. Readers of this document who have access to the necessary data and who have a sufficient level of technical expertise will be able to implement a similar system on their own. For a full exposition of the conceptual framework of the CRI, see Duan and Van Laere (2012).

The system used by the CRI will evolve as new innovations and enhancements are applied. The changes to the 2012 technical report and operational implementation of our model are: (1) RMI's global coverage; (2) extension of the forecast horizon to five years by applying a

Nelson-Siegel type parameterization and using a Sequential Monte Carlo (SMC) method; (3) changes to treatment of financial statements in monthly calibration; (4) exclusion rule for merger and acquisition (M&A) events; (5) changes to treatment of companies after a default event; (6) change from monthly sigma to daily sigma; (7) changes in the treatment of missing values; and (8) changes in the level and trend calculations and (9) changes in the Distance-to-Default computation. This version of the technical report provides an update on the operational implementation of the CRI and includes all changes to the system that had been implemented by September 2013. More specifically, in addition to Version: 2013 update 1, the current version of the technical report specifies some revisions to the monthly parameter updates that went into effect as of the August 2013 calibration. The latest version of the Technical Report and addenda to the latest version are available via the web portal and will include any changes to the system that have been implemented since the publication of this version.

The remainder of this Technical Report is organized as follows. The next section describes the quantitative model that is currently used to compute PDs from the CRI. The model was first described in Duan *et al.* (2012). The description includes calibration procedures, which are performed on a monthly basis, and individual firm PD computations, which are performed on a daily basis.

Section 2 describes the input variables of the model as well as the data used to produce the variables for input into the model. This model uses both input variables that are common to all firms in an economy and input variables that are firm-specific. Another critical component when calibrating a probability of default estimation system is the default data, and this is also described in this section.

While Section 1 provides a broader description of the model, Section 3 describes the implementation details that are necessary for application, given real world issues of, for example, bad or missing data. The specific technical details needed to develop an operational system are also given, including details on the monthly calibration, daily computation of individual firm PDs and aggregation of the individual firm PDs. Distance-to default (DTD) in a Merton-type model is one of the firm-specific variables. The calculation for DTD is not the standard one, and has been modified to allow a meaningful computation of the DTD for financial firms. While most academic studies on default prediction exclude financial firms from consideration, it is important to include them given that the financial sector is a critical component in every economy. The calculation for DTD is detailed in this section.

Section 4 shows an empirical analysis for those economies that are currently covered. While the analysis shows excellent results in several economies, there is room for improvement in a few others. This is because, at the CRI's current stage of development, the economies all use the variables used in the academic study of US firms in Duan *et al.* (2012). Future development within the CRI will deal with variable selection specific to different economies, and the performance is then expected to improve. Other planned developments are discussed in Section 5.

I. MODEL DESCRIPTION

The quantitative model that is currently being used by the CRI is a forward intensity model that was introduced in Duan *et al.* (2012). Certain aspects of the model are taken from Duan and Fulop (2013). This model allows PD forecasts to be made at a range of horizons. In the current CRI implementation of this model, PDs are forecasted from a horizon of one month up to a horizon of five years. At the RMI CRI website, for every firm, the probabilities of that firm defaulting within one month, three months, six months, one year, two years, three years and five years are given. The ability to assess credit quality for different horizons is a useful tool for risk management, credit portfolio management, policy setting and regulatory purposes, since short- and long-term credit risk profiles can differ greatly depending on a firm's liquidity, debt structures and other factors.

The forward intensity model is a reduced form model in which the PD is computed as a function of different input variables. These can be firm-specific or common to all firms within an economy. The other category of the default prediction model is the structural model, whereby the corporate structure of a firm is modeled in order to assess the firm's PD.

A similar reduced form model by Duffie *et al.* (2007) relies on modeling the time series dynamics of the input variables in order to make PD forecasts for different horizons. However, there is little consensus on assumptions for the dynamics of variables such as accounting ratios, and the model output will be highly dependent on these assumptions. In addition, the time series dynamics will be of very high dimension. For example, with the two common variables and two firm-specific variables that Duffie *et al.* (2007) use, a sample of 10,000 firms gives a dimension of the state variables of 20,002.

Given the complexity in modeling the dynamics of variables such as accounting ratios, this model will be difficult to implement if different forecast horizons are required. The key innovation of the forward intensity model is that PD for different horizons can be consistently and efficiently computed based only on the value of the input variables at the time the prediction is made. Thus, the model specification becomes far more tractable.

Fully specifying a reduced form model includes the specification of the function that computes a PD from the input variables. This function is parameterized, and finding appropriate parameter values is called calibrating the model. The forward intensity model can be calibrated by maximizing a pseudo-likelihood function. The calibration is carried out by groups of economies and all firms within a group of economies will use the same parameter values along with each firm's variables in order to compute the firm's PD.

Subsection 1.1 will describe the modeling framework, including the way PDs are computed based on a set of parameter values for the economy and a set of input variables for a firm. Subsection 1.2 explains how the model can be calibrated. Subsection 1.3 details the way parameters are estimated based on the SMC technique.

1.1. Modeling Framework

While the model can be formulated in a continuous time framework, as done in Duan *et al.* (2012), an operational implementation requires discretization in time. Since the model is more easily understood in discrete time, the following exposition of the model will begin in a discrete time framework.

Variables for default prediction can have vastly different update frequencies. Financial statement data is updated only once a quarter or even once a year, while market data like stock prices are available at frequencies of seconds. A way of compromising between these two extremes is to have a fundamental time period Δt of one month in the modeling framework. As will be seen later, this does not preclude updating the PD forecasts on a daily basis. This is important since, for example, large daily changes in a firm's stock price can signal changes in credit quality even when there is no change in financial statement data.

Thus, for the purpose of calibration and subsequently for computing time series of PD, the input variables at the end of each month will be kept for each firm. The input variables associated with the ith firm at the end of the nth month (at time $t = n\Delta t$) is denoted by $X_i(n)$. This is a vector consisting of two parts: $X_i(n) = (W(n), U_i(n))$. Here, $W(n)$ is a vector of variables at the end of month n that is common to all firms in the economy and $U_i(n)$ is a vector of variables specific to firm i.

In the forward intensity model, a firm's default is signaled by a jump in a Poisson process. The probability of a jump in the Poisson process is determined by the intensity of the Poisson process. The forward intensity model draws an explicit dependence of intensities at time periods in the future (that is, forward intensities) to the values of input variables at the time of prediction. With forward intensities, PDs for any forecast horizon can be computed knowing only the values of the input variables at the time of prediction, without needing to simulate future values of the input variables.

There is a direct analogy in interest rate modeling. In spot rate models where dynamics on a short-term spot rate are specified, bond pricing requires expectations on realizations of the short rate. Alternatively, bond prices can be computed directly if the forward rate curve is known.

One issue in default prediction is that firms can exit public exchanges for reasons other than default. For example, in mergers and acquisitions involving two public companies, there will be one company that delists from its stock exchange. This is important in predicting defaults because a default cannot happen if a firm has been previously delisted. An exception is if the exit is a distressed exit and is followed soon after by a credit event. See Subsection 2.4 for details on how this case is handled in the CRI system.

In order to take these other exits into account, defaults and other exits are modeled as two independent Poisson processes, each with their own intensity. While defaults and exits classified as non-defaults are mutually exclusive by definition, the assumption of independent Poisson processes does not pose a problem since the probability of a simultaneous jump in the two Poisson processes is negligible. In the discrete time framework, the probability of simultaneous jumps in the same time interval is non-zero. As a modeling assumption, a simultaneous jump in the same time interval by both the default Poisson process and the non-default type exit Poisson process is considered as a default. In this way, there are three mutually exclusive possibilities during each time interval: survival, default and non-default exit. As with defaults, the forward intensity of the Poisson process for other exits is a function of the input variables. The parameters of this function can also be calibrated.

To further illustrate the discrete framework, the three possibilities for a firm at each time point are diagrammed. Either the firm survives for the next time period Δt, or it defaults within Δt, or it has a non-default exit within Δt. This setup is pictured in Figure 1. Information about firm i is known up until time $t = m\Delta t$ and the figure illustrates possibilities in the future between $t = (n-1)\Delta t$ and $(n+1)\Delta t$. Here, m and n are integers with $m < n$.

The probabilities of each branch are, for example: $p_i(m, n)$ the conditional probability viewed from $t = m\Delta t$ that firm i will default before $(n+1)\Delta t$, conditioned on firm i surviving up until $n\Delta t$. Likewise, $\bar{p}_i(m, n)$ is the conditional probability viewed from $t = m\Delta t$ that firm i will have a non-default exit before $(n+1)\Delta t$, conditioned on firm i surviving up until $n\Delta t$. It is the modeler's objective to determine $p_i(m, n)$ and $\bar{p}_i(m, n)$, but for now it is assumed that these quantities are known. With the conditional default and other exit probabilities known, the corresponding conditional survival probability of firm i is $1 - p_i(m, n) - \bar{p}_i(m, n)$.

With this diagram in mind, the probability that a particular path will be followed is the product of the conditional probabilities along the path. For example, the probability at time $t = m\Delta t$ of firm i surviving until $(n-1)\Delta t$ and then defaulting between $(n-1)\Delta t$ and $n\Delta t$ is:

$$\begin{aligned} &Prob_{t=m\Delta t}[\tau_i = n, \tau_i < \bar{\tau}_i] \\ &= p_i(m, n-1) \prod_{j=m}^{n-2} [1 - p_i(m, j) - \bar{p}_i(m, j)]. \end{aligned} \quad (1)$$

Here, τ_i is the default time for firm i measured in units of months, $\bar{\tau}_i$ is the other exit time measured in units of months, and the product is equal to 1 if there is no term in the product. The condition $\tau_i < \bar{\tau}_i$ is the requirement that the firm defaults before it has a non-default type of exit. Note that by measuring exits in units of months, if, for example, a default occurs at any time in the interval $[(n-1)\Delta t, n\Delta t]$, then $\tau_i = n$.

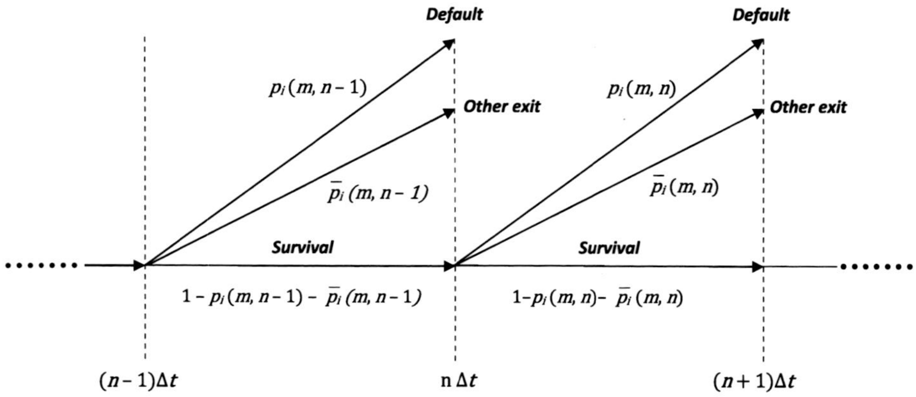

Figure 1. Default-other exit-survival tree for firm i, viewed from time $t = m\Delta t$.

Using Equation (1), cumulative default probabilities can be computed. At $m\Delta t$ the probability of firm i defaulting at or before $n\Delta t$ and not having an other exit before $t = n\Delta t$ is obtained by taking the sum of all of the paths that lead to default at or before $n\Delta t$:

$$\begin{aligned} &Prob_{t=m\Delta t}[m < \tau_i \leq n, \tau_i < \bar{\tau}_i] \\ &= \sum_{k=m}^{n-1} \left\{ p_i(m, k) \prod_{j=m}^{k-1} [1 - p_i(m, j) - \bar{p}_i(m, j)] \right\}. \end{aligned} \quad (2)$$

While it is convenient to derive the probabilities given in Equations (1) and (2) in terms of the conditional probabilities, expressions for these in terms of the forward intensities need to be found, since the forward intensities will be functions of the input variable $X_i(m)$. The forward intensity for the default of firm i that is observed at time $t = m\Delta t$ for the forward time interval from $t = n\Delta t$ to $(n + 1)\Delta t$, is denoted by $h_i(m,n)$, where $m \leq n$. The corresponding forward intensity for a non-default exit is denoted by $\bar{h}_i(m,n)$. Because default is signaled by a jump in a Poisson process, its conditional probability is a simple function of its forward intensity:

$$p_i(m, n) = 1 - \exp[-\Delta t\, h_i(m, n)]. \quad (3)$$

Since joint jumps in the same time interval are assigned as defaults, the conditional other exit probability needs to take this into account:

$$\bar{p}_i(m, n) = \exp[-\Delta t\, h_i(m, n)]\{1 - \exp[-\Delta t\, \bar{h}_i(m, n)]\}. \quad (4)$$

The conditional survival probabilities in Equations (1) and (2) are computed as the conditional probability that the firm does not default in the period and the firm does not have a non-default exit either:

$$\begin{aligned} &Prob_{t=m\Delta t}[\tau_i, \bar{\tau}_i > n + 1 | \tau_i, \bar{\tau}_i > n] \\ &= \exp\{-\Delta t[h_i(m, n) + \bar{h}_i(m, n)]\}. \end{aligned} \quad (5)$$

It remains to be specified the dependence of the forward intensities on the input variable $X_i(m)$. The forward intensities need to be positive so that the conditional probabilities are non-negative. A standard way to impose this constraint is to specify the forward intensities as exponentials of a linear combination of the input variables:

$$\begin{aligned} h_i(m, n) &= \exp[\beta(n - m) \cdot Y_i(m)], \\ \bar{h}_i(m, n) &= \exp[\bar{\beta}(n - m) \cdot Y_i(m)]. \end{aligned} \quad (6)$$

Here, β and $\bar{\beta}$ are coefficient vectors that are functions of the number of months between the observation date and the beginning of the forward period $(n - m)$, and $Y_i(m)$ is simply the vector $X_i(m)$ augmented by a preceding unit element: $Y_i(m) = (1, X_i(m))$. The unit element allows the linear combination in the argument of the exponentials in Equation (6) to have a non-zero intercept.

In the current implementation of the forward intensity model in the CRI, the maximum forecast horizon is 60 months (5 years) and there are 12 input variables plus the intercept, so there are 60 sets of β and $\bar{\beta}$. While this is a large set of parameters, as will be seen in Subsection 1.2 and 1.3, the calibration is tractable because the default parameters can be calibrated separately from the other exit parameters, and the total number of parameters are greatly reduced after constraining the term-structure of the parameter estimates to be Nelson-Siegel functions.

Before expressing the probabilities in Equation (1) and (2) in terms of the forward intensities, a notation H is introduced for the forward intensities so that it becomes clear which parameters the forward intensity depends on:

$$H(\beta(n - m), X_i(m)) = \exp[\beta(n - m) \cdot Y_i(m)]. \quad (7)$$

This is the forward default intensity. The corresponding notation for the forward other exit intensity is then just $H(\bar{\beta}(n - m), X_i(m))$. So, the probability in Equation (1) is expressed in terms of the forward intensities, using Equation (3) as the conditional default probability and Equation (5) as the conditional survival probability:

$$
\begin{aligned}
&Prob_{t=m\Delta t}[\tau_i = n, \tau_i < \bar{\tau}_i] \\
&= \{1-\exp[-\Delta t\, H(\beta(n-1-m), X_i(m))]\} \\
&\quad \times \prod_{j=m}^{n-2} \exp\{-\Delta t\,[H(\beta(j-m), X_i(m)) \\
&\quad + H(\bar{\beta}(j-m), X_i(m))]\} \\
&= \{1-\exp[-\Delta t\, H(\beta(n-m-1), X_i(m))]\} \\
&\quad \times \exp\left\{-\Delta t \sum_{j=m}^{n-2} [H(\beta(j-m), X_i(m)) \right. \\
&\quad \left. + H(\bar{\beta}(j-m), X_i(m))]\right\}.
\end{aligned} \tag{8}
$$

This probability will be relevant in the next part during the calibration. The cumulative default probability given in Equation (2) in terms of the forward intensities is then:

$$
\begin{aligned}
&Prob_{t=m\Delta t}[m < \tau_i \le n, \tau_i < \bar{\tau}_i] \\
&= \sum_{k=m}^{n-1} \left\{ \{1-\exp[-\Delta t\, H(\beta(k-m), X_i(m))]\} \right. \\
&\quad \times \exp\left\{-\Delta t \sum_{j=m}^{k-1} [H(\beta(j-m), X_i(m)) \right. \\
&\quad \left.\left. + H(\bar{\beta}(j-m), X_i(m))] \right\}\right\}.
\end{aligned} \tag{9}
$$

This formula is used to compute the main output of the CRI: an individual firm's PD within various time horizons. The β and $\bar{\beta}$ parameters are obtained when the firm's economy is calibrated, and using those together with the firm's input variables yields the firm's PD.

1.2. Pseudo-Likelihood Function

The empirical data set used for calibration can be described as follows. For the economy as a whole, there are N end of month observations, indexed as $n = 1, \ldots, N$. Of course, not all firms will have observations for each of the N months as they may start later than the start of the economy's data set or they may exit before the end of the economy's data set. There are a total of I firms in the economy, and they are indexed as $i = 1, \ldots, I$. As before, the input variables for the ith firm in the nth month is $X_i(n)$. The set of all observations for all firms is denoted by X.

In addition, the default times τ_i and non-default exit times $\bar{\tau}_i$ for the ith firm are known if the default or other exit occurs after time $t = \Delta t$ and at or before $t = N\Delta t$. The possible values for τ_i and $\bar{\tau}_i$ are integers between 2 and N, inclusive. If a firm exits before the month end, then the exit time is recorded as the first month end after the exit. If the firm does not exit before $t = N\Delta t$, then the convention can be used that both of these values are infinite. If the firm has a default type of exit within the data set, then $\bar{\tau}_i$ can be considered as infinite. If instead the firm has a non-default type of exit within the data set, then τ_i can be considered as infinite. The set of all default times and non-default exit times for all firms is denoted by τ and $\bar{\tau}$, respectively. The first month in which firm i has an observation is denoted by t_{0i}. Except for cases of missing data, these observations continue until the end of the data set if the firm never exits. If the firm does exit, the last needed input variable $X_i(n)$ is for $n = \min(\tau_i, \bar{\tau}_i) - 1$.

The calibration of the β and $\bar{\beta}$ parameters is done by maximizing a pseudo-likelihood function. The function to be maximized violates the standard assumptions of likelihood functions, but Appendix A in Duan *et al.* (2012) derives the large sample properties of the pseudo-likelihood function.

In formulating the pseudo-likelihood function, the assumption is made that the firms are conditionally independent from each other. In other words, correlations arise naturally from shared common factors $W(n)$ and any correlations between different firms' firm-specific variables. With this assumption, the pseudo-likelihood function for the horizon of ℓ months, a set of parameters β and $\bar{\beta}$ and the data set $(\tau, \bar{\tau}, X)$ is:

$$
\mathcal{L}_\ell(\beta, \bar{\beta}; \tau, \bar{\tau}, X) = \prod_{m=1}^{N-1} \prod_{i=1}^{I} P_{\min(N-m,\ell)}(\beta, \bar{\beta}; \tau_i, \bar{\tau}_i, X_i(m)). \tag{10}
$$

Here, $P_{\min(N-m,\ell)}(\beta, \bar{\beta}; \tau_i, \bar{\tau}_i, X_i(m))$ is a probability for the ith firm, with the nature of the probability depending on what happens to the firm during the period from month m to month $m + \min(N - m, \ell)$. This is defined as:

$$
\begin{aligned}
&P_\ell(\beta,\bar{\beta};\tau_i,\bar{\tau}_i,X_i(m))\\
&= 1_{\{t_{0i}\le m,\min(\tau,\bar{\tau})>m+\ell\}}\\
&\quad\times\exp\left\{-\Delta t\sum_{j=0}^{\ell-1}[H(\beta(j),X_i(m))+H(\bar{\beta}(j),X_i(m))]\right\}\\
&\quad+1_{\{t_{0i}\le m,\tau_i\le\bar{\tau}_i,\tau_i\le m+\ell\}}\{1-\exp[-\Delta t\,H(\beta(\tau_i-m-1),X_i(m))]\}\\
&\quad\times\exp\left\{-\Delta t\sum_{j=0}^{\tau_i-m-2}[H(\beta(j),X_i(m))+H(\bar{\beta}(j),X_i(m))]\right\}\\
&\quad+1_{\{t_{0i}\le m,\bar{\tau}_i\le\tau_i,\bar{\tau}_i\le m+\ell\}}\{1-\exp[-\Delta t\,H(\bar{\beta}(\bar{\tau}_i-m-1),X_i(m))]\}\\
&\quad\times\exp[-\Delta t\,H(\beta(\tau_i-m-1),X_i(m))]\\
&\quad\times\exp\left\{-\Delta t\sum_{j=0}^{\bar{\tau}_i-m-2}[H(\beta(j),X_i(m))+H(\bar{\beta}(j),X_i(m))]\right\}\\
&\quad+1_{\{t_{0i}>m\}}+1_{\{\min(\tau_i,\bar{\tau}_i)\le m\}}.
\end{aligned}
\tag{11}
$$

In words, if the ith firm survives from the observation time at month m for the full horizon ℓ until at least $m + \ell$, then the probability is the model-based survival probability for this period. This is the first term in Equation (11). The second term handles the cases where the firm has a default within the horizon, in which case the probability is the model-based probability of the firm defaulting at the month that it ends up defaulting, as given in Equation (8). The third term handles the cases where the firm has a non-default exit within the horizon, in which case the probability is the model-based probability of the firm having a non-default type exit at the month that the exit actually does occur. The expression for this probability uses the conditional non-default type exit probability given in Equation (4). The final two terms handle the cases where the firm is not in the data set at month m — either the first observation for the firm is after m or the firm has already exited. A constant value is assigned in this case so that this firm will not affect the maximization at this time point.

The pseudo-likelihood function given in Equation (10) can be numerically maximized to give estimates for the coefficients β and $\bar{\beta}$. Notice though that the sample observations for the pseudo-likelihood function are overlapping if the horizon is longer than one month. For example, when $\ell = 2$, default over the next two periods from month m is correlated to default over the next two periods from month $m + 1$ due to the common month in the two sample observations. However, in Appendix A of Duan *et al.* (2012), the maximum pseudo-likelihood estimator is shown to be consistent, in the sense that the estimators converge to the "true" parameter value in the large sample limit.

Notice though that each of the terms in Equation (11) can be written as a product of terms containing only β and terms containing only $\bar{\beta}$. This will allow separate maximizations with respect to β and with respect to $\bar{\beta}$, that is, the defaults and other exits.

The β and $\bar{\beta}$ specific versions of Equation (11) are:

$$
\begin{aligned}
&P_\ell^{\beta}(\beta;\tau_i,\bar{\tau}_i,X_i(m))\\
&= 1_{\{t_{0i}\le m,\min(\tau,\bar{\tau}_i)>m+\ell\}}\exp\left\{-\Delta t\sum_{j=0}^{\ell-1}H(\beta(j),X_i(m))\right\}\\
&\quad+1_{\{t_{0i}\le m,\tau_i\le\bar{\tau}_i,\tau_i\le m+\ell\}}\exp\left\{-\Delta t\sum_{j=0}^{\tau_i-m-2}H(\beta(j),X_i(m))\right\}\\
&\quad\times\{1-\exp[-\Delta t\,H(\beta(\tau_i-m-1),X_i(m))]\}\\
&\quad+1_{\{t_{0i}\le m,\bar{\tau}_i\le\tau_i,\bar{\tau}_i\le m+\ell\}}\exp\left\{-\Delta t\sum_{j=0}^{\bar{\tau}_i-m-2}H(\beta(j),X_i(m))\right\}\\
&\quad\times\exp[-\Delta t\,H(\beta(\tau_i-m-1),X_i(m))]\\
&\quad+1_{\{t_{0i}>m\}}+1_{\{\min(\tau_i,\bar{\tau}_i)\le m\}},\\
&P_\ell^{\bar{\beta}}(\bar{\beta};\tau_i,\bar{\tau}_i,X_i(m))\\
&= 1_{\{t_{0i}\le m,\min(\tau,\bar{\tau})>m+\ell\}}\exp\left\{-\Delta t\sum_{j=0}^{\ell-1}H(\bar{\beta}(j),X_i(m))\right\}\\
&\quad+1_{\{t_{0i}\le m,\tau_i\le\bar{\tau}_i,\tau_i\le m+\ell\}}\exp\left\{-\Delta t\sum_{j=0}^{\tau_i-m-2}H(\bar{\beta}(j),X_i(m))\right\}\\
&\quad+1_{\{t_{0i}\le m,\bar{\tau}_i\le\tau_i,\bar{\tau}_i\le m+\ell\}}\exp\left\{-\Delta t\sum_{j=0}^{\bar{\tau}_i-m-2}H(\bar{\beta}(j),X_i(m))\right\}\\
&\quad\times\{1-\exp[-\Delta t\,H(\bar{\beta}(\bar{\tau}_i-m-1),X_i(m))]\}\\
&\quad+1_{\{t_{0i}>m\}}+1_{\{\min(\tau_i,\bar{\tau}_i)\le m\}}.
\end{aligned}
\tag{12}
$$

Then, the β and $\bar{\beta}$ specific versions of the pseudo-likelihood function are given by:

$$\begin{aligned}\mathcal{L}_\ell^\beta(\beta;\tau,\bar{\tau},X) &= \prod_{m=1}^{N-\ell}\prod_{i=1}^{I} P_\ell^\beta(\beta;\tau_i,\bar{\tau}_i,X_i(m))\\ \mathcal{L}_\ell^{\bar{\beta}}(\bar{\beta};\tau,\bar{\tau},X) &= \prod_{m=1}^{N-\ell}\prod_{i=1}^{I} P_\ell^{\bar{\beta}}(\bar{\beta};\tau_i,\bar{\tau}_i,X_i(m)).\end{aligned} \tag{13}$$

With the definitions given in Equation (12) and (13), it can be seen that:

$$\mathcal{L}_\ell(\beta,\bar{\beta};\tau,\bar{\tau},X) = \mathcal{L}_\ell^\beta(\beta;\tau,\bar{\tau},X)\mathcal{L}_\ell^{\bar{\beta}}(\bar{\beta};\tau,\bar{\tau},X). \tag{14}$$

Thus, $\mathcal{L}_\ell^\beta$ and $\mathcal{L}_\ell^{\bar{\beta}}$ can be separately maximized to find their respective parameters. Subsection 1.3 will further explain how the optimal parameters can be estimated.

1.3. Parameter Estimation

Previously, the CRI system produced default predictions up to horizons of two years (RMI, 2012). An extension of the forecast horizon has been implemented as of the PD released on 1 April 2013. With this update, horizons of up to five years are now being computed. Technically speaking, horizons of arbitrary length can be calculated.

This extension to a five-year horizon is done by constraining the term-structure of the parameter estimates to be Nelson-Siegel (Nelson and Siegel, 1987; hereafter NS) functions of the forward-starting time. Horizon-specific parameters β, $\bar{\beta}$ can be obtained from the continuous NS function by using the forward prediction horizon as an input. The term-structures are further constrained so that the effect of risk factors on the forward intensity goes to zero as the horizon increases. This allows tractable and parsimonious extrapolations for horizons beyond five years.

The parameter estimation for the NS functions is based on a new numerical method (a pseudo-Bayesian SMC technique) developed in a working paper by Duan and Fulop (2013). The remainder of this section details the new parameter estimation. 1.3.1 describes the parameterization of the parameters by NS functions, 1.3.2 gives an overview of the SMC method that is used to estimate the NS functions, 1.3.3 details the calculation of the confidence intervals for the parameter estimation, and 1.3.4 describes how the parameters can be re-estimated given new data or updates of old data.

1.3.1. *Smoothed parameters*

Duan *et al.* (2012) formulate the forward intensity model in which the forward default intensity for a firm is a function of a number of covariates. The forward default intensities for different forward starting periods are computed using different sets of parameters.

In Duan *et al.* (2012), the sets of parameters are estimated separately for each forward starting time. Parameters at different forward starting times that are associated with each covariate can be approximated by a function of the forward starting time using NS type term structure functions. Duan *et al.* (2012) show that this approximation by NS functions does not negatively affect prediction performance. The RMI implementation follows Duan and Fulop (2013) to impose the functional restriction during the estimation as opposed to the method used in Duan *et al.* (2012) of fitting the curve after parameter estimates have been obtained. This is done for two reasons.

First, it will significantly reduce the number of parameters. For example, using 12 covariates for forward default intensities up to 60 months would require a joint estimation of $13 \times 60 = 780$ parameters. Here, 13 comes from adding an intercept to the intensity function with 12 covariates. If the coefficients corresponding to each covariate are represented by the NS function of 4 parameters, there will be at most $13 \times 4 = 52$ parameters. In fact, there will be fewer parameters as some of the NS parameters will be constrained to zero.

Second, the NS function will allow extrapolation. For example, the 13 NS functions estimated with predictions up to 60 months can be used for prediction, say, over 72 months.

The NS function with four free parameters is:

$$\begin{aligned} r(t;\varrho_0,\varrho_1,\varrho_2,d) = \varrho_0 + \varrho_1\frac{1-\exp(-t/d)}{t/d} \\ +\varrho_2\left[\frac{1-\exp(-t/d)}{t/d} - \exp(-t/d)\right], \end{aligned} \tag{15}$$

where t is the forecast horizon (measured in years). In the RMI implementation, the horizon is 60 months (5 years) so that t ranges from 0 to 59/12. Once the four NS parameters are estimated, individual horizon-specific parameters β, $\bar{\beta}$ are obtained from the NS function r using the forecast horizon as input to the NS function. In our current implementation with forecast horizons extending to 60 months (5 years), 120 sets of month-specific β and $\bar{\beta}$ are obtained. For all covariates, the restriction $d > 0$ is imposed so that the functions converge to a value for large t. This formulation will be used for forward intensities for both defaults and other types of exit.

For the coefficients of all stochastic covariates, the long-run level ϱ_0 is restricted to zero, because the current value of a stochastic covariate should be uninformative of default or other exits when the forward starting time goes to infinity. In other words, the coefficient of such a stochastic covariate should approach zero when t goes to infinity.

The intercept of the forward intensity function is of course non-stochastic. Thus, ϱ_0 can have non-zero values for the intercept. With these restrictions on the NS parameters, take the example of 12 covariates, there will be a total of $12 \times 3 + 1 \times 4 = 40$ parameters.

In the RMI implementation, the NS function is further constrained to be non-positive for certain covariates: DTD level and trend, liquidity level and trend, and profitability level and trend. Refer to Section 2 for descriptions of these covariates.

1.3.2. *Parameter estimation by SMC*

Reliably estimating a system involving 40 parameters presents a numerical challenge. Moreover, the number of parameters can be greater than 40 if there are more than 12 covariates. The RMI implementation follows Duan and Fulop (2013) who use the SMC pseudo-Bayesian method for estimation and self-normalized statistics for inference.

Due to decomposability, the analysis can be performed separately on the forward default and other exit intensities. The data in the RMI implementation are refreshed with monthly frequency, and the sample likelihood used in estimation relies on default predictions running from 1 month to 60 months with a one month increment. Naturally, default prediction is subjected to data availability. Towards the end of the period with available data, the prediction horizon naturally decreases and stops at one-month predictions.

The following exposition closely follows the appendix in Duan and Fulop (2013). It is important to note that the RMI implementation uses the model described in Duan and Fulop (2013), which does not contain any latent frailty or partial conditioning variable, and hence is technically much simpler in parameter estimation. For example, there is no nonlinear filtering problem.

According to the current modeling framework, where for a particular economy there are N end of month observations, the input variables of the ith firm in the mth month is given by $X_i(m)$. Let θ denote a set of NS parameters and ℓ denote the forecast horizon ($\ell = 60$). Then the pseudo-likelihood function at step m, denoted by $\mathcal{L}_{m,\min(N-m,\ell)}(\theta)$, takes the form:

$$\mathcal{L}_{m,\min(N-m,\ell)}(\theta) = \prod_{i=1}^{I} P_{\min(N-m,\ell)} \left(\beta(\theta), \bar{\beta}(\theta); \tau_i, \bar{\tau}_i, X_i(m)\right), \tag{16}$$

where I is the number of firms, $\beta(\theta)$ and $\bar{\beta}(\theta)$ are the coefficient vectors from Equation (6) generated from the NS functions with parameter θ. One may notice that $\mathcal{L}_{m,\min(N-m,\ell)}(\theta)$ is one of the terms in the outer-most product in Equation (10).

Let $\pi(\theta)$ denote the prior. Following the notation from Section 1.1, consider the following pseudo-posterior distribution at time n after one makes the ℓ-period prediction:

$$\gamma_n(\theta) \propto \prod_{m=1}^{n-1} \mathcal{L}_{m,\min(N-m,\ell)}(\theta)\pi(\theta), \quad \text{for } n = 2, \ldots, N. \tag{17}$$

One can apply the sequential batch-resampling routine of Chopin (2012) together with tempering steps as in Del Moral *et al.* (2006) to advance the system. For each n, this procedure yields a weighted sample of K particles, $(\theta^{(k,n)}, w^{(k,n)})$ with $k = 1, \ldots, K$, whose empirical distribution function will converge to $\gamma_n(\theta)$ as K increases. In the following paragraphs, the superscript k denotes the particle index. Note that in the RMI implementation, $K = 1000$.

Initialization: Draw an initial random sample from the prior: $(\theta^{(k,0)} \sim \pi(\theta), w^{(k,0)} = 1/K)$. Here, the only role of the prior $\pi(\theta)$, is to provide the initial particle cloud from which the algorithm can start. Of course, the support of $\pi(\theta)$ must contain the true parameter value θ_0. In the RMI implementation, normal/truncated normal priors are used. Truncation applies in order to impose the restriction $d > 0$. To obtain the means of the priors for the SMC method, a least square fit of the MLE parameter estimates of the NS function is conducted. The standard deviations of the priors are set to 5.

Recursions and defining the tempering sequence: Assume there is a particle cloud $(\theta^{(k,n)}, w^{(k,n)})$ whose empirical distribution represents $\gamma_n(\theta)$. Then, a cloud representing $\gamma_{n+1}(\theta)$ will be reached by combining importance sampling and the Markov Chain Monte Carlo (MCMC) steps. Sometimes moving directly from $\gamma_n(\theta)$ to $\gamma_{n+1}(\theta)$ is too ambitious as the two distributions are too far from each other. This will be reflected in highly variable importance weights if one resorts to direct importance sampling. Hence, following Duan and Fulop (2013) which in turn followed Del Moral *et al.* (2006), a tempered bridge is built between the two densities and the particles are evolved through the resulting sequence of densities. In particular, assume that at $n + 1$, there are P_{n+1} intermediate densities:

$$\bar{\gamma}_{n+1,p}(\theta) \propto \gamma_n(\theta)\mathcal{L}^{\xi_p}_{n,\min(N-n,\ell)}(\theta), \quad \text{for } p = 1,\ldots,P_{n+1}. \tag{18}$$

This construction defines an appropriate bridge: $\xi_0 = 0$ so that $\bar{\gamma}_{n+1,0}(\theta) = \gamma_n(\theta)$, and $\xi_{P_{n+1}} = 1$ so that $\bar{\gamma}_{n+1,P_{n+1}}(\theta) = \gamma_{n+1}(\theta)$. For p between 0 and P_{n+1}, ξ_p is chosen from a grid of points to evenly distribute the weights, as decribed below. A particle cloud representing $\bar{\gamma}_{n+1,0}(\theta)$ can be initialized as $(\bar{\theta}^{(k,n+1,0)}, \bar{w}^{(k,n+1,0)}) = (\theta^{(k,n)}, w^{(k,n)})$. Then, for $p = 1,\ldots, P_{n+1}$ the sequence proceeds as follows:

- *Reweighting Step*: In order to arrive at a representation of $\bar{\gamma}_{n+1,p}(\theta)$, the particles representing $\bar{\gamma}_{n+1,p-1}(\theta)$ and the importance sampling principle can be used. This leads to:

$$\bar{\theta}^{(k,n+1,p)} = \bar{\theta}^{(k,n+1,p-1)}, \tag{19}$$

$$\begin{aligned}\bar{w}^{(k,n+1,p)} &= \bar{w}^{(k,n+1,p-1)} \times \frac{\bar{\gamma}_{n+1,p}(\bar{\theta}^{(k,n+1,p)})}{\bar{\gamma}_{n+1,p-1}(\bar{\theta}^{(k,n+1,p)})} \\ &= \bar{w}^{(k,n+1,p-1)} \times \mathcal{L}^{\xi_p-\xi_{p-1}}_{n,\min(N-n,\ell)} \\ &\quad (\bar{\theta}^{(k,n+1,p)}).\end{aligned} \tag{20}$$

To avoid particle impoverishment in sequential importance sampling where most of the weight is concentrated in a small number of particles, a resample-move step is run, which is triggered whenever a measure of particle diversity — the efficient sample size (ESS) defined as:

$$\text{ESS} = \frac{\left(\sum_{k=1}^{N} \bar{w}^{(k,n+1,p)}\right)^2}{\sum_{k=1}^{N} (\bar{w}^{(k,n+1,p)})^2}, \tag{21}$$

falls below some preset value B. Here, resampling directs the particle cloud towards more likely areas of the sampling space, while the move step enriches particle diversity. In the RMI implementation, B is set to 50%. Thus, if ESS < 50%, the following resampling and move steps are performed.

- *Resampling Step*: The particles are resampled proportional to their weights. If $I^{(k,n+1,p)} \in (1,\ldots,K)$ are particle indices sampled proportional to $\bar{w}^{(k,n+1,p)}$, the equally weighted particles are obtained as:

$$\bar{\theta}^{(k,n+1,p)} = \bar{\theta}^{(I^{(k,n+1,p)},n+1,p)}, \tag{22}$$

$$\bar{w}^{(k,n+1,p)} = \frac{1}{K}. \tag{23}$$

- *Move Step*: Each particle is passed through a Markov kernel $K_{n+1,p}(\theta^{(k,n+1,p)},\cdot)$ that leaves $\gamma_{n+1,p}(\theta)$ invariant, typically a Metropolis-Hastings kernel:

  1. Propose $\theta^{*(k)} \sim Q_{n+1,p}\left(\cdot \middle| \bar{\theta}^{(k,n+1,p)}\right)$.
  2. Compute the acceptance weight α, where:

$$\alpha = \min\left(1, \frac{\bar{\gamma}_{n+1,p}(\theta^{*(k)})Q_{n+1,p}\left(\bar{\theta}^{(k,n+1,p)} \middle| \theta^{*(k)}\right)}{\bar{\gamma}_{n+1,p}(\bar{\theta}^{(k,n+1,p)})Q_{n+1,p}\left(\theta^{*(k)} \middle| \bar{\theta}^{(k,n+1,p)}\right)}\right). \tag{24}$$

3. With probability α, set $\bar{\theta}^{(k,n+1,p)} = \theta^{*(k)}$, otherwise keep the old particle.

This step will enrich the support of the particle cloud while conserving its distribution. If the particle set is a poor representation of the target distribution, the move step can also help adjust the location of the support. Crucially, given the importance of the sampling setup, the proposal distribution $Q_{n+1,p}\left(\cdot\middle|\bar{\theta}^{(k,n+1,p)}\right)$ can be adapted using the existing particle cloud.

In the RMI implementation, block independent normal distribution proposals using the means and the standard deviations implied by the particle set are fitted to the particle cloud before the move. Three (or four) NS parameters corresponding to each covariate form one block. To ensure that the NS parameter d remains positive, any block with a non-positive value for d is discarded. To ensure the smoothness of the term structure of the forward intensity parameters, any block that does not produce an increasing or decreasing structure of the NS function for the first five months is also discarded. Once some block is discarded, the particle is regenerated until it meets the requirements. Note that the likelihood ratio in the Metropolis-Hastings algorithm is not affected by this because the truncated normal creates a common adjustment term in both the numerator and denominator.

As mentioned previously, the coefficients for some covariates are required to be non-positive over all forward starting times. This is achieved by checking whether the NS curve at a particular set of three (or four) parameters meets the condition. If not, the parameter set will be discarded.

To improve the support of the particle cloud, one can execute multiple such Metropolis-Hastings steps each time. In the RMI implementation, such Metropolis-Hastings steps are consecutively performed in each resampling-move step until the number of unique particles exceeds $K/2$.

When $p = P_{n+1}$ is reached, a representation of $\gamma_{n+1}(\theta)$ is:

$$(\theta^{(k,n+1)}, w^{(k,n+1)}) = (\bar{\theta}^{(k,n+1,P_{n+1})}, \bar{w}^{(k,n+1,P_{n+1})}). \quad (25)$$

Following Duan and Fulop (2013), the tempering sequence ξ_p is automatically set to ensure that the efficient sample size stays close to 50%. This is done by a grid search, where the ESS is evaluated at a grid of candidate ξ_p and the one that produces the closest ESS to 50% is chosen.

After the recursion procedure (i.e., ξ_p reaches 1), additional moves using the means implied by the particle set but with all standard deviations increased by a factor of 30% are further performed to enrich the support and adjust the location of the particle set. The number of such moves is set to 20 for the first time point and exponentially declines to 3 mid-way to the sample period and stays at 3 for the remainder. After that, if the number of unique particles is still below $K/2$, more moves using the means and the standard deviations implied by the particle set (without expansions) are consecutively performed until the particle set meets the requirement. (This case could only happen when ESS$\geq B$ for $\xi_p = 1$.)

1.3.3. *Statistical inference*

The full sample size has N time series data points but one can only make default prediction at $N-1$ time points; for example, at time point 2, the data is only available for making one-period default prediction at time point 1. Denote the pseudo-posterior mean of the parameter of the whole sample by $\bar{\beta}$ and for $n = 2, \ldots, N$,

$$\hat{\theta}_n = \frac{1}{\sum_{k=1}^{K} w^{(k,n)}} \sum_{k=1}^{K} w^{(k,n)} \theta^{(k,n)}. \quad (26)$$

Note that $(\bar{\theta}^{(k,n+1,0)}, \bar{w}^{(k,n+1,0)}) = (\theta^{(k,n)}, w^{(k,n)})$. is not a true posterior because the likelihood function in equation (17) is not a true likelihood function. Thus, it cannot directly provide valid Bayesian inference. But following Duan and Fulop (2013) — which is in turn based on Shao's self-normalized statistic (Shao, 2010) — inference can be performed using the t-like statistic. To test, for example, the hypothesis of the kth element of $\bar{\theta}^{(k,n+1,p)} = \bar{\theta}^{(I^{(k,n+1,p)},n+1,p)}$, denoted by $\bar{w}^{(k,n+1,p)} = \frac{1}{K}$, equal to a, one has:

$$t^* = \frac{\sqrt{N-1}\left(\hat{\theta}_N^{(k)} - a\right)}{\sqrt{\hat{\delta}_{k,N}}} \xrightarrow{d} \frac{W(1)}{\left[\int_0^1 (W(r) - rW(1))^2\, dr\right]^{1/2}}, \quad (27)$$

where $W(r)$ is a Wiener process, is the kth diagonal element of $\theta_0^{(k)}$, and:

$$\hat{C}_N = \frac{1}{(N-1)^2}\sum_{n=2}^{N} n^2(\hat{\theta}_n - \hat{\theta}_N)(\hat{\theta}_n - \hat{\theta}_N)'. \tag{28}$$

The right-hand-side random variable for t^* does not have a known distribution, but can be easily simulated. Kiefer *et al.* (2000) reported that the 95% quantile is 5.374 and the 97.5% quantile is 6.811. These values can also be used to set up confidence intervals.

1.3.4. *Periodic updating*

In reality, portfolio credit risk models need to be updated periodically as new data arrive and/or old data are revised. With one new month of data, this means that the final date index N is increased to $N + 1$. A particular strength of Duan and Fulop's (2013) methodology is that the estimation routine does not need to be re-initialized from the prior as the pseudo-posterior using data up to $N\Delta t$ will provide a much better proposal distribution.

Let the pseudo-posterior at time N (based on the old data set available at time N) be denoted by:

$$\gamma_N^{(N)}(\theta) \propto \prod_{m=1}^{N-1} \mathcal{L}_{m,\min(N-m,\ell)}^{(N)}(\theta)\pi(\theta), \tag{29}$$

and the pseudo-posterior at time $N + 1$ (based on the new data set available at time $N + 1$) by:

$$\gamma_{N+1}^{(N+1)}(\theta) \propto \prod_{m=1}^{N} \mathcal{L}_{m,\min((N+1)-m,\ell)}^{(N+1)}(\theta)\pi(\theta). \tag{30}$$

The superscript is introduced to differentiate the data set available at time N and $N + 1$, respectively. It is important to note that $\mathcal{L}_{m,k}^{(N+1)}(\theta) \neq \mathcal{L}_{m,k}^{(N)}(\theta)$ can be caused by revisions to the old data set. More importantly, there is a generic difference between the pseudo-posterior distribution up to time N under the new data set and the corresponding quantity under the old data set specifically due to multiperiod prediction; that is, $\gamma_{N+1}^{(N)}(\theta) \neq \gamma_N^{(N)}(\theta)$ even without any data revisions to the period covered by the old data set. To put it concretely, using the new data set and at, say, one period before the last (i.e., time $N - 1$), one can make default predictions up to two periods, whereas at the same time point, it was only possible to make one-period predictions under the old data set because there were no data beyond time N. Adjustments to the weights are thus necessary to reflect the change in data set before making any sequential updates.

There are several possible ways of advancing the system. The RMI implementation decomposes the move into two steps. First, we take care of data revision up to time N and then act as if we were making predictions with data only up to time N. Doing it this way is meant to maintain the same default prediction setting; that is, for example, only making one-period default prediction at time $N - 1$ even though the new data set permits predictions up to two periods. Thus, we introduce:

$$\gamma_N^{(N+1,N)}(\theta) \propto \prod_{m=1}^{N-1} \mathcal{L}_{m,\min(N-m,\ell)}^{(N+1)}(\theta)\pi(\theta) \tag{31}$$

to denote this pseudo-posterior when the superscript $(N + 1, N)$ stands for the updated data set available at time $N + 1$ but making default predictions as if the data were only available up to time N.

From the previous run up to time N, one already has a weighted set of particles $(\theta^{(k,N)}, w^{(k,N)})$ representing the pseudo-posterior distribution $\gamma_N^{(N)}(\theta)$. Next, perform a reweighting by:

$$\theta^{*(k,N)} = \theta^{(k,N)}, \tag{32}$$

$$w^{*(k,N)} = w^{(k,N)} \times \frac{\gamma_N^{(N+1,N)}(\theta^{(k,N)})}{\gamma_N^{(N)}(\theta^{(k,N)})}. \tag{33}$$

Since the denominator is available from the previous run, one only needs to compute the numerator using the new data set up to time N. Then, the weighted set $(\theta^{*(k,N)}, w^{*(k,N)})$ represents the revised pseudo-posterior distribution at time N, i.e., $\gamma_N^{(N+1,N)}(\theta)$, specifically to account for data revisions. From this point onward, one can apply the same recursive procedure described in Section 1.3.2, starting from equation (18), to complete the updating task.

Reweighting may substantially alter the ESS of the particle set due to a large volume of data changes. If the reweighting leads to a satisfactory ESS, i.e., ESS $\geq B$, advancing to $N + 1$ continues as usual. Otherwise, the weighted sample will be discarded to prevent the support from degeneration. One can return to the particle set before reweighting and perform resampling to create an equally-weighted particle set. Then, make the Metropolis-Hastings moves by targeting $\gamma_N^{(N+1,N)}(\theta)$ using the Gaussian-type sampler described earlier and starting with the mean and variance implied by the resampled particle set. One should make these Metropolis-Hastings moves until the particle set reaches a desirable level of distinctiveness, and perhaps with a preset minimum number of moves to ensure that the resulting particle set is close enough to the target distribution. In the RMI implementation, the number of moves is set to be 20.

Furthermore, one can update all self-normalized statistics in the way as described earlier to reflect the one additional pseudo-posterior means to the sequence.

The initial parameter estimation is carried out for all calibration groups using the data up to the end of January 2013. Relevant quantities (parameter estimates, the 1000 parameter particles and corresponding weights and sample likelihoods) are saved for periodic updating for all future months. Additional implementation details on the calibration are given in Section 3.

II. INPUT VARIABLES AND DATA

Subsection 2.1 describes the input variables used in the quantitative model. Currently, the same set of input variables is common to all of the economies under the CRI's coverage. Future enhancements to the CRI system will allow different input variables for different economies. The effect of each of the variables on the PD output will be discussed in the empirical analysis of Section 4.

Subsection 2.2 gives the data sources and relevant details of the data sources. There are two categories of data sources: current and historical. Data sources used for current data need to be updated in a timely manner so that daily updates of PD forecasts are meaningful. They also need to be comprehensive in their current coverage of firms. Data sources that are comprehensive for current data may not necessarily have comprehensive historical coverage for different economies. Thus, other data sources are merged in order to obtain comprehensive coverage of historical and current data.

Subsection 2.3 indicates the fields from the data sources that are used to construct the input variables. For some of the fields, proxies need to be used for a firm if the preferred field is not available for that firm.

Subsection 2.4 discusses the definition and sources of defaults and of other exits used in the CRI.

2.1. Input Variables

Following the notation that was introduced in Section 1, firm i's input variables at time $t = n\Delta t$ are represented by the vector $X_i(n) = (W(n), U_i(n))$ consisting of a vector $W(n)$ that is common to all firms in the same economy, and a firm-specific vector $U_i(n)$ which is observable from the date the firm's first financial statement is released, until the month end before the month in which the firm exits, if it does exit.

In Duan *et al.* (2012), different variables that are commonly used in the literature were tested as candidates for the elements of $W(n)$ and $U_i(n)$. Two common variables and ten firm-specific variables, as described below, were selected as having the greatest predictive power for corporate defaults in the United States. In the current stage of development, this same set of twelve input variables is used for all economies. Future development will include variable selection for firms in different economies.

- *Common variables*

  The vector $W(n)$ contains two elements, which are:

  1. Stock index return: the trailing one-year simple return on a major stock index of the economy;
  2. Interest rate: a representative 3-month short term interest rate.

- *Firm-specific variables*

  The ten firm-specific input variables are transformations of measures of six different firm characteristics. The six firm characteristics are:
  1. volatility-adjusted leverage;
  2. liquidity;
  3. profitability;
  4. relative size;
  5. market misvaluation/future growth opportunities; and
  6. idiosyncratic volatility.

Volatility-adjusted leverage is measured as the DTD in a Merton-type model. The calculation of DTD used by the CRI allows a meaningful DTD for financial firms, a critical sector that must be excluded from most DTD computations. This calculation is detailed in Section 3.

Liquidity is measured as a ratio of cash and short term investments to total assets. Profitability is measured as a ratio of net income to total assets. Relative size is measured as the logarithm of the ratio of market capitalization to the economy's median market capitalization.

Duan *et al.* (2012) transformed these first four characteristics into level and trend versions of the measures. For each of these characteristics, the level is computed as the one-year average of the measure, and the trend is computed as the current value of the measure minus the one-year average of the measure. The level and trend of a measure has seldom been used in the academic or industry literature for default prediction, and Duan *et al.* (2012) found that using the level and trend significantly improves the predictive power of the model for short-term horizons.

To understand the intuition behind using the level and trend of a measure as opposed to using just the current value, consider the case of two firms with the same current value for all measures. If the level and trend transformations were not performed, only the current values would be used and the two firms would have identical PD. Suppose that for the first firm the DTD had reached its current level from a high level, and for the second firm the DTD had reached its current level from a lower level (see Figure 2). The first firm's leverage is increasing (worsening) and the second firm's leverage is decreasing (improving). If there is a momentum effect in DTD, then firm 1 should have a higher PD than firm 2.

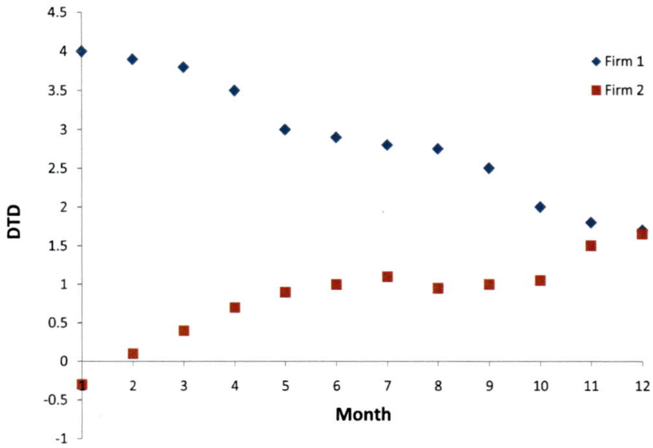

Figure 2. Two firms with all current values equal to each other, but DTD trending in the opposite direction.

Duan *et al.* (2012) found evidence of the momentum effect in DTD, liquidity, profitability and size. For the other two firm characteristics, applying the level and trend transformation did not improve the predictive power of the model.

One of the remaining two firm characteristics is the market mis-valuation/future growth opportunities characteristic, which is taken as the market-to-book asset ratio and measured as a ratio of market capitalization and total liabilities to total assets. One can see whether the market mis-valuation effect or the future growth opportunities effect dominates this measure by looking at whether the parameter for this variable is positive or negative. This will be further discussed in the empirical analysis of Section 4.

The last firm characteristic is the idiosyncratic volatility which is taken as SIGMA, following Shumway (2001). SIGMA is computed by regressing the daily returns of the firm's market capitalization against the daily returns of the economy's stock index, for the previous 250 days. SIGMA is defined to be the standard deviation of the residuals of this regression. Using daily returns is to ensure that SIGMA provides an accurate and timely measure of idiosyncratic risk of individual companies. Shumway (2001) reasons that SIGMA should be logically related to bankruptcy since firms with more variable cash flows and therefore more variable stock returns relative to a market index are likely to have a higher probability of bankruptcy.

Finally, the vector $U_i(n)$ contains ten elements, consisting of:

1. Level of DTD.
2. Trend of DTD.
3. Level of (Cash + Short term investments)/Total assets, abbreviated as CASH/TA.
4. Trend of CASH/TA.
5. Level of Net income/Total assets, abbreviated as NI/TA.
6. Trend of NI/TA.
7. Level of log (Firm market capitalization/ Economy's median market capitalization), abbreviated as SIZE.
8. Trend of SIZE.
9. Current value of (Market capitalization + Total liabilities)/Total asset, abbreviated as M/B.
10. Current value of SIGMA.

The data fields that are needed to compute DTD and short term investments are described in Subsection 2.3. The remaining data fields required are straightforward and standard. The computation for DTD is explained in Section 3.

2.2. Data Sources

There are two data sources that are used for the daily PD forecast updates: Thomson Reuters Datastream and the Bloomberg Data License Back Office Product. Many of the common factors such as short term interest rates and macroeconomic data are retrieved from Datastream.

Firm-specific data comes from Bloomberg's Back Office Product which delivers daily update files by region via FTP after the respective market closes. All relevant data is extracted from the FTP files and uploaded into the CRI database for storage. From this, the necessary fields are extracted and joined with previous months of data.

The Back Office Product includes daily market capitalization data based on closing share prices and also includes new financial statements as companies release them. Firms will often have multiple versions of financial statements within the same period, with different accounting standards, filing statuses (most recent, preliminary, original, reclassified or restated), currencies or consolidated/unconsolidated indicators. A major challenge lies in prioritizing these financial statements to decide which data should be used. The priority rules are described in Section 3.

The firm coverage of the Back Office Product is of sufficient quality that around 34,000 firms can be updated on a daily basis in the 106 economies under the CRI's coverage. While the current coverage is quite comprehensive, historical data from the Back Office Product can be sparse for certain economies. For this reason, various other databases are merged in order to fill out the historical data. The other databases used for historical data are: a database from the Taiwan Economics Journal (TEJ) for Taiwanese firms; a database provided by Korea University for South Korean firms; and data from Prowess for Indian firms.

With all of the databases merged together and for the 106 economies under CRI's coverage, over 60,000 exchange listed firms are in the CRI database. This includes over 30,000 firms that have been delisted at some point in time. The historical coverage of the firm data goes back to the early 1990s. In order to be included in our coverage, a company needs to have common equity traded on a stock exchange. Of these 106 economies, 71 economies have their own stock exchange (see Table A.2). For the other 35 economies under the RMI coverage, we cover companies domiciled in the economy that are quoted on a foreign exchange, either because those economies do not have a stock exchange or because data issues are preventing us from including the companies listed on the local exchange.

2.3. Constructing Input Variables

The chosen stock indices and short term interest rates for the 71 economies with their own stock exchange under the CRI's current coverage are listed in Table A.5 and Table A.6, respectively. All economies are listed by their three letter ISO code given in Table A.4.

Most of the firm-specific variables can be readily constructed from standard fields from firms' financial statements in addition to daily market capitalization values. The only two exceptions are the DTD and the liquidity measure.

The calculation for DTD is explained in Section 3. In the calculation, several variables are required. One variable is a proxy for a one-year risk-free interest rate, and the choices for each of the 71 economies are listed in Table A.7. Total assets, long-term borrowing and total liabilities are also required, but can be obtained from standard financial statement fields easily.

Total current liabilities are also required, and due to the relatively large number of firms that are missing this value, proxies have to be found. The preferred Bloomberg field for this is BS_CUR_LIAB. If this is missing, then the sum of BS_ST_BORROW, BS_OTHER_ST_LIAB and BS_CUST_ACCPT_LIAB_CUSTDY_SEC (customers' acceptance and liabilities/custody securities) is used. If one or two of these are missing, zero is inserted for those fields, but at least one field is required.

The liquidity measure requires different fields for financial and non-financial firms. For non-financial firms, the numerator of the ratio (Cash + Short term investments) is taken as the sum of BS_CASH_NEAR_CASH_ITEM and BS_MKT_SEC_OTHER_ST_INVEST (marketable securities and other short term investments). If BS_MKT_SEC_OTHER_ST_INVEST is missing, substitute zero (but BS_CASH_NEAR_CASH_ITEM is required).

It was found that this sum frequently overstated the liquidity for financial firms. In place of BS_MKT_SEC_OTHER_ST_INVEST, financial firms use the sum of ARD_SEC_PURC_UNDER_AGR_TO_RESELL (securities purchased under agreement to resell), ARD_ST_INVEST and BS_INTERBANK_ASSET. If one or two of these are missing, zero is inserted for those fields, but at least one field is required. The "ARD" prefix indicates that these are "as reported" numbers directly from the financial statements. As such, for some firms these fields may need to be adjusted to the same units before adding them to other fields.

To summarize, the firm-specific variables include: DTD, Cash/TA, NI/TA, SIZE, M/B, and SIGMA, and the statistics grouped by economy are listed in Table A.8.

2.4. Data for Defaults

The CRI database contains credit events of over 4,000 firms from 1990 to the present. The default events come from numerous sources, including Bloomberg, Compustat, CRSP, Moody's reports, TEJ, exchange websites and news sources.

The default events that are recognized by the CRI can be classified under one of the following events:

1. Bankruptcy filing, receivership, administration, liquidation or any other legal impasse to the timely settlement of interest and/or principal payments;
2. A missed or delayed payment of interest and/or principal, excluding delayed payments made within a grace period;
3. Debt restructuring/distressed exchange, in which debt holders are offered a new security or package of securities that result in a diminished financial obligation (e.g., a conversion of debt to equity, debt with lower coupon or par amount, debt with lower seniority, debt with longer maturity).

The more precise sub-categories of default corporate actions are listed in Table A.9.

Delisting due to other reasons such as failure to meet listing requirements, inactive stock prices or M&A are counted as "other exits" and are not considered as default. However, firms that are delisted from an exchange and then experience a default event within 365 calendar days of the delisting will have an exit event reclassified as credit default. Technical defaults such as covenant violations are not included in our definition of default. The exit events that are not considered as defaults in the CRI system are listed in Table A.10.

In addition to the aforementioned events, there are still cases that require special attention and will be assessed on a case-by-case basis, e.g., subsidiary default. As a general rule, the CRI does not consider related party-default (e.g., subsidiary bankruptcy) as a default event. However, when a non-operating holding parent company relies heavily on its subsidiary, bankruptcy by the subsidiary will cause a considerable economic impact on the parent company. Such cases will be reviewed and final classifications made.

Complete statistics of the total number of firms, number of defaults and number of other exits in each of the 71 economies from 1992 to 2012 are listed in Table A.11.

III. IMPLEMENTATION DETAILS

Section 1 described the modeling framework underlying the current implementation of the CRI system. It focused on theory rather than the details encountered in an operational implementation. The present section describes how the CRI system handles more specific issues.

Subsection 3.1 describes implementation details related to data, mainly dealing with data cleaning and missing data. Subsection 3.2 describes the specific computation of DTD used by the CRI system that leads to meaningful DTD for financial firms. Subsection 3.3 explains how the calibration previously described in Subsection 1.2 can be implemented. Subsection 3.4 gives the implementation details relevant to the daily output. This includes an explanation of the various modifications needed to compute daily PD so that the daily PD is consistent with the usual month end PD, and a description of the computation of the aggregate PDs provided by the CRI.

3.1. Data Treatment

Fitting data to monthly frequency: Historical end of month data for every firm in an economy is required to calibrate the model. For daily data such as market capitalization, interest rates and stock index values, the last day of the month for which there is valid data is used.

Up to the October 2012 calibration, financial statement (FS) variables data were used, starting from the period end of the statement lagged by 3 months. This is to ensure that predictions are made based on information that was available at the time the prediction was made. However, this treatment can be over-conservative, and many companies actually release their financial statements quicker than 3 months. Therefore, we implement a new logic and we start using the values in an FS as soon as its latest revision was put into the RMI database, unless the FS' release was delayed for more than 3 months. If there was no revision to a FS, the originally released FS is used. Whenever the latest revision is available more than 3 months after the period end, we revert to the previous logic. We start including the FS before the latest revision is actually available as a compromise, to avoid situations like later minor revisions of the FS holding back more up-to-date information. It should be noted that the new approach was only applied for FS input into the RMI database after February 2011, as the revision dates were not accurately recorded before this date. The CRI considers financial statement variables to be valid for one year without restriction, after they were first used.

Priority of financial statements: As described in Subsection 2.2, data provided in Bloomberg's Back Office Product can include numerous versions of financial statements within the same period. If there are multiple financial statements with the same period end, priority rules must be followed in order to determine which to use. The formulation and implementation of these rules are major challenges and areas of continuing development.

The first rule is to prioritize by consolidated/unconsolidated status. This status is relevant only to firms in India, Japan, South Korea and Taiwan, so this rule is only relevant in those economies. Most firms in these economies issue unconsolidated financial statements more frequently than consolidated ones, so these are given higher priority. This simple prioritization can, however, lead to cases where the financial statements used switch from consolidated statements to unconsolidated statements and back again. A more complex prioritization rule is currently under development, with the intention of avoiding this situation.

If, after the first prioritization rule has been applied, there are still multiple financial statements, the second rule is applied. This is prioritization by fiscal period. In most economies, annual statements are required to be audited, whereas other fiscal periods are not necessarily audited. The order of priority from highest to lowest is, therefore: annual, semi-annual, quarterly, cumulative, and finally other fiscal periods.

The third prioritization rule is based on filing status. The "Most Recent" statement is used before the "Original" statement, which is used before the "Preliminary" statement.

The final prioritization rule is based on the accounting standard. Here, financial statements that are reported using Generally Accepted Accounting Principles (GAAP) are given higher priority than financial statements that are reported using International Financial Reporting Standards (IFRS). If an accounting standard is not indicated at all, the financial statement is not used.

Financial statement entries with all other descriptors the same but with different filing statuses will be grouped together. For each variable separately, the variable value is taken from the highest priority financial statement within the group where the value is non-null.

For example, we may consider two financial statement entries having the same period end, and they both are from annual, consolidated statements, and both use the same accounting standard, but the first entry is classified as the "Most Recent" entry and the second is "Original" entry. Suppose the total assets and total liabilities are reported in the "Original" entry, and in the "Most Recent" entry only the total liabilities have been updated but the total assets have been replaced with a null value, then the total liabilities will be taken from the "Most Recent" entry while the total assets will be taken from the "Original" entry.

The rule mentioned above allows us to group the "Most Recent" and the "Original" entries together, as Bloomberg occasionally only updates values that change without updating other values. If the entries are not grouped, most of the variables would have null values.

One variable that requires special attention is the net income. Net income is a flow variable and needs to be adjusted based on the period of the financial statement. More specifically, we transform the net income into a monthly net income by dividing the net income by the number of months that the financial statement covers. Due to the different coverage periods, several types of net income can still be used. For example, the monthly net income can be computed from the annual net income divided by 12, the semi-annual net income divided by six and the quarterly net income divided by three. When the monthly net income can be obtained from different sources simultaneously, the quarterly net income will have higher priority than any others because it covers a more recent period of time.

Treatment of stale market capitalization prices: The market capitalization of a firm is required in a few input variables: DTD, SIZE, M/B and SIGMA. For most firms, the market capitalization is available from Bloomberg on a daily basis.

A check on the trading volume of shares is used to remove stale prices. Specifically, if there are more than two consecutive days of identical market capitalization prices, subsequent identical prices are removed only if the trading volume is equal to zero. This is to avoid, for example, cases where the shares of a company are under a trading suspension but the market capitalization data is incorrectly carried forward.

An exception is for Indian companies, where it is common for some companies to have market capitalizations reported only once a month with several consecutive months having identical prices and positive trading volume. These prices are very likely not to be accurate reflections of the firms' value. So, the trading volume is not checked for Indian firms and market capitalizations are excluded after more than two repeated prices.

For some firms, there are gaps in the market capitalization data provided by Bloomberg. Previously, the first recourse was to use the share price multiplied by the shares outstanding listed in the balance sheet and multiplied by an adjustment factor that Bloomberg provides to account for splits, dividends, etc. However, this data is frequently in error and using the shares outstanding as the previous available market capitalization divided by the price on that day was found to be more reliable.

If the gap in market capitalization data is more than a year, then the previous computation using the shares outstanding from the balance sheet is again used. If there are still remaining gaps in the data, then shares outstanding from Compustat data is used.

Currency conversion: Currency conversions are required if the market capitalization or any of the financial statement variables are reported in a currency different than the currency of the economy. If a currency conversion is required, the foreign exchange rate used is that reported at the relevant market close. For firms traded in Asia and Asia-Pacific, the Tokyo closing rate is used; for firms traded in Western Europe, the London closing rate is used; and for firms traded in North America, the New York closing rate is used. For market capitalizations, the FX rate used is for the date that the market capitalization is reported. For financial statement variables, the FX rate used is for the date of the period end of the statement.

Provisions for missing values and outliers: Missing values and outliers are dealt with by a three-step procedure. In the first step, the ten firm-specific input variables are computed for all firms and all months. In the second step, outliers are eliminated by winsorization. In the final step, missing values are replaced under certain conditions.

The first step is to compute the input variables and to determine which are missing. As mentioned previously, financial statement variables are carried forward for one year after the date that they are first used. This is generally three months after the period end of the statement. If no financial statement is available for the company within this year, then the financial statement variable will be missing. For market capitalization, if there is no valid market capitalization value within the calendar month, then the value is set to missing.

For illiquid stocks, if there has been no valid market capitalization value for a firm within the last 90 calendar days, then the market capitalization is deemed to not properly reflect the value of the firm. The firm is considered to have exited with a non-default event. Once the firm starts trading again and a new financial statement is released, the firm can enter back into the calibration. With regard to historical PD, the PD can be reported again once there are enough valid variables.

With regard to the level variables, the current month and the last eleven months are averaged to compute the level. A minimum of six observations are required to calculate the level variables. However, this condition is not enforced during the first six months of a firm. In the absence of six valid observations after the initial six months of a company, the level variable will be considered as missing.

To compute the trend variables, the level is subtracted from the current month value. If the current month value is missing, the trend variable is set to be the last valid value during the previous one year.

The value of M/B is set to be missing if any of the following values are missing: market capitalization, total liabilities or total assets of the firm. For the computation of SIGMA, at least 50 valid returns over the last 250 days of possible returns are required for the regression. If there are less than 50 valid returns, SIGMA is set to be missing.

In this way, the eight trend and level variables as well as M/B and SIGMA are computed and identified as missing or present. Winsorization can then be performed as a second step to eliminate outliers. The volume of outliers is too large to be able to determine whether each one is valid or not, so winsorization applies a floor and a cap on each of the variables. The historical 0.1 percentile and 99.9 percentile for all firms in the economy are recorded for each of the ten variables. Any values that exceed these levels are set to equal these boundary values.

With a winsorization level and 0.1 percentile and 99.9 percentile, the boundary values still may not be reasonable. For example, NI/TA levels of nearly –25, meaning an annual net income –25 times larger than the total assets of a firm, have been observed at this stage. In these cases, a more aggressive winsorization level is applied, until the boundary values are reasonable. Thus, the winsorization level is economy- and variable-specific, and will depend on the data quality for that economy and variable. Winsorization levels different from the default of 0.1 percentile and 99.9 percentile are indicated in RMI (2013).

A third and final step can be taken to deal with missing values. If during a particular month, no variable is missing for a particular firm, the PD can then be computed. If six or more of these ten variables are missing, there is deemed to be too many missing observations and no replacement shall be made.

If between one and five variables are missing out of the ten, the first step is to trace back for at most twelve months to use previous values of these variables instead. If this does not succeed in replacing all of the variables, a replacement by sector medians is done. The median is for the financial or non-financial firms (as indicated by their Bloomberg industry sector code) within the economy during that month. Replacement by the sector median should have a neutral effect on the PD of the firm; the firm is assessed by the other variables that it does have values for. This sector median is always performed in calibration. However, when reporting historical PD, the sector replacement is not done if it results in a relative change in PD of 10% or more where the initial PD was at or above

100 bps, or an absolute change in PD of 10 bps or more where the initial PD was below 100 bps.

However, this treatment of missing values is not always meaningful and occasionally results in counter-intuitive patterns in a company's historical PD. Accordingly, the RMI CRI team is reconsidering the treatment of missing values in two stages of development, with the first stage focusing on the replacement of missing values in the initial phase of a company, and the second stage of development focusing on later periods in the company's time series. The first stage has been implemented and is explained below.

In the initial phase of a company — up until six months after IPO — it can be expected that the company's data availability and quality is relatively low due to, for example, a delay in the issuance of financial statements or illiquid trading. So, many companies require missing value replacements during that period. However, as observed in our data, replacing the missing values during these first six months with a sector median affects a company's PD in an unmeaningful way, sometimes resulting in extreme spikes and falls in the company's PD. Since this occurs at the beginning of a company's history, there are no previous PD values to compare to as can be done at later periods in a company's history.

Hence, in order to avoid this, as of the 2013 February calibration, we set a criterion to start the missing value treatment only six months after the beginning of a company's data. Doing so ensures that PDs in the beginning of a company's history are more reflective of the true creditworthiness of that individual company.

The RMI CRI team is currently developing a method to deal with missing values later in the history of a company in a more meaningful way. This second stage of development for treating missing values will be completed in the coming months.

Inclusion/exclusion of companies for calibration: Firms are included within an economy for calibration when the primary listing of the firm is on an exchange in the economy. This ensures that all firms within the economy are subject to the same disclosure and accounting rules.

There are a relatively small number of firms that are dual listed, in which two corporations listed in different exchanges operate as a single entity but retain separate legal status. In the CRI system, a combined company will be assigned to the single economy it is most associated with. An example is the Rio Tinto Group. This consists of Rio Tinto plc, listed in the UK; and Rio Tinto Limited, listed in Australia. Most of Rio Tinto's operations are in Australia rather than the UK, so Rio Tinto is assigned to Australia.

In the US, firms traded on the OTC markets or the Pink Sheets are not considered as exchange listed so are not included in calibration or in the reporting of PD forecasts. Many of these firms are small or start-up firms. Including this large group of companies would skew the calibration and the aggregate results. The TSX Venture Exchange in Canada also contains only small and start-up firms, so firms listed here are also excluded.

Other examples include Taiwan's GreTai Securities Market and Singapore's Catalist. The challenge for markets outside of the US or Canada is that the data on whether firms are listed on the smaller markets rather than the main board is difficult to obtain. For all economies besides the US and Canada, there is continuing work being done in the CRI system to exclude firms that are not listed on major exchanges within a country.

Firms that record an exit (other than due to no trading for 90 calendar days) will not enter back into the calibration even if the firm continues to trade and issues financial statements, as that can happen after the firms declare bankruptcy. There are two exceptions to this exclusion. The first, determined on a case by case basis, is if the firm should be deemed to have re-emerged from bankruptcy. The second exception is for all firms in China, where two situations are prevalent. The first situation is that the firm experiences few repercussions from the default and continues operating normally. The other situation is for one firm to take over a defaulted firm's listing. This happens due to the limited supply of exchange listings. Both of these situations can be considered as emerging from default, so the CRI system enters all of these companies back into the calibration as new companies.

3.2. Distance-to-Default Computation

The DTD computation used in the CRI system is not a standard one. Standard computations exclude financial firms, which is of course a critical part of any economy. Thus, the standard DTD computation must be extended to give meaningful estimates for financial firms as well. Duan and Wang (2012) have provided a review of different DTD calculations with several examples for financial and non-financial firms.

The description of the specialized DTD computation starts with a brief description of the Merton (1974) model. Merton's model makes the simplifying assumption that firms are financed by equity and a single zero-coupon bond with maturity date T and principal L. The asset value of the firm V_t follows a geometric Brownian motion:

$$dV_t = \mu V_t dt + \sigma V_t dB_t. \tag{34}$$

Here, B_t is the standard Brownian motion, μ is the drift of the asset value in the physical measure, and σ is the volatility of the asset value. Equity holders receive the excess value of the firm above the principal of the zero-coupon bond and have limited liability, so the equity value at maturity is: $E_t = \max(V_t - L, 0)$. This is just a call option payoff on the asset value with a strike value of L. Thus, the Black-Scholes option pricing formula can be used to calculate the equity value at times t before T,

$$E_t = V_t N(d_+) - e^{-r(T-t)} L N(d_-), \tag{35}$$

where r is the risk-free rate, $N(\cdot)$ is the standard normal cumulative distribution function, and

$$d_{\pm} = \frac{\log\left(\frac{V_T}{L}\right) + \left(r \pm \frac{\sigma^2}{2}\right)(T-t)}{\sigma\sqrt{T-t}}. \tag{36}$$

Following the Merton (1974) model, the probability of the company's default at time T evaluated at time t is $N(-\mathrm{DTD}_t)$, where DTD at time t is defined as:

$$\mathrm{DTD}_t = \frac{\log\left(\frac{V_T}{L}\right) + \left(\mu - \frac{\sigma^2}{2}\right)(T-t)}{\sigma\sqrt{T-t}}. \tag{37}$$

The standard KMV assumptions given in Crosbie and Bohn (2003) are to set the time to maturity $T - t$ at a value of one year, and the principal of the zero-coupon bond L to a value equal to the firm's current liabilities plus one half of its long-term debt. Here, the current liabilities and long-term debt are taken from the firm's financial statements. If the firm is missing the current liabilities field, then various substitutes for this field can be used, as described in Subsection 2.3.

This is a poor assumption of the debt level for financial firms, since they typically have large liabilities, such as deposit accounts, that are neither classified as current liabilities nor long-term debt. Thus, using these standard assumptions means ignoring a large part of the debt of financial firms.

To properly account for the debt of financial firms, Duan (2010) included a fraction δ of a firm's other liabilities. The other liabilities are defined as the firm's total liabilities minus both the short and long-term debt. The debt level L then becomes the current liabilities plus half of the long-term debt plus the fraction δ multiplied by the other liabilities, so that the debt level is a function of δ. The standard KMV assumptions are then a special case where $\delta = 0$.

The fraction δ can be optimized along with μ and σ in the maximum likelihood estimation method developed in Duan (1994, 2000). Following Duan *et al.* (2012), the firm's market value of assets is standardized by its book value A_t, so that the scaling effect from a major investment or financing by the firm will not distort the time series from which the parameter values are estimated. Thus, the log-likelihood function is:

$$\begin{aligned}
&\mathcal{L}(\mu,\sigma,\delta) \\
&= -\frac{n-1}{2}\log(2\pi) - \frac{1}{2}\sum_{t=2}^{n}\log(\sigma^2 h_t) \\
&\quad - \sum_{t=2}^{n}\log\left(\frac{\hat{V}_t(\sigma,\delta)}{A_t}\right) - \sum_{t=2}^{n}\log[N(\hat{d}_+(\hat{V}_t(\sigma,\delta),\sigma,\delta))] \\
&\quad - \frac{1}{2\sigma^2}\sum_{t=2}^{n}\frac{1}{h_t}\left[\log\left(\frac{\hat{V}_t(\sigma,\delta)}{A_t}\times\frac{A_{t-1}}{\hat{V}_{t-1}(\sigma,\delta)}\right) - \left(\mu - \frac{\sigma^2}{2}\right)h_t\right]^2,
\end{aligned} \tag{38}$$

where n is the number of days with observations of the equity value in the sample, $\hat{V}_t$ is the implied asset value found by solving Equation (35), $\hat{d}_+$ is computed with Equation (36) using the implied asset value, and h_t is the number of trading days as a fraction of the year between observations $t - 1$ and t. Notice that the implied asset value and $\hat{d}_+$ are dependent on δ by virtue of the dependence of L on δ.

Implementation of DTD computation: The DTD at the end of each month is needed for every firm in order to calibrate the forward intensity model. A moving window, consisting of the last one year of data before each month end is used to compute the month end DTD. Daily market capitalization data based on closing prices is used for the equity value in the implied asset value computation of Equation (34). If there are fewer than 50 days of valid observations for the market capitalization, then the DTD value is set to missing. An observation is valid if there is positive trading volume that day. If the trading volume is not available, the observation is assumed to be valid if the value for the market capitalization changes often enough. The precise criterion is as follows: if the market capitalization does not change for three days or more in a row, the first day is taken as a valid observation and the remaining days with the same value are set to missing.

A straightforward idea for the DTD computation is to first estimate the three variables μ, σ and δ via maximizing the log-likelihood function (38) over $\sigma \geq 0$ and $0 \leq \delta \leq 1$ and then to calculate the DTD from Equation (37). Let $(\hat{\mu}, \hat{\sigma}, \hat{\delta})$ be an optimal solution to the maximization problem. By direct calculation, it is not hard to see that:

$$\hat{\mu} = \frac{\hat{\sigma}^2}{2} + \frac{1}{\sum_{t=2}^{n} h_t} \log\left(\frac{\hat{V}_n(\hat{\sigma},\hat{\delta})}{A_n} \times \frac{A_1}{\hat{V}_1(\hat{\sigma},\hat{\delta})} \right). \quad (39)$$

In view of this, maximizing the three dimensional function $\mathcal{L}(\mu, \sigma, \delta)$ can be equivalently reduced to maximizing the two dimensional function $\tilde{\mathcal{L}}(\sigma, \delta)$ taking the form:

$$\begin{aligned}
\tilde{\mathcal{L}}(\sigma,\delta) = & -\frac{n-1}{2}\log(2\pi) - \frac{1}{2}\sum_{t=2}^{n}\log(\sigma^2 h_t) - \sum_{t=2}^{n}\log\left(\frac{\hat{V}_t(\sigma,\delta)}{A_t}\right) \\
& - \sum_{t=2}^{n}\log[N(\hat{d}_+(\hat{V}_t(\sigma,\delta),\sigma,\delta))] \\
& - \frac{1}{2\sigma^2}\left\{ \sum_{t=2}^{n}\frac{1}{h_t}\left[\log\left(\frac{\hat{V}_t(\sigma,\delta)}{A_t} \times \frac{A_{t-1}}{\hat{V}_{t-1}(\sigma,\delta)}\right)\right]^2 \right. \\
& \left. - \frac{1}{\sum_{t=2}^{n} h_t}\left[\log\left(\frac{\hat{V}_n(\sigma,\delta)}{A_n} \times \frac{A_1}{\hat{V}_1(\sigma,\delta)}\right)\right]^2 \right\}.
\end{aligned} \quad (40)$$

However, with quarterly financial statements there will never be more than three changes in the corporate structure (defined in this model by L and A_t) throughout the year, leading to possibly unstable estimates of δ. This problem is mitigated by performing a two-stage optimization for σ and δ.

In the first stage, the maximization of $\tilde{\mathcal{L}}(\sigma, \delta)$ for each firm is performed over both σ and δ. For each firm, at the first month in which DTD can be computed the maximization is constrained in $\sigma \geq 0$ and $0 \leq \delta \leq 1$. Thereafter, at month n, the maximization is still constrained in $\sigma \geq 0$ while δ is constrained in the interval, $[\max(0, \hat{\delta}_{n-1} - 0.05), \min(1, \hat{\delta}_{n-1} + 0.05)]$, where $\hat{\delta}_{n-1}$ is the estimate of δ made in the previous month. In other words, a ten percent band around the previous estimate of δ (where that band is floored with 0 and capped with 1) is applied so that the estimates do not fluctuate too much from month to month.

However, for many firms, the estimate of δ would frequently lie on the boundary of the constraining interval, meaning that the estimates of δ were not stable. Therefore, a second stage is implemented to impose greater stability. All financial sector firms in the same economy are assumed to share the same estimate of δ, chosen to be the average of all its individual estimates. The same is done for non-financial firms. Accordingly, with δ being fixed to be the sector average, the original maximization of $\mathcal{L}(\sigma, \delta)$ is reduced to a one-dimensional maximization in σ. Thus, this maximization is used to perform the estimates of σ for each firm.

Since the first stage is done to obtain a stable sector-average estimate of δ, the criteria used to include a firm-month is more strict. In the first stage, a two-year window is used instead of one year, and a minimum of 250 days of valid observations of the market capitalization are required instead of 50. If a firm has less than 250 days of valid observations within the last two years of a particular month end, δ will not be estimated for that firm and that month end.

It was found that after applying the two-stage procedure described above, the estimate of μ was frequently unstable and could lower the explanatory power of DTD. For example, suppose a firm has a large drop in its implied asset value in January 2011, so that the estimated μ is negative for the DTD calculation at the end of December 2011. If there is little change in the company in January 2012, then the drop in implied asset value in January 2011 is no longer within the observation window for the DTD calculation at the end of January 2012. There will be a large increase in the estimated μ, resulting in a substantial improvement of the DTD just because of the moving observation window. To avoid this problem, we now set μ to be equal to $\sigma^2/2$. So in calculating DTD, the second term in the numerator of Equation (37) is eliminated.

In summary, the DTD for each firm is computed using the economy and sector (financial or non-financial) average for δ in that month, and the estimate of σ based on the last year of data for the firm.

Carrying out this two-stage procedure would take 70 hours of computation time on a single PC, given the millions of firm months that are required. However, each of the stages is parallelizable. In the first stage the DTD can be computed independently between firms. In the second stage, once the sector averages of the δ have been computed for each month, the DTD can again be computed independently between firms. In the current CRI system, by using a computational grid administered by the NUS computer center, the DTD computational time for all firms over the full history of twenty years takes only about 3.5 hours.

3.3. Calibration

Implementation: As shown in Section (1), the calibration of the forward intensity model involves multiple maximum pseudo-likelihood estimations, where the pseudo-likelihood functions are given in Equation (13). The maximizations are on the logarithm of these expressions, and the default parameters' maximization is performed independently from the non-default exit parameters. Parameter estimates for the entire horizon up to five years for the default and non-default exits can be obtained directly from the NS function.

A few input variables have an unambiguous effect on a firm's probability of default. Increments of both the level and trend of DTD, CASH/TA, and NI/TA should indicate that a firm is becoming more credit-worthy and should lead to a decreasing PD. For large and relatively clean data sets such as the US, an unconstrained optimization leads to parameter values which mostly have the expected sign. For each of the DTD level and trend, CASH/TA level and trend, and NI/TA level, the default parameters at all horizons are negative. A negative default parameter at a horizon means that if the variable increases, the forward intensity will decrease (based on Equation (6)), so that the conditional default probability at that horizon will decrease.

Grouping for economies: There are not enough defaults in some small economies and calibrations of these individual economies are not statistically meaningful. In order to ensure that there are enough defaults for calibration, the 71 economies are categorized into groups according to similarities in their stage of development and their geographic locations. Within these groups, the economies are combined and calibrated together.

Starting from the Aug 2012 calibration, Canada and the US remain in the same calibration group, and the developed economies of Asia-Pacific (Australia, Hong Kong, Japan, Singapore, South Korea, Taiwan and New Zealand) form another calibration group. China and India, the two major emerging economies of Asia-Pacific are each calibrated as individual groups. All the European countries covered by the CRI are in a single calibration group, which now includes Israel, Russia and Turkey. The other emerging economies of Asia-Pacific (Kazakhstan, Indonesia, Malaysia, Pakistan, Philippines, Sri Lanka, Thailand and Vietnam) are grouped together with the Latin American economies (Argentina, Brazil, Colombia, Chile, Mexico, Peru, and Venezuela), Middle-East economies (Bahrain, Jordan, Kuwait, Saudi Arabia and United Arab Emirates) and African economies (Egypt, Morocco, Nigeria and South Africa), to form the "emerging markets" calibration group.

All economies in these new calibration groups share the same coefficients for all variables except for the benchmark risk-free interest rate variable. The benchmark interest rates coefficients will be allowed to vary, because different economies based in different currencies naturally have different dependencies on their interest rates and the interest rate levels can differ significantly across economies. After adopting the euro, all eurozone countries use Germany's three-month Bubill rate as this is more reflective of monetary rather than sovereign credit conditions in each economy, which is the intent of this variable. For the period before joining the eurozone, their own interest rates are used.

In addition, the benchmark interest rate is entered as the current value minus the historical month-end mean. This allows the variable to reflect its value relative to the historical average. When an economy does not have enough default events to identify a separate interest rate coefficient, the interest rate variable will be disabled for that economy by inputting a zero value for the whole time series. In fact, that is also why we de-mean all interest rate series so that setting the interest rate series of a particular economy to zero, when necessary, does not induce a bias by the base economy in the same group.

Since all eurozone countries except Germany do not have enough default events prior to joining the eurozone, their benchmark interest rate is entered as zero for that period. Among the non-eurozone members of the European group, Denmark, Norway, Sweden and the UK each have separate coefficients for the benchmark interest rate. Switzerland and Iceland do not use this variable for their whole history.

In the Developed Asia-Pacific group, all economies have their own coefficient for the benchmark interest rate, except for Japan and New Zealand who share the same coefficient. For the North American group, both Canada and the US have their own coefficient for the benchmark interest rate.

In the Emerging Markets group, there are insufficient defaults in the Latin American economies to calibrate individual economy benchmark interest rate coefficients in a statistically significant way, so all Latin American economies share the same benchmark interest rate coefficient. Among the Asian economies in the Emerging Markets group, Indonesia, Malaysia, and Philippines have their own coefficient for the benchmark interest rate, while Vietnam does not use this variable. All the other economies in the Emerging Markets group share the same benchmark interest rate coefficient. Indonesia also has its own intercept and uses its own coefficients for the stock index return, CASH/TA level and Relative Size level. These coefficients are required because these characteristics for defaulting firms in Indonesia are substantially different than in other economies. Separate coefficients are required to improve the accuracy of the PD forecasts.

Relative Size: For the calibration data set, the median market cap of firms in an economy for each month end includes the market cap from the last trading day of each firm in the month. If a firm does not trade in a particular month, the firm's market cap is not included in the median. For certain economies, many firms are illiquid and the median market cap experiences large variations due to the change in composition of firms rather than the market value of the firms. Another problem is data quality at the beginning of the historical sample: if a data provider starts including the market cap for a large number of firms in one month compared to the previous, there can be a large jump in the median market cap.

To avoid this problem, we use a combination of the economy's stock index and the economy's median market cap as the divisor in the Relative Size variable:

1. We choose a recent month where there is a more complete set of firms in the economy that have trading activity, and calculate the ratio of the economy's median market cap to stock index value at the end of the month.
2. For each month, the divisor for the Relative Size variable of firms in the economy is taken as the month end stock index multiplied by that ratio.

3.4. Daily Output

Individual firms' PD: In computing the pseudo-log-likelihood functions in Equation (13), only the end of month data is needed. The data needs to be extended to daily values in order to produce daily PDs.

For the level variables, the last 12 end-of-month observations (before averaging) are combined with the current value. The current value is scaled by a fraction equal to the current day of the month divided by the number of calendar days in the month. The earliest monthly value is scaled by one minus this fraction. The sum is then divided by the number of valid monthly observations, with the current value and the earliest monthly value jointly having the weight of one observation if either or both are not missing. Not performing this scaling can lead to an artificial jump in PD at the beginning of the month. When performing the scaling, the change in level is more gradual throughout the month.

SIGMA is computed by regressing the daily returns of the firm's market capitalization against the daily returns of the economy's stock index for the previous 250 days.

Exclusion rule for Mergers & Acquisitions: Mergers & Acquisitions (M&A) events are common occurrences. When an important M&A deal is closed, the Market Capitalization (MC) of the acquirer changes immediately as the market cap of the acquirer will now reflect the joint value of the acquirer and the target. However, the financial statement will not immediately reflect the new situation. In this case, the Distance-to-Default (DTD) and market-to-book ratio, which are important inputs for the PD computation, will be distorted due to a mismatch in the MC and the financial statement variables. In order to ensure the accuracy and reliability of our PD estimates, we apply a rule to disable PD calculations for companies that are involved in important M&A deals.

An important M&A deal is defined as an M&A event on which all the following three criteria apply:

1. Upon the deal's completion, the acquiring company owns 20% or more of the target company.
2. The size of the deal is material to the acquirer. This is measured in terms of total assets. If α is the percentage of the target that is being acquired, the size is considered material if the product of α and the total assets of the target is greater than or equal to 20% of the total assets of the acquirer.
3. The change in MC is material, with the largest absolute daily MC return, within 20 days of the M&A completion day, larger than or equal to 5%.

In the event of an important M&A, the PDs of the acquirer will be not be computed until we are able to include financial statement variables reflecting the new situation (typically between 3 and 6 months after deal completion). The RMI CRI team is currently developing a method to deal with M&A cases more systematically, and will avoid having to disable PDs for companies involved in an important M&A deal.

Aggregating PD: The CRI provides term structures of the probability distributions for the number of defaults as well as the expected number of defaults for different groups of firms. The companies are grouped by economy (using each firm's country of domicile), by sector (using the firm's Bloomberg industrial sector code) and sectors within economies. With the individual firms' PD, the expected number of defaults is trivial to compute. The algorithm used to compute the probability distribution of the number of defaults was originally reported in Anderson *et al.* (2003). It assumes conditional independence and uses a fast recursive scheme to compute the necessary probability distribution.

Note that while this algorithm is currently used to produce the probability distribution of the number of defaults within an economy or sector, it can easily be generalized to compute loss distributions for a portfolio manager, in which case the portfolio's exposure to each firm should be aggregated.

Inclusion of firms in aggregation: As explained in Subsection 3.1, firms are included in an economy for calibration if the firms' primary listing is on an exchange in that economy. This is to ensure that all firms in an economy are subject to the same disclosure and accounting requirements. In contrast, a firm is included in an economy's aggregate results if the firm is domiciled in that economy. This is because users typically associate firms with their economy of domicile rather than the economy where their primary listing is, if they are different. For example, the Bank of China has its primary listing in Hong Kong, but its economy of domicile is China so the Bank of China is included in the aggregation forecasts for China, and is included under China when searching for the individual PDs.

Treatment of companies after a default event: When a company experiences a default event, the CRI system discontinues the PD calculation for that company. However, if the company resumes operations after some time, it will be treated as a new company, and we continue to generate PD. The new company's PDs are not affected by the financial statement or market cap data prior to the event. So, the PDs calculated are independent of the PDs that were generated before the default event. On our website, the PDs are however displayed on a single graph for the convenience of our users.

In order to implement the treatment, default events are classified into hard defaults and soft defaults (see Table 1).

Table 1. Classification of default events.

Default-Action Type	Subcategory
Hard Defaults (Default events that are typically permanent)	Administration, Arrangement, Canadian CCAA, Chapter 7, Chapter 11, Chapter 15, Conservatorship, Insolvency, Japanese CRL, Judicial Management, Liquidation, Pre-Negotiated Chapter 11, Protection, Receivership, Rehabilitation, Rehabilitation (Thailand 1997), Reorganization, Restructuring, Section 304, Supreme court declaration, Winding Up, Work Out, Other, Unknown
Soft Defaults (Default events that companies can emerge from)	Coupon & Principal Payment, Coupon Payment Only, Debt Restructuring, Interest Payment, Loan Payment, Principal Payment, ADR (Japan only), Declared Sick (India only), Unknown

Hard defaults are default events that are typically permanent. In other words, companies typically cannot emerge from hard defaults. An example of a hard default is a forced liquidation of a company. PDs will not be computed after the default event unless there is an exceptional circumstance that warrants a manual intervention. General Motors is an example of such an event. Although GM filed for Chapter 11 reorganization in June 2009, the company resumed operations in March 2011. As of March 2011, after the company resumed operations, we decided to treat GM as a new company.

Soft defaults are default events that companies can typically emerge from. An example of a soft default is a debt restructuring. More specifically, after a soft default, if there is sufficient data for the company, then the company is assumed to have been able to continue its operations and PDs are computed. The PDs are generated once sufficient history of both the market capitalization data and the new financial statement data (released after the event) becomes available. Take the Australian company Marion Energy Ltd as an example, which had a debt restructuring in April 2010. We stopped calculating PD after 31 March 2010. As debt restructuring is considered as a soft default, we started calculating PD again from 30 Sept 2010 onwards, when data requirements were met.

This treatment does not apply to Chinese companies, based on two reasons: (1) a firm typically experiences few repercussions from the default and continues operating normally; and (2) it is common for another firm to take over a defaulted firm's listing, due to the limited supply of exchange listings. Both of these situations can be considered as emerging from default, so the CRI system enters all of these companies back into the calibration as new companies.

IV. EMPIRICAL ANALYSIS

This section presents an empirical analysis of the CRI outputs for the 71 economies with their own exchange that are currently being covered. In Subsection 4.1, an overview is given of the default parameter estimates. Subsection 4.2 explains and provides the accuracy ratios for the different countries under the CRI coverage.

4.1. Parameter Estimates

With 60 months of forecast horizons, 13 variables and 6 different groups of economies, tables of the parameter estimates occupy over 20 pages and are not included in this Technical Report. In Figures B.1 and B.2, the parameter estimates are from calibrations performed in September 2013 using data up until the end of August 2013. As an example, plots of the default parameters for the US are given in figures included in Figures B.1 and B.2 in Appendix B. In this part, a brief overview is given of the general traits and patterns seen in the default parameter estimations of the economies covered by the CRI.

Recall that if a default parameter for a variable at a particular horizon is estimated to be positive (negative) from the maximum pseudo-likelihood estimate, then an increasing value in the associated variable will lead to an increasing (decreasing) value of the forward intensity at that horizon, which in turn means an increasing (decreasing) value for the conditional default probability at that horizon.

For the stock index one-year trailing return variable, most groups have default parameters that are slightly negative in the shorter horizons and then become positive in the longer horizons. When the equity market performs well, this is only a short-term positive for firms and in the longer term, firms are actually more likely to default. This seemingly counterintuitive result could be due to correlation between the market index and other firm-specific variables. For example, Duffie *et al.* (2009) suggested that a firm's DTD can overstate its creditworthiness after a strong bull market. If this is the case, then the stock index return serves as a correction to the DTD levels at these points in time.

As expected we observe a different relationship between the short-term interest rate and default across economies. This observation possibly indicates different lead-lag relationships between credit conditions and the raising and cutting of short-term interest rates.

DTD is a measure of the volatility-adjusted leverage of a firm. Low or negative DTD indicates high leverage and high DTD indicates low leverage. Therefore, PD would be expected to increase with decreasing DTD. Indeed, almost all of the calibrations for the different groups lead to negative default parameters for the DTD level.

The ratio of the sum of cash and short-term investments to total assets (CASH/TA) measures liquidity of a firm. This indicates the availability of a firm's funds and its ability to make interest and principal payments. As expected, for almost all economies (Indonesia being the only exception) the default parameters for CASH/TA level in shorter horizons are significantly negative. The magnitude of the default parameters typically decreases for longer horizons, indicating that CASH/TA level is a better indicator of a firm's ability to make payments in the short term than the long term.

The ratio of net income to total assets (NI/TA) measures profitability of a firm. The relationship between PD and NI/TA is as expected: the default parameters for NI/TA level is negative for most economies and most horizons.

The logarithm of the market capitalization of a firm over the median market capitalization of firms within the economy (SIZE) does not have a consistent effect on PD across different economies. For example, in the US the default parameters for SIZE level are positive for all horizons, suggesting that the complexity of larger firms outweighs the potential benefits, such as diversified business lines and funding sources. On the other hand, in Europe the default parameters for SIZE level are negative across all horizons. These differences may reflect differences in the business environments in the respective economies.

The default parameters associated with DTD Trend, CASH/TA Trend, SIZE Trend and NI/TA Trend are negative across almost all economies and horizons. The trend variables reflect momentum. The momentum effect is a short-term effect, and evidence of this is seen in the lower magnitude of the default parameters at longer horizons than at shorter horizons. The exception is the NI/TA Trend, which for some calibration groups has a higher magnitude at longer horizons.

The ratio of the sum of market capitalization and total liabilities to total assets (M/B) can either indicate the market mis-valuation effect or the future growth effect. This default parameter is negative in most economies, indicating that higher M/B implies higher PD, and the future growth effect dominates. On the other hand, in China and in the Developed Asia-Pacific calibration group, the default parameter for M/B is positive, indicating that for these economies, the market mis-valuation effect dominates.

Shumway (2001) argued that a high level of the idiosyncratic volatility (SIGMA) indicates highly variable stock returns relative to the market index, which is equivalent to highly variable cash flows. Currently, for the different economies, this variable is no longer significant.

4.2. Prediction Accuracy

In-sample testing: Various tests are carried out to test the prediction accuracy of the RMI PD forecasts. These tests are conducted in-sample.

A single calibration is conducted for the in-sample tests, using data to the end of the data sample. As an example, one-year PD forecasts are made for December 31, 2000 by using the data at or before

December 31, 2000 and the parameters from the calibration. These PD forecasts can be compared to actual defaults that occurred at any time in 2001.

Accuracy Ratio: The accuracy ratio (AR) is one of the most popular and meaningful tests of the discriminatory power of a rating system (BCBS, 2005). The AR and the equivalent Area Under the Receiver Operating Characteristic (AUROC) are described in Duan and Shrestha (2011). In short, if defaulting firms had been assigned among the highest PD of all firms before they defaulted, then the model has discriminated well between safe and distressed firms. This leads to higher values of AR and AUROC. The range of possible AR values is in [0,1], where 0 is a completely random rating system and 1 is a perfect rating system. The range of possible AUROC values is in [0.5, 1]. AUROC and AR values are related by: AR = 2 × AUROC–1.

The AR and AUROC values for different horizons are available in Table B.1 of this technical report. Only economies with more than 20 defaults entering into the AR and AUROC computation are listed. The PD are taken to be non-overlapping. For example, the one-year AR is based on PDs computed on 31/12/2000, 31/12/2001,..., 31/12/2009 and firms defaulting within one year of those dates, while the two-year AR is based on PDs computed on 31/12/2000, 31/12/2002,..., 31/12/2008 and firms defaulting within two years of those dates.

The AUROC values have been provided only for the purpose of comparison, if other rating systems report their results in terms of AUROC. The discussion will focus only on AR. The model is able to achieve strong AR results mostly greater than 0.80 at the one and six-month horizons for developed economies. There is a drop in AR at one, two and five-year horizons, but the AR are still mostly acceptable. Australia, the UK and Singapore have sharp drops in AR at longer horizons. Hong Kong has comparatively worse AR over all horizons as compared to other developed economies.

The AR in emerging market economies such as Brazil, China, India, Indonesia, Malaysia, Philippines, Russia, and Vietnam are noticeably weaker than the results in the developed economies. This can be due to a number of issues. The quality of data is worse in emerging markets, in terms of availability and data errors. This may be due to lower reporting and auditing standards. Also, variable selection is likely to play a more important role in emerging markets. The variables were selected based on the predictive power in a developed economy, the US. Performing variable selections specific to the calibration group are expected to improve predictive accuracy, especially in emerging market economies. Finally, there could be structural differences in how defaults and bankruptcies occur in emerging market economies. If the judicial system is weak and there are no repercussions for default, firms may be less reluctant to default.

The Basel Committee states in BCBS (2004) that banks must also use other quantitative validation tools and comparisons with relevant external data sources. Thus, rating institutions are required to think about further validation of their models using external data sources. We compare the accuracy ratio of the RMI PD with other rating agencies such as Moody's, S&P's and Fitch separately. For a given rating agency, comparisons are made for firms that have both a corporate rating from the rating agency and an RMI PD over the sample period. We expanded our data to monthly data for each firm from the first month a rating is given until the most recent month.

For S&P, this data set has 4580 listed firms from around world. It consists of 393 default events and 439,652 end of month observations from 1990 to January 2013. The 1-year AR for the RMI PD is 0.87 and the AR for the S&P ratings is 0.81. For Moody's, this sample includes 1805 listed firms from different countries. It covers 198 default events and 117,262 end of month observations. The AR for the Moody's ratings is 0.81 and the 1-year RMI PD is 0.88. In the comparison against ratings from Fitch, there are 1490 firms with 49 default events. The end of month data points are 150,917. The Fitch AR and RMI PD are 0.62 and 0.83, respectively. In summary, the RMI PDs have a stronger performance in terms of AR than any of the three major credit rating agencies.

The AR is a test of discriminatory power, or how well the rating system ranks firms in terms of creditworthiness. In a separate article included in Volume 2 of the GCR (2012), we provided a more qualitative check on the RMI PD in which we compare the behaviour of the RMI PD to the rating actions of external credit rating agencies such as Moody's and S&P for some well known default cases.

Aggregate defaults: The time series of aggregate predicted number of defaults and actual number of defaults in each calibration group are also available in Figures B.3 to B.8. For China and India in particular, these figures show that there is room for improvement in the predictive power of the model.

V. ONGOING DEVELOPMENTS

The CRI can be developed along a number of directions. We now comment on obvious ones that in our view are likely to bring meaningful and measurable benefits. Besides modifications to the current modeling framework of the forward intensity, a change in modeling platform will be undertaken if another model proves more promising in terms of accuracy and robustness of results. For this type of development, we also rely on the collective efforts by the worldwide credit research community to challenge and improve the existing modeling platform.

As an example, the CRI will soon start a parallel implementation using the partially-conditioned forward intensity approach proposed in Duan and Fulop (2013) to study its practicality and performance. In fact, the parameter constraints on the forward-intensity function essential to the implementation of that approach has already been incorporated into the current CRI system in making longer-term default predictions.

Within the current modeling framework, future developments involve, for example, variable selection where more experiments are needed to identify common risk factors and company-specific attributes that are more indicative of defaults in emerging markets.

Finally, a series of new applications and tools using the RMI PD as an input are currently being developed. More specifically, RMI plans to actively work with users to discuss the possibility of taking advantage of the world class research infrastructure at the institute to propagate real world applications in credit rating and testing. Some interesting areas include research in counterparty risk management and stress testing of financial systems by policy makers. RMI also remains committed to making its vast resources available for academic research.

****

The RMI Credit Research Initiative is premised on the concept of credit ratings as a "public good". Being a non-profit undertaking allows a high level of transparency and collaboration that other commercial credit rating systems can not replicate. The research and support infrastructure is in place and researchers from around the world are invited to contribute to this initiative. Any methodological improvements that researchers develop will be incorporated into the CRI system. In essence, the initiative operates as a "selective wikipedia" where many can contribute but implementation control is retained.

If you have feedback on this technical report or wish to work with us in this endeavor, please contact us at rmicri@globalcreditreview.com.

REFERENCES

Anderson, L., J. Sidenius and S. Basu (2003), All your Hedges in One Basket. *Risk*, pp. 67–72.

Basel Committee on Banking Supervision (BCBS) (2005), Studies on the Validation of Internal Rating Systems. Working Paper 14.

Chopin, N. (2012), A Sequential Particle Filter Method for Static Models. *Biometrika*, 89, pp. 539–551.

Crosbie, P. and J. Bohn (2003), Modeling Default Risk. Moody's KMV technical document.

Del Moral, P., A. Doucet and A. Jasra (2006), Sequential Monte Carlo Samplers. *Journal of Royal Statistical Society B*, 68, pp. 411–436.

Duan, J.-C. (1994), Maximum Likelihood Estimation Using Price Data of the Derivative Contract. *Mathematical Finance*, 4, pp. 155–167.

Duan, J.-C. (2000), Correction: Maximum Likelihood Estimation Using Price Data of the Derivative Contract. *Mathematical Finance*, 10, pp. 461–462.

Duan, J.-C. (2010), Clustered Defaults. National University of Singapore Working Paper.

Duan, J.-C. and A. Fulop (2013), Multiperiod Corporate Default Prediction with the Partially-Conditioned Forward Intensity. National University of Singapore Working Paper.

Duan, J.-C. and K. Shrestha (2011), Statistical Credit Rating Methods. *Global Credit Review*, 1, pp. 43–64.

Duan, J.-C. and E. Van Laere (2012), A Public Good Approach to Credit Ratings: From Concept to Reality. *Journal of Banking & Finance*, 36, pp. 3239–3247.

Duan, J.-C. and T. Wang (2012), Measuring Distance-to-Default for Financial and Non-Financial Firms. *Global Credit Review*, 2, pp. 95–108.

Duan, J.-C., J. Sun and T. Wang (2012), Multiperiod Corporate Default Prediction — A Forward Intensity Approach. *Journal of Econometrics*, 170, pp. 191–209.

Duffie, D., L. Saita and K. Wang (2007), Multi-Period Corporate Default Prediction with Stochastic Covariates. *Journal of Financial Economics*, 83, pp. 635–665.

Duffie, D., A. Eckner, G. Horel and L. Saita (2009), Frailty Correlated Default. *Journal of Finance*, pp. 2089–2123.

Kiefer, N. M., T. J. Vogelsang and H. Bunzel (2000), Simple Robust Testing of Regression Hypotheses. *Econometrica*, 68, pp. 695–714.

Merton, R. C. (1974), On the Pricing of Corporate Debt: The Risk Structure of Interest Rates. *Journal of Finance*, 29, pp. 449–470.

Nelson, C. R. and A. F. Siegel (1987), Parsimonious Modeling of Yield Curves. *Journal of Business*, 60, pp. 473–489.

RMI (2012), NUS-RMI Credit Research Initiative Technical Report. Version: 2012 Update 2, *Global Credit Review*, 2, pp. 109–167.

RMI (2013), NUS-RMI Credit Research Initiative Technical Report. Version: 2013 Update 1.

Shao, X. (2010), A Self-Normalized Approach to Confidence Interval Construction in Time Series. *Journal of the Royal Statistical Society: Series B*, 72, pp. 343–366.

Shumway, T. (2001), Forecasting Bankruptcy More Accurately: A Simple Hazard Model. *Journal of Business*, 74, pp. 101–124.

APPENDIX A: DATA

Table A.1. All countries under the RMI coverage.

Region	Economy
Asia-Pacific (21)	Australia, China, Hong Kong, Indonesia, India, Japan, Kazakhstan, Malaysia, Pakistan, Philippines, Singapore, South Korea, Sri Lanka, Taiwan, Thailand, Vietnam, New Zealand, Cambodia, Macau, Mongolia and Papua New Guinea.
North America (2)	Canada, the United States.
Europe (43)	Austria, Belgium, Bermuda, Bulgaria, Croatia, Cyprus, Czech Republic, Denmark, Estonia, Finland, France, Germany, Greece, Hungary, Iceland, Ireland, Italy, Latvia, Lithuania, Luxembourg, Macedonia, Malta, Netherlands, Norway, Poland, Portugal, Romania, Russian Federation, Slovakia, Slovenia, Spain, Sweden, Switzerland, Turkey, the United Kingdom, Ukraine, Faeroe Island, Gibraltar, Guernsey, Isle of Man, Jersey, Liechtenstein and Monaco.
Latin America (17)	Argentina, Brazil, Columbia, Chile, Mexico, Peru, Venezuela, Bahamas, Belize, Cayman Islands, Curacao, Dominican Republic, Falkland Islands, Panama, Puerto Rico, Virgin Islands and Virgin Islands, British.
Middle-East (10)	Bahrain, Israel, Jordan, Kuwait, Saudi Arabia, United Arab Emirates, Azerbaijan, Iraq, Qatar and Sudan.
Africa (13)	Angola, Egypt, Morocco, Nigeria, South Africa, Gabon, Mauritius, Mozambique, Namibia, Sierra Leone, Tanzania, United Republic of Togo and Zambia.

Table A.2. The 71 countries under the RMI coverage for which we cover companies listed on the exchange.

Region	Economy
Asia-Pacific (17)	Australia, China, Hong Kong, Indonesia, India, Japan, Kazakhstan, Malaysia, Pakistan, Philippines, Singapore, South Korea, Sri Lanka, Taiwan, Thailand, Vietnam and New Zealand.
North America (2)	Canada and the United States.
Europe (35)	Austria, Belgium, Bulgaria, Croatia, Cyprus, Czech Republic, Denmark, Estonia, Finland, France, Germany, Greece, Hungary, Iceland, Ireland, Italy, Latvia, Lithuania, Luxembourg, Macedonia, Malta, Netherlands, Norway, Poland, Portugal, Romania, Russian Federation, Slovakia, Slovenia, Spain, Sweden, Switzerland, Turkey and the United Kingdom, Ukraine.
Latin America (7)	Argentina, Brazil, Columbia, Chile, Mexico, Peru and Venezuela.
Middle-East (6)	Bahrain, Israel, Jordan, Kuwait, Saudi Arabia and United Arab Emirates.
Africa (4)	Egypt, Morocco, Nigeria and South Africa.

Table A.3. The 35 countries under the RMI coverage for which we cover companies domiciled in the economy but listed on a foreign exchange included in Table A.2. The bolded text indicate that these economies also have their own local stock exchange.

Angola	**Gibraltar**	**Panama**
Azerbaijan	**Guernsey**	**Papua New Guinea**
Bahamas	**Iraq**	Puerto Rico
Belize	Isle of Man	**Qatar**
Bermuda	**Jersey**	**Sierra Leone**
Cambodia	Liechtenstein	**Sudan**
Cayman Islands	Macau	**Tanzania, United Republic of**
Curacao	**Mauritius**	Togo
Dominican Republic	Monaco	Virgin Islands
Faeroe Island	**Mongolia**	Virgin Islands, British
Falkland Islands	**Mozambique**	**Zambia**
Gabon	**Namibia**	

Table A.4. ISO codes for economies currently covered by the CRI and the group that each economy is calibrated in.

ISO Code	Economy	Calibration Group
ARE	United Arab Emirates	Emerging
ARG	Argentina	Emerging
AUS	Australia	Developed Asia-Pacific
AUT	Austria	Europe
BEL	Belgium	Europe
BGR	Bulgaria	Europe
BHR	Bahrain	Emerging
BRA	Brazil	Emerging
CAN	Canada	North America
CHE	Switzerland	Europe
CHL	Chile	Emerging
CHN	China	China
COL	Colombia	Emerging
CYP	Cyprus	Europe
CZE	Czech Republic	Europe
DEU	Germany	Europe
DNK	Denmark	Europe
EGY	Egypt	Emerging
ESP	Spain	Europe
EST	Estonia	Europe
FIN	Finland	Europe
FRA	France	Europe
GBR	United Kingdom	Europe
GRC	Greece	Europe
HKG	Hong Kong	Developed Asia-Pacific
HRV	Croatia	Europe
HUN	Hungary	Europe
IDN	Indonesia	Emerging
IND	India	India
IRL	Ireland	Europe
ISL	Iceland	Europe
ISR	Israel	Europe
ITA	Italy	Europe
JOR	Jordan	Emerging
JPN	Japan	Developed Asia-Pacific
KAZ	Kazakhstan	Emerging
KOR	South Korea	Developed Asia-Pacific
KWT	Kuwait	Emerging
LKA	Sri Lanka	Emerging
LTU	Lithuania	Europe
LUX	Luxembourg	Europe
LVA	Latvia	Europe
MAR	Morocco	Emerging
MEX	Mexico	Emerging

(Continued)

Table A.4. (*Continued*)

ISO Code	Economy	Calibration Group
MKD	Macedonia	Europe
MLT	Malta	Europe
MYS	Malaysia	Emerging
NGA	Nigeria	Emerging
NLD	Netherlands	Europe
NOR	Norway	Europe
NZL	New Zealand	Developed Asia-pacific
PAK	Pakistan	Emerging
PER	Peru	Emerging
PHL	Philippines	Emerging
POL	Poland	Europe
PRT	Portugal	Europe
ROM	Romania	Europe
RUS	Russian Federation	Europe
SAU	Saudi Arabia	Emerging
SGP	Singapore	Developed Asia-Pacific
SVK	Slovakia	Europe
SVN	Slovenia	Europe
SWE	Sweden	Europe
THA	Thailand	Emerging
TUR	Turkey	Europe
TWN	Taiwan	Developed Asia-Pacific
UKR	Ukraine	Emerging
USA	United States	North America
VEN	Venezuela	Emerging
VNM	Vietnam	Emerging
ZAF	South Africa	Emerging

Table A.5. The stock indices used for each economy in computing the first common variable.

Country	Stock Exchange	Period Used
ARE	FTSE NASDAQ DUB UAE 20	6/28/2006–Present
ARG	Buenos Aires Stock Exchange Merval Index	
AUS	All Ordinaries Index	
AUT	Austrian Traded ATX Index	
BEL	Belgian All Shares Return Index	
BGR	Bulgaria Stock Exchange Sofix Index	10/24/2000–Present
BHR	Bahrain Bourse All Share Index	7/8/2004–Present
BRA	Brazil Bovespa Stock Index	
CAN	S&P/TSX Composite Index	
CHE	SPI Swiss Performance Index	
CHL	Santiago Stock Exchange IPSA Index	
CHN	Shanghai Stock Exchange Composite Index	
COL	FTSE All World Series Colombia Local	

(*Continued*)

Table A.5. (*Continued*)

Country	Stock Exchange	Period Used
CYP	Cyprus Stock Exchange General Index	9/3/2004–Present
	Cyprus Stock Exchange General	4/2/1996–9/2/2004
CZE	Prague Stock Exch Index	4/5/1994–Present
DEU	CDAX Performance Index	
DNK	OMX Copenhagen 20 Index	
EGY	EGX 100 Index	5/1/2006–Present
ESP	IBEX 35 Index	
EST	OMX Tallinn OMXT	
FIN	OMX Helsinki Index	
FRA	CAC 40 Index	
GBR	FTSE 100 Index	
GRC	Athex Composite Share Price Index	
HKG	Hang Seng Index	
HRV	Croatia Zagreb CROBEX	6/14/2002–Present
HUN	Budapest Stock Exch Index	1/2/1991–Present
IDN	Jakarta Composite Index	
IND	BSE Sensex 30 Index	
IRL	Irish Overall Index	
ISL	OMX Iceland All-Share Price Index	
ISR	Tel Aviv 100 Index	12/31/1991–Present
ITA	Italy Stock Market BCI Comit Global	
JOR	Jordan Traded Value Index	11/10/2005–Present
JPN	Nikkei 500	
KAZ	Kazakhstan Stock Exchange Index KASE	7/12/2000–Present
KOR	KOSPI Index	
KWT	Kuwait SE Weighted Index	1/2/2012–Present
	Kuwait Global General Index	1/2/1984–1/2/2012
LKA	Sri Lanka Colombo All-Share Index	1/2/1985–Present
LTU	OMX Vilnius OMXV	1/4/2000–Present
LUX	Luxembourg Stock Exchange LuxX Index	1/4/1999–Present
	Luxembourg Stock Exchange 13 'Dead'	1/2/1998–1/3/1999
LVA	OMX GIRA OMXR	1/2/2000–Present
MAR	CFG 25	12/31/1993–Present
MEX	Mexico Bolsa Index	
MKD	Macedonian Stock Exchange MBI 10	12/30/2004–Present
MLT	Malta Stock Exchange	
MYS	FTSE Bursa Malaysia KLCI	
NGA	NIGERIA STCK EXC ALL SHR	1/30/1998–Present
NLD	AEX Index	
NOR	OBX Price Index	
NZL	NZX All Index	3/30/1992–Present
PAK	Karachi All Share Index	3/11/1998–Present
PER	Bolsa de Valores de Lima General Sector Index	
PHL	PSEI-Philippine Stock Exchange Index	
POL	WSE WIG Index	4/16/1991–Present

(*Continued*)

Table A.5. (*Continued*)

Country	Stock Exchange	Period Used
PRT	PSI General Index	
ROM	BSE COMPOSITE INDEX	4/17/1998–Present
RUS	MICEX INDEX	9/22/1997–Present
SAU	TADAWUL ALL SHARE INDEX	1/31/1994–Present
SGP	Straits Times Index	1/10/2008–Present
	Straits Times Old Index	8/31/1999–1/9/2008
SVK	Slovak Share Index	
SVN	HSBC Slovenia Dollar	
SWE	OMX Stockholm All-Share Index	
THA	Stock Exchange of Thailand Index	
TUR	Istanbul Stock Exchange National 100 Index	1/4/1988–Present
TWN	Taiwan Taiex Index	
UKR	Ukraine PFTS Index	1/12/1998–Present
USA	S&P 500 Index	
VEN	Caracas Stock Exchange Stock Market Index	
VNM	Ho Chi Minh Stock Index	7/28/2000–Present
ZAF	MSCI South Africa Index	12/31/1992–Present

Note: *A blank Period Used column indicates that there is only a single index that is used throughout the whole period.

Table A.6. The interest rates used for each economy as the second common variable.

Country	Short-Term Interest Rate	Period Used
ARE	UAE Ibor 3 Month	5/15/2000–Present
ARG	Argentina Deposit 90 Day	
AUS	Australia Dealer Bill 90 Day	
AUT	Germany 3 Month Bubill	1/1/1999–Present
	—	–12/31/1998
BEL	Germany 3 Month Bubill	1/1/1999–Present
	—	–12/31/1998
BGR	Bulgaria Interbank 3 Month	2/17/2003–Present
BHR	Bahrain Ibor 3 Month	12/14/2006
BRA	Andima Brazil Govt Bond Fixed Rate 3 Months	4/3/2000–Present
	Brazil CDB (up to 30 Days)	10/10/1994–3/31/2000
CAN	Canada Treasury Bill 3 Month	
CHE	—	
CHL	Chile TAB UF Interbank Rate 90 Days	
CHN	China Time Deposit Rate 3 Month	
COL	Colombia CD Rate 90-Day	
CYP	Germany 3 Month Bubill	1/1/2008–Present
	—	–12/31/2007
CZE	Czech Republic Interbank 3 MTH	4/22/1992–Present
DEU	Germany 3 Month Bubill	5/25/1993–Present
	Germany Interbank 3 Month	1/2/1986–5/24/1993
DNK	Denmark Interbank 3 Month	
EGY	Egypt 91 Day T-Bill	7/6/2004–Present
ESP	Germany 3 Month Bubill	1/1/1999–Present
	—	–12/31/1998
EST	Germany 3 Month Bubill	1/1/2011–Present
	—	–12/31/2010
FIN	Germany 3 Month Bubill	1/1/1999–Present
	—	–12/31/1998
FRA	Germany 3 Month Bubill	1/1/1999–Present
	—	–12/31/1998
GBR	UK Treasury Bill Tender 3 Month	
GRC	Germany 3 Month Bubill	1/1/2001–Present
	—	–12/31/2000
HKG	Hong Kong Exchange Fund Bill 3 Month	
HRV	Croatia Zibor Rate 3 Month	6/2/1997–Present
HUN	Hungary Interbank 3 Month	9/7/1995–Present
IDN	Indonesia SBI 90 Day	7/10/2003–Present
	Indonesia SBI/DISC 90 Day	1/1/1985–7/9/2003
IND	India T-Bill Secondary 91 Day	
IRL	Germany 3 Month Bubill	1/1/1999–Present
	—	–12/31/1998
ISL	—	
ISR	Israel T-Bill Secondary 3 Month	5/30/1995–Present
ITA	Germany 3 Month Bubill	1/1/1999–Present

(Continued)

Table A.6. *(Continued)*

Country	Short-Term Interest Rate	Period Used
	—	–12/31/1998
JOR	Amman Interbank 3 Month	3/9/2001–Present
JPN	Japan Treasury Discount Bills 3 Month	7/10/1992–Present
	Japanese Government Bond Interest Rate-1 Year Maturity	9/24/1974–7/9/1992
KAZ	Kazakhstan KIBOR/KIBID 90 Days Interbank	9/29/2001–Present
KOR	Korea Commercial Paper 91 Day	
KWT	Kuwait Interbank 3 Month	8/17/1983–Present
LKA	Sri Lanka Treasury Bill 3 Month	1/6/1989–Present
LTU	VILNIUS Interbank Three Month	1/6/1999–Present
LUX	Germany 3 Month Bubill	1/1/1999–Present
	—	–12/31/1998
LVA	Treasury Bill Rate 3 Month	5/11/1994–Present
MAR	Morocco Deposit Rate 3 Month	6/6/2003–Present
MEX	Mexico Cetes 2ND MKT. 90 Day	6/26/1996 – Present
	Mexico Cetes 91 Dat AVG.RET.AT AUC.	3/9/1989–6/25/1996
MKD	Macedonia Skibor 3 Months	7/2/2007 – Present
MLT	Germany 3 Month Bubill	1/1/2008–Present
	—	–12/31/2007
MYS	Malaysia Deposit 3 Month	
NGA	Nigeria Interbank Offered Rate 3 Month	1/30/2004–Present
NLD	Germany 3 Month Bubill	1/1/1999–Present
	—	–12/31/1998
NOR	Norway Govt Treasury Bills 3 Month	6/27/1995–Present
	Norway Interbank 3 Month(effective)	1/2/1986–6/26/1995
NZL	New Zealand Dollar Deposit 3 Month	9/27/1988–Present
PAK	PKR 3 Month Repo	10/29/1999–Present
PER	Peru Savings Rate	
PHL	Philippine Treasury Bill 91 Day	
POL	Poland Interbank 3 Month (EOD)	6/4/1993–Present
PRT	Germany 3 Month Bubill	1/1/1999–Present
	—	–12/31/1998
ROM	Romanian Interbank 3 Month	8/1/1995–Present
RUS	Russian Federation Interbank 31–90 Day	9/1/1994–Present
SAU	Saudi Interbank 3 Month	1/1/1987–Present
SGP	Singapore T-Bill 3 Month	
SVK	Germany 3 Month Bubill	1/1/2009–Present
	—	–12/31/2008
SVN	Germany 3 Month Bubill	1/1/2007–Present
	—	–12/31/2006
SWE	Sweden T-Bill 3 Month	5/25/1993–Present
	Sweden Treasury Bill 90 Day	4/25/1989–5/24/1993
THA	Thailand Repo 3 Month(BOT)	
TUR	Turkish Interbank 3 Month	8/1/2002–Present
TWN	Taiwan Money Market 90 Day	
UKR	Ukraine Interbank 3 Months	3/1/2001–Present

(Continued)

Table A.6. *(Continued)*

Country	Short-Term Interest Rate	Period Used
USA	US Generic Govt 3-Month Yield	
VEN	Venezuela Overnight	
VNM	Vietnam Interbank 3 Month	12/11/1998–Present
ZAF	South Africa T-Bill 91 Days (Tender Rates)	12/31/1980–Present

Note: *A blank Period Used column indicates that there is only a single interest rate that is used throughout the whole period.

Table A.7. The interest rates used for each economy in the DTD calculation.

Country	Interest Rate Name	Period Used
ARE	UAE Ibor 1 Year	5/15/2000–Present
ARG	Aregentina Deposit 90 Day (PA.)	
AUS	Australia Govt. Bonds Generic Mid Yield 1 Year	
AUT	German Government Bonds 1 Year BKO	1/1/1999–Present
	Austria VIBOR 12 Month	6/10/1991–12/31/1998
BEL	German Government Bonds 1 Year BKO	1/1/1999–Present
	Belgium Treasury Bill 1 Year	4/2/1991–12/31/1998
BGR	Bulgaria Interbank 3 Month	2/17/2003–Present
BHR	Bahrain Ibor 1 Year	12/14/2006
BRA	Andima Brazil Govt Bond Fixed Rate 1 Year	4/3/2000–Present
	BRAZIL CDB (UP TO 30 DAYS)	10/10/1994–3/31/2000
CAN	Canada Treasury Bill 1 Year	
CHE	Swiss Interbank 1 Year (ZRC:SNB)	
CHL	Chile TAB UF Interbank Rates 360 Days	8/1/1996– Present
	Chile TAB UF Interbank Rate 90 Days	11/2/1992–7/30/1996
CHN	China Household Savings Deposits 1-Year Rate	
COL	Colombia Government Generic Bond 1 Year Yield	3/1/2001 – Present
	Colombia CD Rate 360-Dat	7/12/1993– 2/8/2001
CYP	Cyprus Treasury Bill Rate — 13 Week	
CZE	Czech Republic Interbank 3 MTH	4/22/1992–Present
DEU	German Government Bonds 1 Year BKO	1/10/1995–Present
	Germany Interbank 12 Month	11/2/1990–1/9/1995
DNK	Denmark Government Bonds 1 Year Note Generic Bid Yield	6/1/2008–Present
	Denmark Euro-Krone 1 Year(FT/ICAP/TR)	6/14/1985–5/31/2008
EGY	Egypt 364 Day T-Bill	7/6/2004–Present
ESP	German Government Bonds 1 Year BKO	1/1/1999–Present
	Spain 12 Month Treasury Bill Yield	11/30/1992–12/31/1998
	Spain Interbank 12 Month	12/19/1991–11/29/1992
EST	Estonia, Interest Rates, Prices, Production & Labour, Interest Rates, Deposit Rate	
FIN	German Government Bonds 1 Year BKO	1/1/1999–Present
	Finland Interbank Close 12 Month	4/2/1992–12/31/1998
FRA	German Government Bonds 1 Year BKO	1/1/1999–Present
	France Treasury Bill 12 Months	1/3/1989–12/31/1998
GBR	UK Govt. Bonds 1 Year Note Generic	9/12/2001–Present

(Continued)

Table A.7. *(Continued)*

Country	Interest Rate Name	Period Used
	UK Govt. Liability Nominal Spot Curve 12 Month	12/13/1985–9/11/2001
GRC	German Government Bonds 1 Year BKO	1/1/2001–Present
	Greece Treasury Bill 1 Year	1/2/1990–12/31/2000
HKG	HKMA Hong Kong Exchange Fund Bill 12 Month	
HRV	Croatia Zibor Rate 3 Month	6/2/1997–Present
HUN	Hungary Interbank 3 Month	9/7/1995–Present
IDN	Indonesia SBI 90 Day	7/10/2003–Present
	Indonesia SBI/DISC 90 Day	1/1/1985–7/9/2003
IND	India T-Bill Secondary 1 Year	
IRL	UK Govt. Liability Nominal Spot Curve 12 Month	
ISL	Iceland Interbank 12 Month	2/1/2000–Present
	Iceland Interbank 3 Month	8/4/1998–1/31/2000
	Iceland 90-day CB Notes	5/12/1987–8/3/1998
ISR	Israel T-Bill Secondary 1 Year	11/15/1994–Present
ITA	German Government Bonds 1 Year BKO	1/1/1999–Present
	Italy Bots Treasury Bill 12 Month Gross Yields	9/5/1994–12/31/1998
	Italy T-Bill Auction Gross 12 Month	3/31/1987–9/4/1994
JOR	Amman Interbank 1 Year	3/9/2001–Present
JPN	Japan Treasury Bills 12 Month	12/14/1999–Present
	Japanese Government Bond Interest Rate-1 Year Maturity	9/24/1979–12/13/1999
KAZ	Kazakhstan KIBOR/KIBID 90 Days Interbank	9/29/2001–Present
KOR	Korea Monetary Stabilization Bonds 1 Year	
KWT	Kuwait Interbank 1 Year	8/17/1983–Present
LKA	Sri Lanka Fixed Deposit 1 Year	3/31/1988–Present
LTU	Vilnius Interbank 12 Month	3/29/2000–Present
LUX	Long-Term Government Bond Yields — Maastricht Definition (Avg.)	
LVA	Treasury Bill Rate 1 Year	4/3/1998–Present
MAR	Morocco Deposit Rate 1 Year	6/6/2003–Present
MKD	Macedonia Skibor 3 Month	7/2/2007–Present
MEX	Mexico Cetes 2ND MKT. 360 Day	6/26/1996 –Present
	Mexico Cete 91 DAY AVG.RET.AT AUC.	3/9/1989– 6/25/1996
MLT	Long-Term Government Bond Yields — Maastricht Definition (Avg.)	
MYS	Bank Negara Malaysia 1 Year Govt. Securities Indicative YTM	6/21/2005–Present
	Malaysia Deposit 1 Year	1/1/1985–6/20/2005
NGA	Nigeria Interbank Offered Rate 3 Month	1/30/2004–Present
NLD	German Government Bonds 1 Year BKO	1/1/1999–Present
	Netherlands Interbank 1 Year	1/2/1987–12/31/1998
NOR	Norway Govt Treasury Bills 12 Month	7/1/1997–Present
	Norway Interbank 1 Year	1/2/1986–6/30/1997
NZL	New Zealand Dollar Deposit 1 Year	9/27/1988–Present
PAK	PKR 12 Month Repo	10/29/2004–Present
PER	Peru Savings Rate	
PHL	Philippine Treasury Bill 364 Day	
POL	Poland Interbank 1 Year (EOD)	10/11/1995–Present
PRT	German Government Bonds 1 Year BKO	1/1/1999–Present

(Continued)

Table A.7. *(Continued)*

Country	Interest Rate Name	Period Used
	Portugal 1-Year-LISBOR-Act/365 Day convention	8/16/1993–12/31/1998
ROM	Romanian Interbank 12 Month	8/1/1995–Present
RUS	Russian Federation Interbank 31–90 Day	9/1/1994–Present
SAU	Saudi Interbank 1 Year	1/1/1987–Present
SGP	Singapore T-Bill 3 Month	
SVK	Slovak Rep.Interbank 1 Year	
SVN	Slovenia Treasury Bill 3 Month 'Dead'	
SWE	Sweden Interbank 1 Year	5/25/1993–Present
	Sweden Treasury Bill 1 Year Note	4/25/1989–5/24/1993
THA	Thailand Govt. Bond 1 Year Note	8/7/2000–Present
	Thailand Deposit 12 Month(KT)	1/2/1991–8/6/2000
TUR	Turkish Interbank 12 Month	8/1/2002–Present
TWN	Taiwan Deposit 12 Month	
UKR	UAE Ibor 1 Year	5/15/2000–Present
USA	US Treasury Constant Maturities 1 Year	
VEN	Venezuela Overnight	
VNM	Vietnam Interbank 3 Month	12/11/1998–Present
ZAF	South Africa T-Bill 91 Days (Tender Rates)	12/31/1980–Present

Note: *A blank Period Used column indicates that there is only a single interest rate that is used throughout the whole period.

Table A.8. Summary statistics of input variables (based on data from January 1991 to August 2013).

	DTD Level							
	Min	25%	Median	75%	Max	Mean	StdDev	# Observations
ARE	−0.80	1.77	2.76	3.83	13.33	3.07	1.88	5040
ARG	−1.75	1.37	2.68	3.89	19.82	2.89	2.25	12432
AUS	−1.43	1.85	2.98	4.20	18.39	3.29	2.18	279166
AUT	−2.68	1.95	3.12	5.02	27.36	4.06	4.11	20255
BEL	−2.68	2.52	4.38	6.73	27.36	5.03	3.77	28803
BGR	−1.78	1.07	2.01	3.20	27.36	2.43	2.26	9953
BHR	−0.27	1.69	2.73	4.57	18.32	3.60	2.97	1344
BRA	−1.85	0.71	1.84	3.35	24.67	2.39	2.69	49196
CAN	−1.13	1.91	3.26	4.93	24.77	3.69	2.57	212877
CHE	−2.68	2.69	4.08	5.90	23.69	4.53	2.85	50300
CHL	−1.85	3.58	5.22	6.77	25.75	5.62	3.44	28137
CHN	0.05	3.09	4.17	5.74	16.75	4.66	2.29	261715
COL	−1.35	2.34	3.86	5.70	20.21	4.31	3.03	5590
CYP	−1.19	0.89	1.54	2.46	23.81	2.07	2.28	16037
CZE	−2.68	1.30	2.42	3.70	20.27	2.71	2.21	5949
DEU	−2.68	1.62	2.89	4.38	27.36	3.31	2.68	174121

(Continued)

Table A.8. (*Continued*)

	DTD Level							
	Min	**25%**	**Median**	**75%**	**Max**	**Mean**	**StdDev**	**# Observations**
DNK	−1.92	1.88	3.17	4.70	27.36	3.65	2.96	41358
EGY	−1.85	1.78	2.80	4.07	25.75	3.11	2.09	13226
ESP	−2.68	2.07	3.46	4.98	27.36	3.87	3.11	34401
EST	−0.30	1.40	2.89	3.99	11.63	3.27	2.53	714
FIN	−2.68	2.27	3.44	4.93	16.52	3.79	2.34	27721
FRA	−2.68	1.83	3.01	4.59	27.36	3.48	2.71	157441
GBR	−2.68	2.23	3.57	5.29	27.36	4.03	2.72	373188
GRC	−2.68	1.38	2.40	3.73	23.59	2.72	2.13	54384
HKG	−1.43	1.52	2.54	3.97	18.39	3.03	2.29	204365
HRV	−2.68	1.15	2.29	3.60	18.21	2.64	2.17	10054
HUN	−1.53	1.62	2.74	4.31	27.36	3.14	2.41	7000
IDN	−1.85	0.65	1.66	2.80	25.55	1.98	2.08	57698
IND	−1.73	0.82	1.70	2.84	17.86	2.10	2.09	440591
IRL	−1.73	1.96	3.26	4.78	14.51	3.49	2.23	9861
ISL	−1.48	1.76	2.96	4.31	20.01	3.29	2.31	4305
ISR	−2.19	1.26	2.35	3.61	27.36	2.73	2.40	71614
ITA	−2.68	1.61	2.83	4.36	27.36	3.20	2.52	57802
JOR	−1.09	2.37	3.46	4.93	15.49	3.99	2.49	11234
JPN	−1.43	2.08	3.13	4.49	18.39	3.53	2.19	792157
KAZ	−1.59	0.54	1.24	2.99	25.75	2.49	4.13	781
KOR	−1.43	1.23	2.16	3.32	18.39	2.50	2.10	278669
KWT	−0.44	2.28	3.23	4.47	25.75	3.70	2.30	21036
LKA	−1.85	1.61	2.41	3.73	16.12	2.80	1.94	16090
LTU	−1.30	1.43	3.13	5.21	20.95	3.68	3.19	4158
LUX	−0.17	3.06	4.75	7.40	27.36	6.02	4.48	2800
LVA	−1.45	1.30	2.27	3.89	27.36	2.90	2.54	2873
MAR	−0.69	2.62	3.90	5.34	21.53	4.18	2.45	6959
MEX	−1.85	2.01	3.64	5.50	25.75	4.13	3.19	18307
MKD	−1.09	1.35	1.93	2.84	16.51	2.59	2.56	1826
MLT	−0.65	2.30	3.52	4.86	14.99	4.11	3.01	892
MYS	−1.85	1.56	2.83	4.59	25.75	3.49	2.91	183585
NGA	−1.78	1.20	2.28	3.22	25.75	2.81	3.50	13202
NLD	−2.68	2.44	3.96	5.77	27.36	4.38	3.00	35364
NOR	−2.63	1.24	2.36	3.79	20.49	2.63	2.04	42178
NZL	−1.30	2.87	4.88	6.94	18.39	5.21	3.20	16703
PAK	−1.85	0.42	1.59	3.23	14.52	2.03	2.26	21899
PER	−1.85	1.96	3.11	4.55	22.71	3.55	2.53	11048
PHL	−1.85	1.11	2.25	3.65	25.75	2.66	2.30	37197

(*Continued*)

Table A.8. *(Continued)*

	DTD Level							
	Min	25%	Median	75%	Max	Mean	StdDev	# Observations
POL	−1.94	1.37	2.31	3.46	27.36	2.63	2.06	55811
PRT	−2.68	1.10	2.29	3.82	20.10	2.73	2.37	13389
ROM	−2.68	0.98	1.80	2.38	27.36	1.92	1.60	15254
RUS	−2.27	1.33	2.61	4.03	27.36	3.27	4.01	20091
SAU	−1.52	3.59	5.23	7.49	25.75	6.05	3.67	13908
SGP	−1.19	1.54	2.65	4.28	18.39	3.17	2.36	113973
SVK	−0.39	1.62	2.41	3.04	27.36	3.36	5.06	905
SVN	−2.47	2.10	3.39	5.49	16.88	3.92	2.95	6426
SWE	−2.68	1.72	3.02	4.54	27.36	3.37	2.50	77340
THA	−1.71	1.65	2.89	4.40	25.75	3.29	2.53	91012
TUR	−2.34	1.61	2.87	4.57	22.59	3.47	2.82	37376
TWN	−1.43	2.62	3.72	5.07	18.39	4.04	2.21	225465
UKR	−1.69	0.98	1.70	2.76	21.52	1.89	1.53	4847
USA	−1.13	1.79	3.04	4.70	24.77	3.53	2.62	1454952
VEN	−1.85	0.35	1.21	2.65	17.01	2.05	3.01	3393
VNM	−1.85	0.99	1.74	2.83	25.75	2.08	1.74	33109
ZAF	−1.85	1.33	2.76	4.52	25.75	3.35	3.12	76694

	DTD Trend							
	Min	25%	Median	75%	Max	Mean	StdDev	# Observations
ARE	−4.43	−0.37	0.02	0.38	6.00	−0.02	0.84	5040
ARG	−7.73	−0.51	−0.01	0.41	7.38	−0.04	1.01	12432
AUS	−5.68	−0.47	−0.02	0.38	5.40	−0.05	0.98	279166
AUT	−8.45	−0.56	−0.03	0.42	7.80	−0.14	1.58	20255
BEL	−8.45	−0.61	−0.01	0.59	7.80	−0.02	1.51	28803
BGR	−8.45	−0.44	0.00	0.30	7.80	−0.08	1.01	9953
BHR	−7.73	−0.35	0.01	0.26	4.36	−0.10	0.91	1344
BRA	−7.73	−0.33	0.01	0.37	7.38	0.02	1.00	49196
CAN	−6.37	−0.53	−0.02	0.45	5.44	−0.05	1.10	212877
CHE	−8.45	−0.59	0.01	0.62	7.80	0.02	1.28	50300
CHL	−7.73	−0.64	0.05	0.61	7.38	−0.01	1.49	28137
CHN	−5.93	−0.56	−0.02	0.47	5.41	−0.06	1.03	261715
COL	−7.73	−0.42	0.04	0.65	7.38	0.11	1.29	5590
CYP	−8.45	−0.35	−0.07	0.17	7.80	−0.12	0.77	16037
CZE	−7.78	−0.34	0.00	0.38	5.78	0.00	0.87	4949
DEU	−8.45	−0.49	−0.03	0.42	7.80	−0.03	1.10	174121
DNK	−8.45	−0.50	−0.01	0.43	7.80	−0.03	1.19	41358
EGY	−7.73	−0.46	−0.01	0.45	7.38	−0.01	0.98	13226

(Continued)

Table A.8. (*Continued*)

	DTD Trend							
	Min	25%	Median	75%	Max	Mean	StdDev	# Observations
ESP	−8.45	−0.49	0.01	0.47	7.80	−0.00	1.26	34401
EST	−3.42	0.00	0.30	0.87	3.80	0.43	0.81	714
FIN	−8.45	−0.45	0.04	0.54	7.80	0.04	1.04	27721
FRA	−8.45	−0.46	0.00	0.45	7.80	−0.01	1.08	157441
GBR	−8.45	−0.54	−0.02	0.42	7.80	−0.08	1.25	373188
GRC	−8.45	−0.53	−0.08	0.32	7.80	−0.10	0.96	54384
HKG	−5.68	−0.47	0.00	0.45	5.40	−0.02	0.97	204365
HRV	−4.96	−0.55	−0.03	0.26	7.80	−0.12	0.93	10054
HUN	−6.80	−0.43	0.00	0.40	7.80	−0.06	0.91	7000
IDN	−7.73	−0.30	0.02	0.33	7.38	−0.00	0.77	57698
IND	−6.55	−0.36	−0.03	0.33	5.21	−0.02	0.82	440591
IRL	−6.45	−0.48	0.00	0.46	7.23	−0.04	1.01	9861
ISL	−8.45	−0.69	−0.06	0.42	6.70	−0.17	1.35	4305
ISR	−8.45	−0.43	0.00	0.40	7.80	−0.03	1.05	71614
ITA	−8.45	−0.56	−0.02	0.47	7.80	−0.05	1.13	57802
JOR	−7.38	−0.34	0.00	0.36	7.38	0.03	0.92	11234
JPN	−5.68	−0.46	−0.01	0.43	5.40	−0.01	0.88	792157
KAZ	−7.73	−0.50	0.00	0.40	7.38	0.01	1.16	781
KOR	−5.68	−0.43	0.00	0.42	5.40	−0.01	0.91	278669
KWT	−7.73	−0.44	0.00	0.40	7.38	−0.04	1.06	21036
LKA	−7.73	−0.34	0.00	0.41	7.38	0.04	0.87	16090
LTU	−6.02	−0.64	−0.01	0.65	7.80	0.01	1.35	4158
LUX	−8.45	−0.64	0.01	0.55	7.80	−0.09	1.40	2800
LVA	−8.45	−0.37	0.03	0.37	7.80	−0.04	1.11	2873
MAR	−7.73	−0.59	−0.08	0.39	7.38	−0.10	1.09	6959
MEX	−7.73	−0.42	0.06	0.61	7.38	0.07	1.18	18307
MKD	−6.14	−0.37	−0.05	0.34	6.55	0.04	0.84	1826
MLT	−6.66	−0.60	−0.04	0.55	4.26	0.02	1.27	892
MYS	−7.73	−0.47	−0.01	0.42	7.38	−0.04	1.07	183585
NGA	−7.73	−0.39	0.00	0.39	7.38	−0.01	1.42	13202
NLD	−8.45	−0.63	−0.03	0.55	7.80	−0.05	1.22	35364
NOR	−8.45	−0.41	−0.00	0.38	7.80	−0.03	0.90	42178
NZL	−5.68	−0.57	0.03	0.63	5.40	0.02	1.42	16703
PAK	−5.24	−0.26	0.03	0.35	6.17	0.04	0.74	21899
PER	−7.73	−0.43	0.00	0.50	7.38	0.03	1.21	11048
PHL	−7.73	−0.34	0.00	0.34	7.38	0.01	0.92	37197
POL	−8.45	−0.49	−0.03	0.37	7.80	−0.08	0.91	55811
PRT	−8.45	−0.43	−0.02	0.33	7.34	−0.04	0.94	13389

(*Continued*)

Table A.8. *(Continued)*

	DTD Trend							
	Min	25%	Median	75%	Max	Mean	StdDev	# Observations
ROM	−8.45	−0.27	0.00	0.23	7.80	−0.01	0.73	15254
RUS	−8.45	−0.46	0.00	0.42	7.80	−0.12	1.54	20091
SAU	−7.73	−0.74	0.13	1.01	7.38	0.10	1.83	13908
SGP	−5.68	−0.44	−0.01	0.41	5.40	−0.03	0.96	113973
SVK	−8.45	−0.15	0.06	0.31	7.80	0.04	1.39	905
SVN	−5.13	−0.57	−0.10	0.20	7.80	−0.17	1.00	6426
SWE	−8.45	−0.47	−0.02	0.44	7.80	−0.02	1.04	77340
THA	−7.73	−0.51	−0.01	0.45	7.38	−0.04	1.05	91012
TUR	−8.45	−0.50	0.09	0.66	7.80	0.09	1.31	37376
TWN	−5.68	−0.53	0.00	0.56	5.40	0.01	1.02	225465
UKR	−5.71	−0.51	−0.00	0.33	6.49	−0.14	0.90	4847
USA	−6.37	−0.47	0.00	0.47	5.44	−0.01	0.99	1454952
VEN	−6.72	−0.29	−0.00	0.28	7.38	0.00	0.90	3393
VNM	−7.73	−0.39	−0.05	0.24	7.38	−0.07	0.66	33109
ZAF	−7.73	−0.45	−0.01	0.37	7.38	−0.06	1.18	76694

	CASH/TA Level							
	Min	25%	Median	75%	Max	Mean	StdDev	# Observations
ARE	0.00	0.07	0.15	0.23	0.94	0.17	0.14	6142
ARG	0.00	0.02	0.05	0.11	0.69	0.08	0.08	12964
AUS	0.00	0.04	0.13	0.35	0.97	0.23	0.25	289939
AUT	0.00	0.03	0.07	0.15	0.96	0.11	0.13	21975
BEL	0.00	0.03	0.07	0.18	0.99	0.14	0.18	31291
BGR	0.00	0.01	0.03	0.08	0.58	0.06	0.08	10253
BHR	0.00	0.09	0.18	0.27	0.91	0.20	0.15	2778
BRA	0.00	0.02	0.08	0.17	0.94	0.12	0.13	52443
CAN	0.00	0.01	0.06	0.21	0.99	0.16	0.21	218264
CHE	0.00	0.05	0.10	0.20	0.99	0.15	0.16	54975
CHL	0.00	0.01	0.03	0.08	0.94	0.06	0.09	29891
CHN	0.00	0.08	0.14	0.25	0.89	0.19	0.16	267324
COL	0.00	0.03	0.06	0.09	0.76	0.07	0.08	6101
CYP	0.00	0.01	0.05	0.15	0.93	0.11	0.14	16617
CZE	0.00	0.02	0.05	0.11	0.99	0.09	0.13	6647
DEU	0.00	0.03	0.08	0.19	0.99	0.14	0.18	181477
DNK	0.00	0.03	0.09	0.18	0.99	0.14	0.17	45170
EGY	0.00	0.04	0.12	0.23	0.94	0.16	0.14	14709
ESP	0.00	0.02	0.05	0.11	0.82	0.08	0.10	38443
EST	0.00	0.03	0.05	0.12	0.53	0.09	0.09	2467

(Continued)

Table A.8. *(Continued)*

	CASH/TA Level							
	Min	25%	Median	75%	Max	Mean	StdDev	# Observations
FIN	0.00	0.03	0.08	0.16	0.99	0.12	0.14	29245
FRA	0.00	0.03	0.08	0.17	0.99	0.13	0.14	163863
GBR	0.00	0.03	0.09	0.22	0.99	0.17	0.21	378789
GRC	0.00	0.02	0.06	0.13	0.83	0.10	0.11	56058
HKG	0.00	0.06	0.14	0.26	0.97	0.19	0.17	210091
HRV	0.00	0.01	0.02	0.05	0.52	0.05	0.08	11945
HUN	0.00	0.02	0.06	0.13	0.74	0.09	0.10	7476
IDN	0.00	0.03	0.08	0.17	0.90	0.12	0.12	61228
IND	0.00	0.01	0.03	0.07	0.81	0.06	0.09	602790
IRL	0.00	0.05	0.09	0.21	0.97	0.15	0.17	10353
ISL	0.00	0.02	0.04	0.08	0.53	0.06	0.06	4725
ISR	0.00	0.03	0.10	0.22	0.99	0.18	0.21	72757
ITA	0.00	0.03	0.06	0.14	0.99	0.10	0.11	61244
JOR	0.00	0.01	0.04	0.14	0.94	0.11	0.15	13308
JPN	0.00	0.08	0.13	0.22	0.97	0.17	0.14	795679
KAZ	0.00	0.08	0.14	0.18	0.36	0.13	0.07	922
KOR	0.00	0.04	0.09	0.18	0.97	0.13	0.13	282260
KWT	0.00	0.03	0.07	0.20	0.94	0.15	0.18	22089
LKA	0.00	0.02	0.04	0.10	0.94	0.09	0.13	16415
LTU	0.00	0.01	0.03	0.07	0.51	0.06	0.09	4325
LUX	0.00	0.05	0.11	0.18	0.97	0.15	0.14	3191
LVA	0.00	0.01	0.04	0.12	0.44	0.08	0.09	3146
MAR	0.00	0.01	0.05	0.13	0.78	0.09	0.11	10481
MEX	0.00	0.03	0.06	0.11	0.77	0.08	0.08	19948
MKD	0.00	0.02	0.04	0.16	0.59	0.11	0.13	2324
MLT	0.00	0.04	0.08	0.21	0.50	0.14	0.14	1330
MYS	0.00	0.02	0.07	0.16	0.94	0.12	0.13	186337
NGA	0.00	0.03	0.07	0.20	0.73	0.13	0.15	14526
NLD	0.00	0.02	0.05	0.12	0.99	0.10	0.13	37561
NOR	0.00	0.04	0.09	0.19	0.99	0.15	0.18	44342
NZL	0.00	0.01	0.03	0.10	0.97	0.10	0.17	17600
PAK	0.00	0.01	0.05	0.14	0.90	0.10	0.12	28455
PER	0.00	0.01	0.04	0.13	0.71	0.09	0.11	11736
PHL	0.00	0.02	0.08	0.18	0.94	0.13	0.15	38970
POL	0.00	0.03	0.06	0.14	0.99	0.11	0.12	57259
PRT	0.00	0.01	0.03	0.07	0.54	0.06	0.08	14419
ROM	0.00	0.01	0.03	0.08	0.73	0.07	0.10	15955

(Continued)

Table A.8. *(Continued)*

	CASH/TA Level							
	Min	25%	Median	75%	Max	Mean	StdDev	# Observations
RUS	0.00	0.02	0.06	0.15	0.99	0.11	0.12	22186
SAU	0.00	0.04	0.09	0.18	0.94	0.15	0.18	14598
SGP	0.00	0.06	0.13	0.24	0.97	0.17	0.15	115827
SVK	0.00	0.02	0.05	0.11	0.59	0.08	0.09	1414
SVN	0.00	0.01	0.04	0.08	0.41	0.06	0.07	7000
SWE	0.00	0.04	0.09	0.20	0.99	0.16	0.19	79823
THA	0.00	0.02	0.06	0.14	0.88	0.10	0.12	93020
TUR	0.00	0.02	0.06	0.15	0.99	0.11	0.14	60029
TWN	0.00	0.06	0.11	0.21	0.95	0.16	0.14	227903
UKR	0.00	0.01	0.02	0.07	0.88	0.06	0.12	5636
USA	0.00	0.03	0.07	0.24	0.99	0.18	0.22	1509399
VEN	0.00	0.04	0.07	0.18	0.94	0.12	0.11	3937
VNM	0.00	0.03	0.08	0.17	0.93	0.13	0.14	34586
ZAF	0.00	0.03	0.08	0.16	0.94	0.12	0.14	80493

	CASH/TA Trend							
	Min	25%	Median	75%	Max	Mean	StdDev	# Observations
ARE	−0.36	−0.02	−0.00	0.01	0.40	−0.01	0.06	6142
ARG	−0.36	−0.01	0.00	0.01	0.40	−0.00	0.04	12964
AUS	−0.42	−0.03	−0.00	0.01	0.44	−0.01	0.09	289939
AUT	−0.46	−0.01	0.00	0.00	0.46	−0.00	0.04	21975
BEL	−0.46	−0.01	0.00	0.00	0.46	−0.00	0.05	31291
BGR	−0.25	−0.00	0.00	0.00	0.46	−0.00	0.03	10253
BHR	−0.36	−0.02	0.00	0.01	0.40	−0.00	0.07	2778
BRA	−0.36	−0.01	0.00	0.01	0.40	−0.00	0.05	52443
CAN	−0.44	−0.02	0.00	0.01	0.42	−0.00	0.07	218264
CHE	−0.46	−0.01	0.00	0.01	0.46	−0.00	0.04	54975
CHL	−0.36	−0.01	−0.00	0.00	0.40	−0.00	0.04	29891
CHN	−0.30	−0.03	−0.00	0.01	0.30	−0.01	0.05	267324
COL	−0.36	−0.01	0.00	0.01	0.40	0.00	0.04	6101
CYP	−0.46	−0.01	0.00	0.00	0.46	−0.00	0.04	16617
CZE	−0.33	−0.00	0.00	0.00	0.46	0.00	0.04	6647
DEU	−0.46	−0.01	0.00	0.00	0.46	−0.00	0.06	181477
DNK	−0.46	−0.01	−0.00	0.01	0.46	−0.00	0.06	45170
EGY	−0.36	−0.02	−0.00	0.01	0.40	−0.00	0.05	14709
ESP	−0.46	−0.01	0.00	0.01	0.46	−0.00	0.04	38443
EST	−0.25	−0.01	0.00	0.01	0.17	−0.00	0.03	2467
FIN	−0.46	−0.01	−0.00	0.01	0.46	−0.00	0.05	29245

(Continued)

Table A.8. *(Continued)*

	CASH/TA Trend							
	Min	25%	Median	75%	Max	Mean	StdDev	# Observations
FRA	−0.46	−0.01	0.00	0.01	0.46	−0.00	0.04	163863
GBR	−0.46	−0.02	0.00	0.01	0.46	−0.01	0.07	378789
GRC	−0.46	−0.01	−0.00	0.01	0.46	−0.00	0.05	56058
HKG	−0.42	−0.02	0.00	0.01	0.44	−0.00	0.07	210091
HRV	−0.18	−0.01	−0.00	0.00	0.44	−0.00	0.03	11945
HUN	−0.46	−0.01	−0.00	0.01	0.46	−0.00	0.04	7476
IDN	−0.36	−0.01	0.00	0.01	0.40	−0.00	0.04	61228
IND	−0.35	−0.00	0.00	0.00	0.36	−0.00	0.04	602790
IRL	−0.46	−0.01	0.00	0.01	0.46	−0.00	0.05	10353
ISL	−0.36	−0.01	0.00	0.00	0.40	−0.00	0.03	4725
ISR	−0.46	−0.02	−0.00	0.01	0.46	−0.00	0.08	72757
ITA	−0.46	−0.01	−0.00	0.01	0.46	−0.00	0.04	61244
JOR	−0.36	−0.01	0.00	0.00	0.40	−0.00	0.04	13308
JPN	−0.42	−0.01	0.00	0.01	0.44	−0.00	0.04	795679
KAZ	−0.17	−0.02	0.00	0.01	0.30	−0.00	0.04	922
KOR	−0.42	−0.02	−0.00	0.01	0.44	−0.00	0.06	282260
KWT	−0.36	−0.01	−0.00	0.01	0.40	−0.00	0.06	22089
LKA	−0.36	−0.01	0.00	0.01	0.40	0.00	0.05	16415
LTU	−0.20	−0.01	−0.00	0.00	0.31	−0.00	0.03	4325
LUX	−0.39	−0.01	0.00	0.00	0.26	0.00	0.04	3191
LVA	−0.21	−0.01	0.00	0.01	0.32	−0.00	0.04	3146
MAR	−0.36	−0.01	0.00	0.01	0.40	−0.00	0.04	10481
MEX	−0.30	−0.01	−0.00	0.01	0.40	−0.00	0.03	19948
MKD	−0.18	−0.00	0.00	0.00	0.31	0.00	0.04	2324
MLT	−0.32	−0.01	0.00	0.00	0.18	−0.00	0.03	1330
MYS	−0.36	−0.01	0.00	0.01	0.40	−0.00	0.05	186337
NGA	−0.36	−0.01	0.00	0.00	0.40	−0.00	0.06	14526
NLD	−0.46	−0.01	0.00	0.00	0.46	−0.00	0.04	37561
NOR	−0.46	−0.02	−0.00	0.01	0.46	−0.00	0.06	44342
NZL	−0.42	−0.01	0.00	0.00	0.44	−0.00	0.06	17600
PAK	−0.36	−0.01	0.00	0.00	0.40	−0.00	0.04	28455
PER	−0.32	−0.01	0.00	0.01	0.39	0.00	0.04	11736
PHL	−0.36	−0.01	0.00	0.01	0.40	−0.00	0.06	38970
POL	−0.46	−0.01	−0.00	0.00	0.46	−0.00	0.05	57259
PRT	−0.40	−0.01	0.00	0.00	0.46	−0.00	0.03	14419
ROM	−0.46	−0.00	0.00	0.00	0.46	−0.00	0.03	15955
RUS	−0.46	−0.01	0.00	0.01	0.46	0.00	0.06	22186

(Continued)

Table A.8. *(Continued)*

	CASH/TA Trend							
	Min	25%	Median	75%	Max	Mean	StdDev	# Observations
SAU	−0.36	−0.01	0.00	0.01	0.40	−0.00	0.06	14598
SGP	−0.42	−0.02	0.00	0.01	0.44	−0.00	0.06	115827
SVK	−0.13	−0.01	0.00	0.00	0.15	−0.00	0.02	1414
SVN	−0.30	−0.00	0.00	0.00	0.28	−0.00	0.02	7000
SWE	−0.46	−0.01	−0.00	0.01	0.46	−0.00	0.06	79823
THA	−0.36	−0.01	−0.00	0.01	0.40	−0.00	0.04	93020
TUR	−0.46	−0.01	0.00	0.01	0.46	−0.00	0.06	60029
TWN	−0.42	−0.02	0.00	0.02	0.44	0.00	0.05	227903
UKR	−0.23	−0.00	0.00	0.00	0.32	0.00	0.03	5636
USA	−0.44	−0.02	−0.00	0.01	0.42	−0.00	0.06	1509399
VEN	−0.18	−0.01	0.00	0.00	0.31	−0.00	0.03	3937
VNM	−0.36	−0.02	−0.00	0.01	0.40	−0.00	0.05	34586
ZAF	−0.36	−0.01	0.00	0.01	0.40	−0.00	0.05	80493

	NI/TA Level							
	Min	25%	Median	75%	Max	Mean	StdDev	# Observations
ARE*	−0.04	0.00	0.00	0.01	0.03	0.00	0.01	6180
ARG*	−0.04	−0.00	0.00	0.01	0.03	0.00	0.01	13017
AUS	−0.47	−0.02	−0.00	0.00	0.10	−0.02	0.05	290464
AUT	−0.56	0.00	0.00	0.00	0.08	−0.00	0.02	22103
BEL	−0.35	0.00	0.00	0.01	0.08	0.00	0.01	31396
BGR	−0.19	−0.00	0.00	0.01	0.08	0.00	0.01	11193
BHR*	−0.03	0.00	0.00	0.01	0.03	0.01	0.01	2825
BRA*	−0.04	−0.00	0.00	0.01	0.03	0.00	0.01	52496
CAN	−0.39	−0.01	0.00	0.00	0.20	−0.01	0.04	218860
CHE	−0.56	0.00	0.00	0.00	0.08	0.00	0.02	55184
CHL*	−0.04	0.00	0.00	0.01	0.03	0.00	0.01	29989
CHN	−0.17	0.00	0.00	0.01	0.13	0.00	0.01	267646
COL*	−0.04	0.00	0.00	0.01	0.03	0.00	0.01	6149
CYP	−0.56	−0.00	0.00	0.00	0.08	−0.00	0.03	17142
CZE	−0.29	0.00	0.00	0.00	0.04	0.00	0.01	6688
DEU	−0.56	−0.00	0.00	0.00	0.08	−0.00	0.02	182385
DNK	−0.56	0.00	0.00	0.00	0.08	−0.00	0.03	45393
EGY*	−0.04	0.00	0.00	0.01	0.03	0.01	0.01	14769
ESP	−0.56	0.00	0.00	0.00	0.08	0.00	0.03	38509
EST	−0.09	0.00	0.00	0.01	0.05	0.00	0.01	2489
FIN	−0.22	0.00	0.00	0.01	0.08	0.00	0.01	29292
FRA	−0.56	0.00	0.00	0.00	0.08	0.00	0.02	164611

*Winsorization levels are at 1 and 99 percentiles instead of 0.1 and 99.9 percentiles.

(Continued)

Table A.8. (*Continued*)

	NI/TA Level							
	Min	25%	Median	75%	Max	Mean	StdDev	# Observations
GBR	−0.56	−0.00	0.00	0.01	0.08	−0.01	0.04	379983
GRC	−0.56	−0.00	0.00	0.01	0.08	0.00	0.01	56167
HKG	−0.47	−0.00	0.00	0.01	0.10	−0.00	0.03	210117
HRV	−0.11	−0.00	0.00	0.00	0.08	0.00	0.01	12210
HUN	−0.13	−0.00	0.00	0.01	0.03	0.00	0.01	7500
IDN*	−0.04	0.00	0.00	0.01	0.03	0.00	0.01	61292
IND*	−0.04	0.00	0.00	0.01	0.03	0.00	0.01	608425
IRL	−0.56	−0.00	0.00	0.01	0.08	0.00	0.02	10395
ISL	−0.13	0.00	0.00	0.01	0.02	0.00	0.01	4758
ISR	−0.56	−0.00	0.00	0.00	0.08	−0.01	0.05	72805
ITA	−0.23	−0.00	0.00	0.00	0.08	0.00	0.01	61297
JOR*	−0.04	−0.00	0.00	0.00	0.03	0.00	0.01	13325
JPN	−0.47	0.00	0.00	0.00	0.10	0.00	0.01	795722
KAZ*	−0.04	0.00	0.00	0.00	0.03	0.00	0.01	935
KOR	−0.47	−0.00	0.00	0.01	0.10	−0.00	0.02	285324
KWT*	−0.04	0.00	0.00	0.01	0.03	0.00	0.01	22170
LKA*	−0.04	0.00	0.00	0.01	0.03	0.00	0.01	16489
LTU	−0.05	−0.00	0.00	0.01	0.05	0.00	0.01	4335
LUX	−0.36	0.00	0.00	0.01	0.08	−0.00	0.04	3341
LVA	−0.06	−0.00	0.00	0.01	0.08	0.00	0.01	3266
MAR*	−0.04	0.00	0.00	0.01	0.03	0.00	0.01	10552
MEX*	−0.04	0.00	0.00	0.01	0.03	0.00	0.01	20085
MKD	−0.50	0.00	0.00	0.00	0.03	−0.00	0.03	2421
MLT	−0.14	0.00	0.00	0.00	0.04	0.00	0.01	1334
MYS*	−0.04	0.00	0.00	0.01	0.03	0.00	0.01	186385
NGA*	−0.04	0.00	0.00	0.01	0.03	0.00	0.01	14838
NLD	−0.56	0.00	0.00	0.01	0.08	0.00	0.02	37588
NOR	−0.56	−0.00	0.00	0.00	0.08	−0.00	0.03	44583
NZL	−0.47	0.00	0.00	0.01	0.10	−0.01	0.05	17627
PAK*	−0.04	0.00	0.00	0.01	0.03	0.00	0.01	28534
PER*	−0.04	0.00	0.00	0.01	0.03	0.01	0.01	11808
PHL*	−0.04	−0.00	0.00	0.01	0.03	0.00	0.01	39045
POL	−0.36	−0.00	0.00	0.01	0.08	0.00	0.02	57462
PRT	−0.22	−0.00	0.00	0.00	0.06	0.00	0.01	14528
ROM	−0.56	−0.00	0.00	0.01	0.08	0.00	0.02	17822
RUS	−0.56	0.00	0.00	0.01	0.08	0.00	0.02	22582
SAU*	−0.04	0.00	0.00	0.01	0.03	0.00	0.01	14649

*Winsorization levels are at 1 and 99 percentiles instead of 0.1 and 99.9 percentiles.

(*Continued*)

Table A.8. *(Continued)*

	NI/TA Level							
	Min	25%	Median	75%	Max	Mean	StdDev	# Observations
SGP	−0.47	0.00	0.00	0.01	0.10	0.00	0.02	115917
SVK	−0.02	0.00	0.00	0.00	0.03	0.00	0.01	1503
SVN	−0.08	0.00	0.00	0.00	0.03	0.00	0.01	7072
SWE	−0.56	−0.01	0.00	0.01	0.08	−0.01	0.03	80221
THA*	−0.04	0.00	0.00	0.01	0.03	0.00	0.01	93064
TUR	−0.56	−0.00	0.00	0.01	0.08	0.00	0.03	60041
TWN	−0.29	0.00	0.00	0.01	0.10	0.00	0.01	227950
UKR	−0.10	−0.00	0.00	0.01	0.06	0.00	0.01	5789
USA	−0.39	−0.00	0.00	0.01	0.20	−0.00	0.03	1508765
VEN*	−0.04	0.00	0.00	0.01	0.03	0.00	0.01	3971
VNM*	−0.04	0.00	0.00	0.01	0.03	0.01	0.01	34835
ZAF*	−0.04	0.00	0.01	0.01	0.03	0.00	0.01	80780

	NI/TA Trend							
	Min	25%	Median	75%	Max	Mean	StdDev	# Observations
ARE*	−0.03	−0.00	0.00	0.00	0.03	−0.00	0.01	6180
ARG*	−0.03	−0.00	0.00	0.00	0.03	−0.00	0.01	13017
AUS	−0.37	−0.00	0.00	0.00	0.28	−0.00	0.04	290464
AUT	−0.33	−0.00	0.00	0.00	0.29	−0.00	0.01	22103
BEL	−0.33	−0.00	0.00	0.00	0.29	−0.00	0.01	31396
BGR	−0.33	−0.00	0.00	0.00	0.29	−0.00	0.02	11193
BHR*	−0.03	−0.00	0.00	0.00	0.03	−0.00	0.00	2825
BRA*	−0.03	−0.00	0.00	0.00	0.03	−0.00	0.01	52496
CAN	−0.31	−0.00	0.00	0.00	0.24	0.00	0.03	218860
CHE	−0.33	−0.00	0.00	0.00	0.29	−0.00	0.01	55184
CHL*	−0.03	−0.00	0.00	0.00	0.03	−0.00	0.01	29989
CHN	−0.20	−0.00	−0.00	0.00	0.14	−0.00	0.01	267646
COL*	−0.03	−0.00	0.00	0.00	0.03	−0.00	0.00	6149
CYP	−0.33	−0.00	0.00	0.00	0.29	−0.00	0.02	17142
CZE	−0.27	−0.00	0.00	0.00	0.26	−0.00	0.01	6688
DEU	−0.33	−0.00	0.00	0.00	0.29	−0.00	0.02	182385
DNK	−0.33	−0.00	0.00	0.00	0.29	−0.00	0.02	45393
EGY*	−0.03	−0.00	0.00	0.00	0.03	−0.00	0.01	14769
ESP	−0.33	−0.00	0.00	0.00	0.29	−0.00	0.02	38509
EST	−0.32	−0.00	0.00	0.00	0.11	−0.00	0.02	2489
FIN	−0.20	−0.00	0.00	0.00	0.29	−0.00	0.01	29292
FRA	−0.33	−0.00	0.00	0.00	0.29	−0.00	0.01	164611

*Winsorization levels are at 1 and 99 percentiles instead of 0.1 and 99.9 percentiles.

(Continued)

Table A.8. (*Continued*)

	NI/TA Trend							
	Min	25%	Median	75%	Max	Mean	StdDev	# Observations
GBR	−0.33	−0.00	0.00	0.00	0.29	−0.00	0.03	379983
GRC	−0.33	−0.00	−0.00	0.00	0.29	−0.00	0.01	56167
HKG	−0.37	−0.00	0.00	0.00	0.28	−0.00	0.03	210117
HRV	−0.22	−0.00	0.00	0.00	0.10	−0.00	0.01	12210
HUN	−0.10	−0.00	0.00	0.00	0.11	−0.00	0.01	7500
IDN*	−0.03	−0.00	0.00	0.00	0.03	−0.00	0.01	61292
IND	−0.13	−0.00	0.00	0.00	0.11	−0.00	0.01	608425
IRL	−0.33	−0.00	0.00	0.00	0.29	−0.00	0.02	10395
ISL	−0.12	−0.00	0.00	0.00	0.13	−0.00	0.01	4758
ISR	−0.33	−0.00	0.00	0.00	0.29	−0.00	0.03	72805
ITA	−0.33	−0.00	0.00	0.00	0.29	−0.00	0.01	61297
JOR*	−0.03	−0.00	0.00	0.00	0.03	−0.00	0.01	13325
JPN	−0.37	−0.00	0.00	0.00	0.28	−0.00	0.01	795722
KAZ*	−0.03	−0.00	0.00	0.00	0.03	−0.00	0.01	935
KOR	−0.37	−0.00	0.00	0.00	0.28	−0.00	0.03	285324
KWT*	−0.03	−0.00	0.00	0.00	0.03	−0.00	0.01	22170
LKA*	−0.03	−0.00	0.00	0.00	0.03	0.00	0.01	16489
LTU	−0.12	−0.00	0.00	0.00	0.11	−0.00	0.01	4335
LUX	−0.09	−0.00	0.00	0.00	0.22	0.00	0.01	3341
LVA	−0.19	−0.00	0.00	0.00	0.08	−0.00	0.01	3266
MAR*	−0.03	−0.00	0.00	0.00	0.03	−0.00	0.00	10552
MEX*	−0.03	−0.00	0.00	0.00	0.03	0.00	0.01	20085
MKD	−0.33	−0.00	0.00	0.00	0.29	−0.00	0.02	2421
MLT	−0.04	−0.00	−0.00	0.00	0.03	−0.00	0.00	1334
MYS*	−0.03	−0.00	−0.00	0.00	0.03	−0.00	0.01	186385
NGA*	−0.03	−0.00	0.00	0.00	0.03	−0.00	0.01	14838
NLD	−0.33	−0.00	0.00	0.00	0.29	−0.00	0.02	37588
NOR	−0.33	−0.00	0.00	0.00	0.29	−0.00	0.02	44583
NZL	−0.37	−0.00	0.00	0.00	0.28	−0.00	0.03	17627
PAK*	−0.03	−0.00	0.00	0.00	0.03	0.00	0.01	28534
PER*	−0.03	−0.00	0.00	0.00	0.03	−0.00	0.01	11808
PHL*	−0.03	−0.00	0.00	0.00	0.03	−0.00	0.01	39045
POL	−0.33	−0.00	0.00	0.00	0.29	−0.00	0.02	57462
PRT	−0.33	−0.00	0.00	0.00	0.21	−0.00	0.01	14528
ROM	−0.33	−0.00	0.00	0.00	0.29	−0.00	0.02	17822
RUS	−0.33	−0.00	0.00	0.00	0.29	0.00	0.02	22582
SAU*	−0.03	−0.00	0.00	0.00	0.03	0.00	0.01	14649
SGP	−0.37	−0.00	−0.00	0.00	0.28	−0.00	0.02	115917

*Winsorization levels are at 1 and 99 percentiles instead of 0.1 and 99.9 percentiles.

(*Continued*)

Table A.8. *(Continued)*

	NI/TA Trend							
	Min	25%	Median	75%	Max	Mean	StdDev	# Observations
SVK	−0.05	−0.00	0.00	0.00	0.06	−0.00	0.01	1503
SVN	−0.17	−0.00	0.00	0.00	0.06	−0.00	0.01	7072
SWE	−0.33	−0.00	0.00	0.00	0.29	−0.00	0.03	80221
THA*	−0.03	−0.00	0.00	0.00	0.03	−0.00	0.01	93064
TUR	−0.33	−0.00	−0.00	0.00	0.29	−0.00	0.02	60041
TWN	−0.37	−0.00	−0.00	0.00	0.28	−0.00	0.01	227950
UKR	−0.11	−0.00	0.00	0.00	0.13	−0.00	0.01	5789
USA	−0.31	−0.00	0.00	0.00	0.24	−0.00	0.02	1508765
VEN*	−0.03	−0.00	0.00	0.00	0.03	−0.00	0.00	3971
VNM*	−0.03	−0.00	−0.00	0.00	0.03	−0.00	0.01	34835
ZAF*	−0.03	−0.00	0.00	0.00	0.03	−0.00	0.01	80780

	SIZE Level							
	Min	25%	Median	75%	Max	Mean	StdDev	# Observations
ARE	−4.78	−0.86	0.09	1.15	4.25	0.15	1.50	7005
ARG	−6.58	−1.42	0.26	1.58	7.06	0.14	2.07	14330
AUS	−6.46	−1.22	−0.11	1.54	6.96	0.31	2.05	312426
AUT	−6.75	−1.37	−0.12	1.32	4.50	−0.07	2.00	23602
BEL	−6.75	−1.39	0.10	1.52	6.91	0.12	2.26	37742
BGR	−6.75	−1.70	−0.33	0.91	8.06	−0.37	1.84	16735
BHR	−3.60	−1.16	−0.29	0.98	3.26	−0.12	1.50	3451
BRA	−6.58	−1.74	−0.08	1.31	7.45	−0.15	2.58	59280
CAN	−5.98	−1.50	−0.22	1.26	6.00	−0.08	2.08	239767
CHE	−6.75	−1.26	−0.02	1.30	6.31	0.10	1.95	54559
CHL	−6.58	−1.09	0.10	1.28	4.30	0.01	1.83	33043
CHN	−2.48	−0.74	−0.25	0.30	3.79	−0.15	0.88	289226
COL	−5.42	−1.45	−0.09	1.09	4.43	−0.25	1.68	7196
CYP	−4.64	−1.04	0.00	1.02	6.87	0.01	1.63	20496
CZE	−6.75	−1.51	−0.16	0.89	5.36	−0.23	1.91	8939
DEU	−6.75	−0.37	1.13	2.78	8.06	1.19	2.50	210512
DNK	−6.75	−0.27	0.91	2.23	7.41	1.04	1.89	46094
EGY	−6.58	−1.01	0.05	1.52	5.40	0.24	1.75	17615
ESP	−6.75	−1.66	−0.27	1.15	5.31	−0.31	2.11	40961
EST	−3.55	−0.45	0.40	1.59	5.24	0.54	1.73	2663
FIN	−6.36	−1.78	−0.49	1.08	6.40	−0.33	1.97	29719
FRA	−6.75	−1.32	0.12	1.87	7.66	0.36	2.31	190957
GBR	−6.75	−1.14	0.24	1.86	8.06	0.46	2.23	412607
GRC	−6.08	−0.44	0.50	1.59	6.55	0.65	1.60	59060

*Winsorization levels are at 1 and 99 percentiles instead of 0.1 and 99.9 percentiles.

(Continued)

Table A.8. (*Continued*)

	SIZE Level							
	Min	25%	Median	75%	Max	Mean	StdDev	# Observations
HKG	−8.79	−1.51	−0.50	0.86	6.96	−0.21	1.85	224713
HRV	−6.75	−0.70	0.42	1.63	6.10	0.48	1.79	15242
HUN	−6.75	−0.87	0.88	2.43	6.49	0.83	2.26	8352
IDN	−6.58	−1.04	0.13	1.40	6.08	0.24	1.83	68953
IND	−5.23	−1.20	0.23	2.04	8.38	0.55	2.32	531335
IRL	−6.75	−2.05	−0.83	0.62	4.79	−0.72	1.95	10816
ISL	−6.75	−2.00	−1.07	−0.12	2.76	−1.08	1.53	5886
ISR	−6.75	−0.76	0.30	1.60	8.06	0.51	1.84	95397
ITA	−6.75	−0.90	0.22	1.64	6.36	0.41	1.92	61869
JOR	−3.72	−0.80	0.01	1.18	6.76	0.27	1.57	16405
JPN	−9.57	−0.79	0.25	1.54	6.96	0.48	1.73	817152
KAZ	−6.07	−2.18	−0.62	1.17	5.50	−0.56	1.92	1465
KOR	−11.49	−0.50	0.29	1.34	6.96	0.48	1.82	333045
KWT	−2.55	−0.30	0.61	1.44	5.14	0.68	1.34	24561
LKA	−6.58	−0.79	0.15	1.30	5.26	0.28	1.53	18554
LTU	−4.47	−0.87	0.19	1.18	4.08	0.17	1.53	5661
LUX	−6.75	−2.49	−0.95	0.19	4.33	−1.09	2.07	4479
LVA	−5.38	−1.46	−0.22	2.18	5.91	0.24	2.40	4654
MAR	−6.58	−1.28	−0.15	1.66	4.76	0.10	1.81	11086
MEX	−6.58	−1.19	0.19	1.55	5.16	0.11	1.97	21875
MKD	−6.46	−1.30	0.19	1.34	5.35	0.09	1.87	4151
MLT	−4.07	−1.00	−0.20	0.98	2.31	−0.07	1.32	1873
MYS	−4.25	−0.18	0.69	1.80	6.47	0.85	1.56	198058
NGA	−6.58	−1.39	−0.17	1.65	6.16	0.01	2.16	17787
NLD	−6.75	−1.89	−0.37	1.09	5.99	−0.28	2.17	38059
NOR	−6.75	−0.92	0.15	1.39	6.65	0.26	1.73	47416
NZL	−5.78	−1.54	−0.08	1.05	5.12	−0.22	1.88	19565
PAK	−6.58	−1.08	0.86	2.82	7.45	0.83	2.55	46403
PER	−6.58	−1.02	0.34	1.82	5.54	0.35	2.02	14133
PHL	−6.58	−1.43	−0.31	1.04	5.06	−0.11	1.80	42721
POL	−5.28	−1.01	0.20	1.59	8.06	0.35	2.00	67405
PRT	−6.75	−1.95	−0.32	1.28	4.56	−0.43	2.47	16343
ROM	−6.75	−0.99	0.26	1.59	8.06	0.26	2.11	45558
RUS	−6.75	−1.72	−0.25	1.28	8.06	−0.06	2.45	29503
SAU	−4.48	−0.76	0.15	1.46	5.34	0.41	1.59	16068
SGP	−4.35	−0.61	0.36	1.60	6.96	0.59	1.70	124879
SVK	−6.14	−0.30	1.17	3.08	8.00	1.56	2.57	3941

(*Continued*)

Table A.8. *(Continued)*

	SIZE Level							
	Min	25%	Median	75%	Max	Mean	StdDev	# Observations
SVN	−6.75	−0.50	0.86	2.37	8.06	1.16	2.44	10856
SWE	−6.75	−0.67	1.02	2.62	8.06	1.09	2.38	85358
THA	−5.98	−0.88	0.09	1.23	6.49	0.29	1.61	102574
TUR	−5.21	−1.22	−0.03	1.24	5.62	0.09	1.84	64054
TWN	−5.78	−0.70	0.26	1.28	6.89	0.37	1.51	250096
UKR	−6.75	−0.99	0.10	1.06	8.06	−0.01	1.63	8699
USA	−5.98	−2.00	−0.67	0.77	6.00	−0.54	2.00	1569893
VEN	−6.58	−1.52	−0.08	1.18	7.45	−0.33	2.55	5337
VNM	−4.93	−1.16	−0.22	0.81	6.29	−0.06	1.61	40028
ZAF	−6.58	−1.57	0.17	1.87	6.55	0.16	2.34	86314

	SIZE Trend							
	Min	25%	Median	75%	Max	Mean	StdDev	# Observations
ARE	−1.83	−0.13	−0.01	0.09	2.06	−0.00	0.24	7005
ARG	−1.87	−0.15	−0.02	0.11	2.06	−0.02	0.33	14330
AUS	−1.58	−0.18	−0.00	0.17	1.82	0.00	0.38	312426
AUT	−2.03	−0.12	−0.01	0.09	2.12	−0.02	0.27	23602
BEL	−2.03	−0.11	−0.02	0.07	2.12	−0.02	0.26	37742
BGR	−2.03	−0.15	0.00	0.16	2.12	0.02	0.37	16735
BHR	−0.80	−0.06	0.01	0.09	2.03	0.03	0.17	3451
BRA	−1.87	−0.15	0.00	0.15	2.06	−0.00	0.36	59280
CAN	−1.90	−0.16	0.00	0.16	1.83	−0.00	0.37	239767
CHE	−2.03	−0.11	−0.01	0.08	2.12	−0.02	0.24	54559
CHL	−1.87	−0.10	−0.00	0.09	2.06	−0.00	0.22	33043
CHN	−0.97	−0.10	−0.01	0.10	1.12	0.01	0.19	289226
COL	−1.34	−0.09	0.00	0.10	1.93	0.01	0.22	7196
CYP	−2.03	−0.18	−0.00	0.16	2.12	−0.00	0.35	20496
CZE	−2.03	−0.13	0.00	0.12	2.12	−0.01	0.26	8939
DEU	−2.03	−0.17	−0.03	0.09	2.12	−0.06	0.35	210512
DNK	−2.03	−0.15	−0.02	0.09	2.12	−0.03	0.27	46094
EGY	−1.87	−0.13	−0.01	0.11	2.06	0.02	0.28	17615
ESP	−2.03	−0.11	−0.00	0.10	2.12	0.00	0.26	40961
EST	−2.03	−0.13	−0.01	0.13	2.12	−0.00	0.32	2663
FIN	−2.03	−0.12	0.00	0.14	2.12	0.00	0.27	29719
FRA	−2.03	−0.12	0.00	0.12	2.12	0.00	0.28	190957
GBR	−2.03	−0.15	−0.00	0.13	2.12	−0.02	0.34	412607
GRC	−2.03	−0.19	−0.03	0.13	2.12	−0.02	0.32	59060
HKG	−1.58	−0.18	−0.02	0.14	1.82	−0.00	0.35	224713

(Continued)

Table A.8. *(Continued)*

	SIZE Trend							
	Min	25%	Median	75%	Max	Mean	StdDev	# Observations
HRV	−2.03	−0.14	−0.02	0.08	2.12	−0.02	0.24	15242
HUN	−1.80	−0.20	−0.05	0.08	2.12	−0.06	0.30	8352
IDN	−1.87	−0.18	−0.03	0.13	2.06	−0.01	0.35	68953
IND	−1.71	−0.22	−0.04	0.13	2.06	−0.03	0.36	531335
IRL	−2.03	−0.10	0.02	0.13	2.12	0.01	0.29	10816
ISL	−2.03	−0.11	0.00	0.12	2.12	0.01	0.30	5886
ISR	−2.03	−0.15	−0.02	0.10	2.12	−0.03	0.31	95397
ITA	−2.03	−0.12	−0.01	0.09	2.12	−0.00	0.24	61869
JOR	−1.87	−0.15	0.11	0.35	2.06	0.09	0.44	16405
JPN	−1.58	−0.12	−0.01	0.09	1.82	−0.01	0.22	817152
KAZ	−1.87	−0.11	0.00	0.13	2.06	0.03	0.41	1465
KOR	−1.58	−0.18	−0.03	0.13	1.82	−0.02	0.34	333045
KWT	−1.87	−0.12	−0.02	0.10	2.06	−0.01	0.24	24561
LKA	−1.73	−0.13	−0.01	0.10	2.06	0.00	0.24	18554
LTU	−2.03	−0.14	−0.01	0.12	2.12	−0.01	0.32	5661
LUX	−2.03	−0.08	0.00	0.11	2.12	0.03	0.28	4479
LVA	−2.03	−0.12	0.01	0.17	2.12	0.04	0.32	4654
MAR	−1.87	−0.09	−0.00	0.08	2.06	−0.00	0.20	11086
MEX	−1.87	−0.13	−0.01	0.09	2.06	−0.02	0.25	21875
MKD	−1.45	−0.10	0.00	0.07	1.26	−0.01	0.19	4151
MLT	−1.23	−0.07	0.00	0.08	2.05	0.02	0.24	1873
MYS	−1.87	−0.14	−0.03	0.09	2.05	−0.02	0.26	198058
NGA	−1.87	−0.16	−0.01	0.14	2.05	0.01	0.35	17787
NLD	−2.03	−0.11	0.00	0.11	2.12	−0.01	0.26	38059
NOR	−2.03	−0.13	−0.00	0.13	2.12	0.00	0.33	47416
NZL	−1.58	−0.09	0.01	0.11	1.82	0.02	0.25	19565
PAK	−1.87	−0.19	−0.04	0.09	2.06	−0.03	0.29	46403
PER	−1.87	−0.14	0.00	0.12	2.06	0.00	0.28	14133
PHL	−1.87	−0.15	−0.01	0.13	2.06	0.01	0.32	42721
POL	−2.03	−0.21	−0.04	0.12	2.12	−0.05	0.36	67405
PRT	−2.03	−0.14	−0.02	0.08	2.12	−0.02	0.25	16343
ROM	−2.03	−0.13	0.00	0.21	2.12	0.06	0.39	45558
RUS	−2.03	−0.13	0.00	0.12	2.12	−0.01	0.30	29503
SAU	−1.87	−0.11	−0.00	0.11	2.06	0.01	0.23	16068
SGP	−1.58	−0.14	−0.02	0.10	1.82	−0.02	0.26	124879
SVK	−2.03	−0.05	0.02	0.13	2.12	0.05	0.31	3941
SVN	−2.03	−0.16	−0.03	0.07	1.98	−0.06	0.30	10856

(Continued)

Table A.8. *(Continued)*

	SIZE Trend							
	Min	**25%**	**Median**	**75%**	**Max**	**Mean**	**StdDev**	**# Observations**
SWE	−2.03	−0.15	−0.01	0.14	2.12	−0.01	0.34	85358
THA	−1.87	−0.15	−0.02	0.12	2.06	−0.00	0.28	102574
TUR	−2.03	−0.17	−0.03	0.12	2.12	−0.01	0.30	64054
TWN	−1.58	−0.14	−0.02	0.11	1.82	−0.01	0.24	250096
UKR	−2.03	−0.16	0.00	0.18	2.12	0.01	0.42	8699
USA	−1.90	−0.15	−0.01	0.13	1.83	−0.02	0.33	1569893
VEN	−1.87	−0.17	−0.02	0.11	2.06	0.00	0.41	5337
VNM	−1.87	−0.20	−0.05	0.08	2.06	−0.06	0.26	40028
ZAF	−1.87	−0.16	−0.01	0.13	2.06	−0.03	0.36	86314

	M/B							
	Min	**25%**	**Median**	**75%**	**Max**	**Mean**	**StdDev**	**# Observations**
ARE	0.36	0.86	1.02	1.30	8.35	1.18	0.62	6100
ARG	0.18	0.82	1.00	1.26	520.99	1.74	8.92	12709
AUS*	0.19	0.93	1.33	2.37	14.61	2.26	2.62	286945
AUT	0.20	0.94	1.06	1.37	83.80	1.35	1.93	20902
BEL	0.14	0.93	1.09	1.45	119.97	1.53	3.60	29960
BGR	0.14	0.66	0.92	1.29	50.58	1.24	1.86	10258
BHR	0.40	0.93	1.06	1.26	5.54	1.18	0.48	2754
BRA	0.18	0.83	1.07	1.60	553.67	12.50	67.96	51292
CAN	0.22	0.98	1.31	2.09	58.66	2.22	3.99	215521
CHE	0.16	0.99	1.14	1.61	119.97	1.58	1.87	51024
CHL	0.18	0.86	1.14	1.68	553.67	2.99	22.06	29461
CHN	0.66	1.47	2.08	3.13	41.43	2.69	2.42	266200
COL	0.23	0.79	1.03	1.27	553.67	1.53	13.45	5967
CYP	0.14	0.61	0.80	1.04	46.50	1.10	1.98	16601
CZE	0.15	0.66	0.92	1.16	9.28	1.02	0.59	6492
DEU	0.14	1.00	1.21	1.66	119.97	1.81	4.06	177136
DNK	0.14	0.96	1.06	1.41	119.97	1.57	2.65	42732
EGY	0.21	0.98	1.24	1.83	92.90	1.71	2.46	14608
ESP	0.14	0.95	1.10	1.46	119.97	1.45	2.58	36987
EST	0.17	0.94	1.17	1.81	43.24	1.80	2.54	2463
FIN	0.20	1.01	1.23	1.73	119.97	1.65	2.24	28147
FRA	0.14	0.94	1.13	1.56	119.97	1.68	4.15	159530
GBR	0.14	0.97	1.33	2.07	119.97	2.25	5.15	375674
GRC	0.14	0.87	1.10	1.62	119.97	1.82	4.61	55498
HKG*	0.19	0.72	0.99	1.55	14.61	1.53	1.89	209618

*Winsorization levels are at 0.1 and 99.5 percentiles instead of 0.1 and 99.9 percentiles.

(Continued)

Table A.8. *(Continued)*

	M/B							
	Min	25%	Median	75%	Max	Mean	StdDev	# Observations
HRV	0.14	0.71	0.93	1.19	24.60	1.10	1.21	11831
HUN	0.14	0.74	1.00	1.36	119.97	1.25	2.57	7323
IDN	0.18	0.87	1.07	1.49	553.67	1.51	6.89	60466
IND**	0.19	0.77	0.99	1.49	11.46	1.47	1.60	455646
IRL	0.14	0.99	1.22	1.71	45.56	1.71	2.07	10069
ISL	0.31	1.09	1.27	1.63	119.97	2.10	6.86	4718
ISR	0.14	0.91	1.04	1.36	119.97	1.92	7.01	72419
ITA	0.19	0.95	1.06	1.35	119.97	1.38	3.40	59035
JOR	0.18	0.79	1.02	1.31	70.95	1.25	1.97	13254
JPN*	0.19	0.85	1.00	1.24	14.61	1.21	1.00	795167
KAZ	0.23	0.90	1.01	1.23	9.35	1.17	0.63	882
KOR*	0.19	0.80	0.99	1.32	14.61	1.33	1.36	282862
KWT	0.18	0.90	1.17	1.58	38.02	1.38	0.95	22003
LKA	0.24	0.95	1.15	1.62	553.67	1.70	6.59	16193
LTU	0.31	0.81	1.00	1.37	5.32	1.18	0.61	4326
LUX	0.14	0.74	0.97	1.18	9.28	1.08	0.67	3090
LVA	0.14	0.55	0.75	1.01	5.86	0.85	0.53	3140
MAR	0.18	1.07	1.28	1.84	15.95	1.65	1.00	10386
MEX	0.18	0.78	1.03	1.43	10.84	1.21	0.71	19295
MKD	0.15	0.68	0.92	1.20	119.97	3.29	15.24	2317
MLT	0.25	0.98	1.08	1.41	15.76	1.34	0.94	1330
MYS	0.18	0.77	0.99	1.41	553.67	1.44	5.88	185867
NGA	0.18	0.91	1.21	1.85	179.42	1.86	5.00	14547
NLD	0.14	1.00	1.22	1.68	119.97	1.68	2.55	36129
NOR	1.14	0.95	1.14	1.71	119.97	1.87	3.66	42915
NZL*	0.19	0.97	1.27	1.96	14.61	1.90	2.10	17458
PAK	0.18	0.84	1.00	1.32	50.46	1.32	1.71	28051
PER	0.18	0.80	1.12	1.67	29.63	1.51	1.37	11472
PHL	0.18	0.76	1.05	1.69	553.67	6.15	43.72	38165
POL	0.14	0.86	1.11	1.64	119.97	1.79	5.05	56985
PRT	0.14	0.90	1.02	1.25	27.99	1.16	0.72	14088
ROM	0.14	0.67	0.91	1.25	119.97	1.85	9.20	15944
RUS	0.14	0.84	1.11	1.64	119.97	4.56	19.01	20892
SAU	0.19	1.18	1.71	2.84	49.17	2.45	2.32	14590
SGP*	0.19	0.82	1.04	1.45	14.61	1.37	1.29	115458
SVK	0.26	0.73	0.90	1.05	3.18	0.92	0.33	1382
SVN	0.14	0.67	0.85	1.03	4.99	0.92	0.47	6981

*Winsorization levels are at 0.1 and 99.5 percentiles instead of 0.1 and 99.9 percentiles.
**Winsorization levels are at 1 and 99 percentiles instead of 0.1 and 99.9 percentiles.

(Continued)

Table A.8. *(Continued)*

	M/B							
	Min	25%	Median	75%	Max	Mean	StdDev	# Observations
SWE	0.14	1.03	1.37	2.16	119.97	2.19	4.14	77958
THA	0.18	0.85	1.06	1.45	109.43	1.31	1.10	92653
TUR	0.14	076	0.99	1.32	119.97	1.30	3.23	59875
TWN*	0.29	0.93	1.16	1.65	14.61	1.48	1.06	227830
UKR	0.14	0.88	1.22	1.94	66.21	1.83	2.68	5506
USA	0.22	1.02	1.30	2.09	58.66	2.10	3.14	1506686
VEN	0.18	0.58	0.87	1.06	553.67	25.05	85.55	3817
VNM	0.18	0.82	0.95	1.19	18.99	1.15	0.79	34541
ZAF	0.18	0.89	1.19	1.84	553.67	2.41	14.85	79989

	SIGMA							
	Min	25%	Median	75%	Max	Mean	StdDev	# Observations
ARE	0.01	0.09	0.11	0.16	0.43	0.13	0.06	6132
ARG	0.03	0.09	0.11	0.14	0.64	0.12	0.06	13011
AUS	0.02	0.13	0.22	0.32	0.93	0.24	0.15	295702
AUT	0.01	0.06	0.09	0.13	1.14	0.12	0.10	21775
BEL	0.02	0.07	0.09	0.12	1.41	0.11	0.08	33381
BGR	0.02	0.14	0.18	0.28	1.09	0.22	0.13	11218
BHR	0.03	0.07	0.09	0.12	0.24	0.10	0.03	2761
BRA	0.01	0.10	0.14	0.20	1.19	0.18	0.13	52177
CAN	0.03	0.11	0.17	0.27	1.01	0.21	0.15	227954
CHE	0.01	0.07	0.09	0.13	1.41	0.11	0.07	51919
CHL	0.01	0.06	0.08	0.10	0.71	0.09	0.06	29731
CHN	0.03	0.08	0.10	0.13	0.43	0.11	0.05	281900
COL	0.01	0.06	0.09	0.12	0.47	0.10	0.06	6078
CYP	0.02	0.15	0.21	0.28	1.41	0.25	0.17	17602
CZE	0.03	0.09	0.13	0.17	0.42	0.13	0.05	7145
DEU	0.01	0.10	0.14	0.24	1.41	0.21	0.22	194443
DNK	0.01	0.07	0.10	0.15	1.24	0.13	0.10	43321
EGY	0.01	0.09	0.13	0.19	1.19	0.15	0.09	15577
ESP	0.01	0.06	0.09	0.12	0.93	0.10	0.06	37885
EST	0.01	0.08	0.13	0.20	0.65	0.16	0.10	2522
FIN	0.03	0.08	0.11	0.15	1.41	0.13	0.09	28691
FRA	0.01	0.08	0.11	0.16	1.41	0.13	0.09	172286
GBR	0.01	0.08	0.12	0.18	1.28	0.15	0.10	385233
GRC	0.01	0.10	0.14	0.18	0.90	0.15	0.08	57250
HKG	0.02	0.11	0.16	0.24	0.93	0.19	0.11	217971

*Winsorization levels are at 0.1 and 99.5 percentiles instead of 0.1 and 99.9 percentiles.

(Continued)

Table A.8. *(Continued)*

	SIGMA							
	Min	25%	Median	75%	Max	Mean	StdDev	# Observations
HRV	0.01	0.11	0.14	0.18	0.75	0.16	0.08	12104
HUN	0.02	0.09	0.13	0.18	0.66	0.15	0.09	7647
IDN	0.01	0.13	0.18	0.27	1.19	0.22	0.13	62258
IND	0.05	0.15	0.19	0.24	0.99	0.22	0.13	480192
IRL	0.03	0.08	0.11	0.17	1.41	0.15	0.14	10151
ISL	0.03	0.08	0.11	0.14	0.60	0.12	0.07	4985
ISR	0.01	0.10	0.13	0.20	1.13	0.16	0.09	80390
ITA	0.01	0.07	0.09	0.13	0.75	0.11	0.05	60334
JOR	0.01	0.10	0.12	0.14	0.80	0.13	0.05	14836
JPN	0.02	0.08	0.11	0.16	0.93	0.13	0.07	802610
KAZ	0.01	0.11	0.15	0.23	1.01	0.19	0.13	877
KOR	0.02	0.11	0.15	0.21	0.79	0.17	0.08	324689
KWT	0.01	0.10	0.12	0.16	0.76	0.13	0.05	22313
LKA	0.03	0.11	0.15	0.20	0.98	0.17	0.09	17127
LTU	0.03	0.09	0.13	0.18	1.00	0.15	0.10	5179
LUX	0.02	0.07	0.09	0.12	0.51	0.10	0.05	3189
LVA	0.03	0.11	0.15	0.22	0.95	0.17	0.09	3222
MAR	0.02	0.08	0.09	0.12	0.53	0.10	0.05	10524
MEX	0.01	0.07	0.10	0.13	1.17	0.11	0.07	19681
MKD	0.01	0.08	0.12	0.17	0.53	0.14	0.07	2401
MLT	0.02	0.05	0.07	0.09	0.54	0.08	0.05	1401
MYS	0.02	0.10	0.14	0.21	1.19	0.17	0.11	193736
NGA	0.01	0.11	0.14	0.17	0.54	0.14	0.06	15500
NLD	0.02	0.07	0.09	0.13	1.24	0.11	0.08	37092
NOR	0.03	0.10	0.14	0.20	1.08	0.17	0.10	43879
NZL	0.02	0.07	0.09	0.13	0.93	0.12	0.11	18063
PAK	0.03	0.11	0.15	0.24	1.19	0.22	0.20	37075
PER	0.02	0.09	0.12	0.16	0.61	0.13	0.07	11549
PHL	0.01	0.12	0.17	0.25	0.89	0.20	0.12	39128
POL	0.01	0.12	0.16	0.23	1.41	0.19	0.12	63844
PRT	0.01	0.07	0.10	0.14	1.16	0.12	0.08	14347
ROM	0.01	0.17	0.22	0.33	1.41	0.26	0.15	20711
RUS	0.01	0.10	0.12	0.20	1.22	0.16	0.11	20998
SAU	0.02	0.07	0.10	0.14	0.63	0.11	0.06	15520
SGP	0.02	0.10	0.15	0.23	0.93	0.19	0.14	120940
SVK	0.01	0.08	0.11	0.16	0.58	0.13	0.08	1368
SVN	0.01	0.07	0.10	0.14	1.12	0.13	0.11	8391

(Continued)

Table A.8. *(Continued)*

	SIGMA							
	Min	25%	Median	75%	Max	Mean	StdDev	# Observations
SWE	0.01	0.10	0.14	0.25	1.41	0.20	0.16	81508
THA	0.01	0.09	0.13	0.18	1.19	0.15	0.10	99419
TUR	0.01	0.10	0.14	0.19	1.25	0.15	0.07	62680
TWN	0.02	0.09	0.11	0.14	0.86	0.12	0.05	242951
UKR	0.01	0.15	0.19	0.29	1.03	0.24	0.15	5468
USA	0.03	0.09	0.15	0.23	1.01	0.18	0.12	1532110
VEN	0.01	0.13	0.18	0.23	0.68	0.19	0.10	4065
VNM	0.01	0.11	0.14	0.19	0.67	0.16	0.07	36605
ZAF	0.01	0.09	0.13	0.22	1.19	0.19	0.18	81441

Table A.9. Exits classified as "Defaults".

Default	
Action Type	**Subcategory**
Bankruptcy filling	Administration, Arrangement, Canadian CCAA, Chapter 7, Chapter 11, Chapter 15, Conservatorship, Insolvency, Japanese CRL, Judicial Management, Liquidation, Pre-Negotiation Chapter 11, Protection, Receivership, Rehabilitation, Rehabilitation (Thailand 1997), Reorganization, Restructuring, Section 304, Supreme Court declaration, Winding up, Work out, Other, Unknown
Delisting	Bankruptcy
Default Corporate Action	Bankruptcy, Coupon & Principal Payment, Coupon Payment Only, Debt Restructuring, Interest Payment, Loan Payment, Principal Payment, ADR (Japan only), Declared Sick (India Only), Unknown

Table A.10. Exits classified as "Other Exits".

Other Exits	
Action Type	**Subcategory**
Delisting	Unknown, Acquired/Merged, Assimilated with underlying shares, Bid price below minimum, Cancellation of listing, End of When-issued trading, Expired, Failure to meet listing requirements, Failure to pay listing fees, Inactive security, Insufficient assets, Insufficient capital and surplus, Insufficient number of market makers, Issue postponed, Lack of market maker interest, Lack of public interest, Liquidated, Matured, Not available, Not current in required filings, NP/FP finished, Privatized, Reorganization security called for redemptions, the company's request, Scheme of arrangement, Insufficient spread of holders, Selective capital reduction of the company

Table A.11. Number of defaults and other exits of 71 economies from 1992 to 2012.

Economy:ARE

		Defaults		Others	
Year	Active	#	%	#	%
1992	0	0	NaN	0	NaN
1993	0	0	NaN	0	NaN
1994	0	0	NaN	0	NaN
1995	0	0	NaN	0	NaN
1996	0	0	NaN	0	NaN
1997	0	0	NaN	0	NaN
1998	0	0	NaN	0	NaN
1999	0	0	NaN	0	NaN
2000	0	0	NaN	0	NaN
2001	0	0	NaN	0	NaN
2002	0	0	NaN	0	NaN
2003	0	0	NaN	0	NaN
2004	0	0	NaN	0	NaN
2005	0	0	NaN	0	NaN
2006	70	0	0.00	10	12.50
2007	85	0	0.00	10	10.53
2008	78	0	0.00	20	20.41
2009	81	0	0.00	19	19.00
2010	80	0	0.00	27	25.23
2011	83	0	0.00	21	20.19
2012	82	1	0.96	21	20.19

Economy:ARG

		Defaults		Others	
Year	Active	#	%	#	%
1992	1	0	0.00	0	0.00
1993	1	0	0.00	0	0.00
1994	23	0	0.00	2	8.00
1995	87	0	0.00	18	17.14
1996	95	0	0.00	22	18.80
1997	78	0	0.00	31	28.44
1998	66	2	1.87	39	36.45
1999	71	1	1.06	22	23.40
2000	68	1	1.10	22	24.18
2001	51	2	2.30	34	39.08
2002	65	9	10.23	14	15.91
2003	69	2	2.41	12	14.46
2004	64	0	0.00	13	16.88
2005	69	0	0.00	4	5.48
2006	71	0	0.00	8	10.13
2007	75	0	0.00	10	11.76
2008	65	0	0.00	17	20.73
2009	65	1	1.35	8	10.81
2010	69	1	1.35	4	5.41
2011	65	0	0.00	9	12.16
2012	66	0	0.00	7	9.59

Economy:AUS

		Defaults		Others	
Year	Active	#	%	#	%
1992	696	0	0.00	117	14.39
1993	828	0	0.00	48	5.48
1994	915	0	0.00	93	9.23
1995	953	1	0.10	82	7.92
1996	1002	1	0.09	65	6.09
1997	1012	3	0.27	102	9.13
1998	1009	1	0.09	109	9.74
1999	1073	2	0.17	99	8.43
2000	1187	11	0.84	105	8.06
2001	1164	27	2.08	109	8.38
2002	1180	9	0.70	101	7.83
2003	1226	8	0.60	94	7.08
2004	1348	3	0.21	76	5.33
2005	1461	6	0.39	87	5.60
2006	1578	5	0.29	117	6.88
2007	1752	5	0.27	114	6.09
2008	1685	27	1.45	149	8.01
2009	1670	30	1.65	115	6.34
2010	1690	4	0.22	137	7.48
2011	1682	0	0.00	178	9.57
2012	1663	3	0.16	164	8.96

Economy:AUT

		Defaults		Others	
Year	Active	#	%	#	%
1992	87	0	0.00	3	3.33
1993	101	0	0.00	9	8.18
1994	111	0	0.00	1	0.89
1995	118	0	0.00	2	1.67
1996	117	1	0.81	5	4.07
1997	118	0	0.00	6	4.84
1998	112	0	0.00	15	11.81
1999	108	0	0.00	17	13.60
2000	119	0	0.00	15	11.19
2001	113	2	1.39	29	20.14
2002	109	0	0.00	14	11.38
2003	108	0	0.00	21	16.28
2004	100	0	0.00	23	18.70
2005	99	0	0.00	18	15.38
2006	104	0	0.00	10	8.77
2007	106	0	0.00	11	9.40
2008	105	2	1.71	10	8.55
2009	100	1	0.88	13	11.40
2010	94	1	0.87	20	17.39
2011	84	0	0.00	16	16.00
2012	81	1	1.08	11	11.83

(*Continued*)

Table A.11. (*Continued*)

Economy:BEL

Year	Active	Defaults #	Defaults %	Others #	Others %
1992	134	0	0.00	8	5.63
1993	139	0	0.00	6	4.14
1994	146	0	0.00	12	7.59
1995	151	0	0.00	10	6.21
1996	164	0	0.00	11	6.29
1997	163	0	0.00	18	9.94
1998	175	0	0.00	17	8.85
1999	191	2	1.01	6	3.02
2000	192	0	0.00	10	4.95
2001	186	2	1.00	12	6.00
2002	176	3	1.55	15	7.73
2003	177	1	0.52	14	7.29
2004	170	1	0.54	13	7.07
2005	172	2	1.08	12	6.45
2006	183	2	1.03	9	4.64
2007	217	1	0.36	61	21.86
2008	201	1	0.36	79	28.11
2009	201	2	0.78	52	20.39
2010	203	0	0.00	54	21.01
2011	175	1	0.42	63	26.36
2012	185	1	0.44	39	17.33

Economy:BGR

Year	Active	Defaults #	Defaults %	Others #	Others %
1992	0	0	NaN	0	NaN
1993	0	0	NaN	0	NaN
1994	0	0	NaN	0	NaN
1995	0	0	NaN	0	NaN
1996	0	0	NaN	0	NaN
1997	0	0	NaN	0	NaN
1998	0	0	NaN	0	NaN
1999	0	0	NaN	0	NaN
2000	14	0	0.00	10	41.67
2001	23	0	0.00	8	25.81
2002	28	0	0.00	7	20.00
2003	31	0	0.00	9	22.50
2004	36	0	0.00	3	7.69
2005	127	1	0.65	25	16.34
2006	236	0	0.00	36	13.24
2007	241	2	0.64	71	22.61
2008	211	0	0.00	101	32.37
2009	198	0	0.00	88	30.77
2010	175	1	0.37	91	34.08
2011	168	0	0.00	78	31.71
2012	158	0	0.00	69	30.40

Economy:BHR

Year	Active	Defaults #	Defaults %	Others #	Others %
1992	0	0	NaN	0	NaN
1993	0	0	NaN	0	NaN
1994	0	0	NaN	0	NaN
1995	0	0	NaN	0	NaN
1996	0	0	NaN	0	NaN
1997	0	0	NaN	0	NaN
1998	0	0	NaN	0	NaN
1999	0	0	NaN	0	NaN
2000	0	0	NaN	0	NaN
2001	0	0	NaN	0	NaN
2002	0	0	NaN	0	NaN
2003	0	0	NaN	0	NaN
2004	28	0	0.00	2	6.67
2005	37	0	0.00	1	2.63
2006	30	0	0.00	10	25.00
2007	36	0	0.00	5	12.20
2008	31	0	0.00	10	24.39
2009	32	0	0.00	13	28.89
2010	31	0	0.00	14	31.11
2011	27	0	0.00	19	41.30
2012	29	0	0.00	19	39.58

Economy:BRA

Year	Active	Defaults #	Defaults %	Others #	Others %
1992	0	0	NaN	0	NaN
1993	0	0	NaN	0	NaN
1994	261	0	0.00	26	9.06
1995	273	0	0.00	92	25.21
1996	282	0	0.00	99	25.98
1997	259	0	0.00	133	33.93
1998	284	2	0.45	158	35.59
1999	323	2	0.47	104	24.24
2000	294	1	0.24	122	29.26
2001	274	1	0.24	145	34.52
2002	241	2	0.54	126	34.15
2003	264	2	0.56	90	25.28
2004	271	0	0.00	83	23.45
2005	266	1	0.30	71	21.01
2006	282	0	0.00	55	16.32
2007	350	0	0.00	40	10.26
2008	331	0	0.00	56	14.47
2009	334	0	0.00	35	9.49
2010	326	0	0.00	42	11.41
2011	317	1	0.28	40	11.17
2012	297	4	1.17	41	11.99

(*Continued*)

Table A.11. (*Continued*)

Economy:CAN

Year	Active	Defaults		Others	
		#	%	#	%
1992	946	1	0.10	103	9.81
1993	1156	0	0.00	72	5.86
1994	1328	0	0.00	54	3.91
1995	1449	0	0.00	83	5.42
1996	1635	0	0.00	80	4.66
1997	1781	5	0.26	144	7.46
1998	1752	8	0.40	254	12.61
1999	1194	10	0.52	716	37.29
2000	1105	8	0.61	196	14.97
2001	949	20	1.68	223	18.71
2002	936	5	0.49	74	7.29
2003	934	14	1.36	81	7.87
2004	993	5	0.47	74	6.90
2005	1044	3	0.26	86	7.59
2006	1096	3	0.25	100	8.34
2007	1131	3	0.24	125	9.93
2008	1110	13	1.05	115	9.29
2009	1039	14	1.17	143	11.96
2010	1073	5	0.43	97	8.26
2011	1079	6	0.50	122	10.11
2012	1053	9	0.76	127	10.68

Economy:CHE

Year	Active	Defaults		Others	
		#	%	#	%
1992	143	0	0.00	31	17.82
1993	174	0	0.00	10	5.43
1994	177	0	0.00	20	10.15
1995	189	0	0.00	15	7.35
1996	210	0	0.00	15	6.67
1997	221	1	0.43	11	4.72
1998	227	0	0.00	14	5.81
1999	243	0	0.00	15	5.81
2000	262	0	0.00	12	4.38
2001	258	2	0.72	16	5.80
2002	250	0	0.00	17	6.37
2003	244	2	0.77	13	5.02
2004	238	1	0.40	12	4.78
2005	247	1	0.39	7	2.75
2006	251	0	0.00	17	6.34
2007	255	0	0.00	9	3.41
2008	253	0	0.00	16	5.95
2009	256	0	0.00	16	5.88
2010	251	0	0.00	18	6.69
2011	247	1	0.38	18	6.77
2012	376	1	0.22	87	18.75

Economy:CHL

Year	Active	Defaults		Others	
		#	%	#	%
1992	0	0	NaN	0	NaN
1993	0	0	NaN	0	NaN
1994	141	0	0.00	9	6.00
1995	166	0	0.00	26	13.54
1996	168	0	0.00	46	21.50
1997	181	0	0.00	35	16.20
1998	168	0	0.00	56	25.00
1999	177	0	0.00	41	18.81
2000	168	0	0.00	43	20.38
2001	168	1	0.47	43	20.28
2002	155	1	0.48	54	25.71
2003	152	0	0.00	57	27.27
2004	164	0	0.00	32	16.33
2005	166	0	0.00	39	19.02
2006	171	0	0.00	41	19.34
2007	187	0	0.00	27	12.62
2008	146	0	0.00	52	26.26
2009	167	0	0.00	28	14.36
2010	161	0	0.00	41	20.30
2011	170	0	0.00	36	17.48
2012	167	0	0.00	53	24.09

Economy:CHN

Year	Active	Defaults		Others	
		#	%	#	%
1992	45	0	0.00	2	4.26
1993	165	0	0.00	0	0.00
1994	283	1	0.35	1	0.35
1995	317	6	1.85	1	0.31
1996	522	10	1.88	0	0.00
1997	727	15	2.02	2	0.27
1998	841	34	3.88	2	0.23
1999	935	23	2.40	1	0.10
2000	1079	26	2.35	1	0.09
2001	1151	51	4.21	8	0.66
2002	1203	49	3.85	21	1.65
2003	1266	46	3.45	23	1.72
2004	1353	110	7.39	26	1.75
2005	1351	100	6.79	21	1.43
2006	1372	73	4.82	70	4.62
2007	1457	65	4.02	93	5.76
2008	1581	45	2.68	55	3.27
2009	1681	54	3.06	31	1.76
2010	1992	42	2.02	46	2.21
2011	2272	14	0.60	61	2.60
2012	2425	18	0.72	57	2.28

(*Continued*)

Table A.11. (*Continued*)

Economy:COL

Year	Active	Defaults #	Defaults %	Others #	Others %
1992	0	0	NaN	0	NaN
1993	0	0	NaN	0	NaN
1994	1	0	0.00	0	0.00
1995	49	0	0.00	29	37.18
1996	43	0	0.00	46	51.69
1997	45	0	0.00	43	48.86
1998	58	0	0.00	64	52.46
1999	47	0	0.00	55	53.92
2000	39	0	0.00	40	50.63
2001	49	0	0.00	19	27.94
2002	50	0	0.00	21	29.58
2003	53	0	0.00	15	22.06
2004	53	0	0.00	12	18.46
2005	55	0	0.00	17	23.61
2006	47	0	0.00	18	27.69
2007	50	0	0.00	16	24.24
2008	35	0	0.00	24	40.68
2009	42	0	0.00	10	19.23
2010	44	0	0.00	14	24.14
2011	40	0	0.00	11	21.57
2012	40	1	1.96	10	19.61

Economy:CYP

Year	Active	Defaults #	Defaults %	Others #	Others %
1992	0	0	NaN	0	NaN
1993	0	0	NaN	0	NaN
1994	0	0	NaN	0	NaN
1995	0	0	NaN	0	NaN
1996	35	0	0.00	3	7.89
1997	43	0	0.00	0	0.00
1998	48	0	0.00	2	4.00
1999	58	0	0.00	2	3.33
2000	116	0	0.00	4	3.33
2001	137	0	0.00	6	4.20
2002	144	0	0.00	10	6.49
2003	134	0	0.00	21	13.55
2004	134	0	0.00	29	17.79
2005	139	0	0.00	22	13.66
2006	137	0	0.00	11	7.43
2007	137	0	0.00	8	5.52
2008	121	0	0.00	31	20.39
2009	109	0	0.00	26	19.26
2010	107	0	0.00	27	20.15
2011	83	0	0.00	50	37.59
2012	75	0	0.00	55	42.31

Economy:CZE

Year	Active	Defaults #	Defaults %	Others #	Others %
1992	0	0	NaN	0	NaN
1993	0	0	NaN	0	NaN
1994	1	0	0.00	0	0.00
1995	50	0	0.00	3	5.66
1996	148	0	0.00	6	3.90
1997	263	0	0.00	369	58.39
1998	235	1	0.36	42	15.11
1999	142	4	1.60	104	41.60
2000	101	6	3.45	67	38.51
2001	75	2	1.33	73	48.67
2002	46	1	0.98	55	53.92
2003	33	0	0.00	38	53.52
2004	42	0	0.00	25	37.31
2005	25	0	0.00	25	50.00
2006	19	0	0.00	18	48.65
2007	12	0	0.00	13	52.00
2008	15	0	0.00	7	31.82
2009	13	0	0.00	8	38.10
2010	20	0	0.00	2	9.09
2011	16	1	4.35	6	26.09
2012	15	0	0.00	4	21.05

Economy:DEU

Year	Active	Defaults #	Defaults %	Others #	Others %
1992	399	0	0.00	38	8.70
1993	420	0	0.00	28	6.25
1994	574	0	0.00	63	9.89
1995	592	0	0.00	65	9.89
1996	623	4	0.58	63	9.13
1997	630	2	0.28	74	10.48
1998	727	2	0.26	53	6.78
1999	905	1	0.10	51	5.33
2000	1036	2	0.18	56	5.12
2001	1033	26	2.33	55	4.94
2002	952	37	3.40	100	9.18
2003	893	16	1.62	76	7.72
2004	886	8	0.85	47	4.99
2005	915	4	0.42	41	4.27
2006	1076	4	0.36	35	3.14
2007	1222	5	0.39	60	4.66
2008	1277	17	1.20	120	8.49
2009	1247	11	0.77	170	11.90
2010	1298	0	0.00	153	10.54
2011	1315	5	0.30	336	20.29
2012	954	9	0.62	485	33.49

(*Continued*)

Table A.11. (*Continued*)

Economy:DNK

Year	Active	Defaults #	Defaults %	Others #	Others %
1992	157	0	0.00	19	10.80
1993	173	0	0.00	12	6.49
1994	176	0	0.00	24	12.00
1995	202	1	0.46	16	7.31
1996	219	0	0.00	11	4.78
1997	212	0	0.00	21	9.01
1998	213	0	0.00	29	11.98
1999	210	0	0.00	24	10.26
2000	208	1	0.44	20	8.73
2001	191	5	2.20	31	13.66
2002	175	3	1.44	30	14.42
2003	174	1	0.52	19	9.79
2004	170	1	0.54	14	7.57
2005	169	0	0.00	9	5.06
2006	190	0	0.00	6	3.06
2007	216	1	0.45	4	1.81
2008	213	1	0.43	16	6.96
2009	208	3	1.36	9	4.09
2010	198	0	0.00	15	7.04
2011	187	2	1.00	12	5.97
2012	176	2	1.06	11	5.82

Economy:EGY

Year	Active	Defaults #	Defaults %	Others #	Others %
1992	0	0	NaN	0	NaN
1993	0	0	NaN	0	NaN
1994	0	0	NaN	0	NaN
1995	0	0	NaN	0	NaN
1996	0	0	NaN	0	NaN
1997	0	0	NaN	0	NaN
1998	0	0	NaN	0	NaN
1999	0	0	NaN	0	NaN
2000	0	0	NaN	0	NaN
2001	0	0	NaN	0	NaN
2002	0	0	NaN	0	NaN
2003	0	0	NaN	0	NaN
2004	0	0	NaN	0	NaN
2005	0	0	NaN	0	NaN
2006	171	0	0.00	78	31.33
2007	200	0	0.00	124	38.27
2008	254	0	0.00	141	35.70
2009	208	0	0.00	90	30.20
2010	198	0	0.00	59	22.96
2011	235	0	0.00	11	4.47
2012	214	0	0.00	51	19.25

Economy:ESP

Year	Active	Defaults #	Defaults %	Others #	Others %
1992	148	0	0.00	39	20.86
1993	113	0	0.00	96	45.93
1994	239	0	0.00	18	7.00
1995	237	0	0.00	97	29.04
1996	265	0	0.00	64	19.45
1997	273	0	0.00	59	17.77
1998	232	0	0.00	104	30.95
1999	214	0	0.00	78	26.71
2000	213	0	0.00	55	20.52
2001	195	0	0.00	79	28.83
2002	207	2	0.74	60	22.30
2003	172	0	0.00	81	32.02
2004	162	0	0.00	41	20.20
2005	160	0	0.00	47	22.71
2006	163	0	0.00	44	21.26
2007	154	1	0.51	41	20.92
2008	144	2	1.16	27	15.61
2009	141	0	0.00	24	14.55
2010	144	1	0.63	15	9.38
2011	142	0	0.00	15	9.55
2012	137	2	1.27	18	11.46

Economy:EST

Year	Active	Defaults #	Defaults %	Others #	Others %
1992	0	0	NaN	0	NaN
1993	0	0	NaN	0	NaN
1994	0	0	NaN	0	NaN
1995	0	0	NaN	0	NaN
1996	0	0	NaN	0	NaN
1997	17	0	0.00	0	0.00
1998	19	0	0.00	1	5.00
1999	19	0	0.00	1	5.00
2000	16	0	0.00	4	20.00
2001	14	0	0.00	2	12.50
2002	11	0	0.00	3	21.43
2003	11	0	0.00	0	0.00
2004	11	0	0.00	0	0.00
2005	13	0	0.00	1	7.14
2006	13	0	0.00	2	13.33
2007	16	0	0.00	0	0.00
2008	17	0	0.00	0	0.00
2009	15	0	0.00	2	11.76
2010	15	0	0.00	1	6.25
2011	15	0	0.00	0	0.00
2012	16	0	0.00	0	0.00

(*Continued*)

Table A.11. *(Continued)*

Economy:FIN

		Defaults		Others	
Year	Active	#	%	#	%
1992	92	0	0.00	0	0.00
1993	94	0	0.00	2	2.08
1994	96	0	0.00	6	5.88
1995	102	0	0.00	5	4.67
1996	110	0	0.00	3	2.65
1997	124	0	0.00	1	0.80
1998	127	1	0.75	6	4.48
1999	146	0	0.00	8	5.19
2000	153	0	0.00	12	7.27
2001	148	1	0.62	13	8.02
2002	142	1	0.65	10	6.54
2003	138	1	0.68	9	6.08
2004	131	0	0.00	11	7.75
2005	132	0	0.00	6	4.35
2006	132	0	0.00	8	5.71
2007	130	0	0.00	5	3.70
2008	127	1	0.76	3	2.29
2009	125	1	0.78	2	1.56
2010	123	0	0.00	4	3.15
2011	121	1	0.81	1	0.81
2012	119	0	0.00	5	4.03

Economy:FRA

		Defaults		Others	
Year	Active	#	%	#	%
1992	626	0	0.00	72	10.32
1993	640	0	0.00	78	10.86
1994	691	0	0.00	102	12.86
1995	718	0	0.00	119	14.22
1996	780	0	0.00	116	12.95
1997	802	1	0.11	142	15.03
1998	812	0	0.00	193	19.20
1999	855	0	0.00	93	9.81
2000	917	2	0.20	97	9.55
2001	915	8	0.79	93	9.15
2002	870	5	0.51	113	11.44
2003	860	4	0.41	102	10.56
2004	841	3	0.32	106	11.16
2005	846	5	0.53	98	10.33
2006	913	6	0.60	75	7.55
2007	951	7	0.66	101	9.54
2008	904	12	1.13	149	13.99
2009	891	6	0.58	142	13.67
2010	849	2	0.20	169	16.57
2011	801	2	0.21	153	16.00
2012	776	0	0.00	154	16.56

Economy:GBR

		Defaults		Others	
Year	Active	#	%	#	%
1992	1079	0	0.00	89	7.62
1993	1192	0	0.00	39	3.17
1994	1284	0	0.00	49	3.68
1995	1415	0	0.00	63	4.26
1996	1623	0	0.00	62	3.68
1997	1721	0	0.00	114	6.21
1998	1688	0	0.00	198	10.50
1999	1560	2	0.11	295	15.89
2000	1675	2	0.11	210	11.13
2001	1686	12	0.65	148	8.02
2002	1641	13	0.71	169	9.27
2003	1600	6	0.33	187	10.43
2004	1786	2	0.10	151	7.79
2005	2036	2	0.09	205	9.14
2006	2186	0	0.00	251	10.30
2007	2225	2	0.08	264	10.60
2008	2029	30	1.24	355	14.71
2009	1827	32	1.47	318	14.61
2010	1788	3	0.15	253	12.38
2011	1666	11	0.56	278	14.22
2012	1582	19	1.05	211	11.64

Economy:GRC

		Defaults		Others	
Year	Active	#	%	#	%
1992	90	0	0.00	0	0.00
1993	97	0	0.00	0	0.00
1994	162	0	0.00	2	1.22
1995	182	0	0.00	2	1.09
1996	196	0	0.00	6	2.97
1997	208	0	0.00	4	1.89
1998	231	0	0.00	5	2.12
1999	264	0	0.00	6	2.22
2000	308	0	0.00	8	2.53
2001	312	0	0.00	14	4.29
2002	309	0	0.00	19	5.79
2003	313	0	0.00	9	2.80
2004	313	0	0.00	10	3.10
2005	299	0	0.00	21	6.56
2006	285	0	0.00	16	5.32
2007	279	0	0.00	13	4.45
2008	274	0	0.00	18	6.16
2009	265	0	0.00	24	8.30
2010	257	0	0.00	30	10.45
2011	232	0	0.00	35	13.11
2012	223	0	0.00	42	15.85

(Continued)

Table A.11. (*Continued*)

Economy:HKG

Year	Active	Defaults #	Defaults %	Others #	Others %
1992	356	0	0.00	11	3.00
1993	423	0	0.00	7	1.63
1994	464	0	0.00	13	2.73
1995	491	0	0.00	9	1.80
1996	529	0	0.00	15	2.76
1997	601	0	0.00	24	3.84
1998	628	2	0.30	30	4.55
1999	661	6	0.87	21	3.05
2000	743	4	0.52	21	2.73
2001	813	9	1.06	30	3.52
2002	908	4	0.42	36	3.80
2003	957	4	0.40	51	5.04
2004	995	0	0.00	56	5.33
2005	1028	3	0.27	65	5.93
2006	1080	2	0.18	44	3.91
2007	1170	2	0.17	24	2.01
2008	1174	8	0.66	33	2.72
2009	1233	3	0.24	23	1.83
2010	1309	1	0.07	28	2.09
2011	1366	1	0.07	26	1.87
2012	1409	2	0.14	43	2.96

Economy:HRV

Year	Active	Defaults #	Defaults %	Others #	Others %
1992	0	0	NaN	0	NaN
1993	0	0	NaN	0	NaN
1994	0	0	NaN	0	NaN
1995	0	0	NaN	0	NaN
1996	0	0	NaN	0	NaN
1997	0	0	NaN	0	NaN
1998	0	0	NaN	0	NaN
1999	0	0	NaN	0	NaN
2000	0	0	NaN	0	NaN
2001	0	0	NaN	0	NaN
2002	28	0	0.00	4	12.50
2003	34	0	0.00	8	19.05
2004	48	0	0.00	9	15.79
2005	54	0	0.00	8	12.90
2006	211	0	0.00	20	8.66
2007	240	0	0.00	62	20.53
2008	164	0	0.00	120	42.25
2009	160	0	0.00	72	31.03
2010	162	1	0.47	50	23.47
2011	133	0	0.00	65	32.83
2012	127	1	0.56	50	28.09

Economy:HUN

Year	Active	Defaults #	Defaults %	Others #	Others %
1992	0	0	NaN	0	NaN
1993	0	0	NaN	0	NaN
1994	0	0	NaN	0	NaN
1995	34	0	0.00	2	5.56
1996	38	0	0.00	7	15.56
1997	39	0	0.00	10	20.41
1998	46	0	0.00	4	8.00
1999	53	0	0.00	7	11.67
2000	50	1	1.72	7	12.07
2001	47	0	0.00	8	14.55
2002	39	0	0.00	11	22.00
2003	40	0	0.00	6	13.04
2004	38	0	0.00	7	15.56
2005	36	0	0.00	6	14.29
2006	37	0	0.00	5	11.90
2007	35	0	0.00	4	10.26
2008	37	0	0.00	1	2.63
2009	40	0	0.00	0	0.00
2010	45	0	0.00	1	2.17
2011	44	0	0.00	6	12.00
2012	46	1	1.96	4	7.84

Economy:IDN

Year	Active	Defaults #	Defaults %	Others #	Others %
1992	124	0	0.00	30	19.48
1993	155	0	0.00	23	12.92
1994	184	0	0.00	49	21.03
1995	204	0	0.00	41	16.73
1996	236	0	0.00	26	9.92
1997	255	0	0.00	33	11.46
1998	250	17	5.48	43	13.87
1999	257	15	5.07	24	8.11
2000	262	6	1.99	34	11.26
2001	272	8	2.43	49	14.89
2002	270	2	0.60	63	18.81
2003	297	1	0.31	28	8.59
2004	286	1	0.28	64	18.23
2005	277	0	0.00	77	21.75
2006	303	0	0.00	53	14.89
2007	321	0	0.00	71	18.11
2008	281	0	0.00	93	24.87
2009	323	4	1.04	56	14.62
2010	360	2	0.50	40	9.95
2011	386	0	0.00	42	9.81
2012	414	1	0.22	37	8.19

(*Continued*)

Table A.11. *(Continued)*

Economy:IND

Year	Active	Defaults #	Defaults %	Others #	Others %
1992	1495	1	0.06	143	8.72
1993	1842	0	0.00	201	9.84
1994	2801	0	0.00	270	8.79
1995	4073	2	0.05	349	7.89
1996	4078	5	0.10	1060	20.61
1997	3011	11	0.22	1958	39.32
1998	2685	8	0.19	1469	35.30
1999	3060	13	0.31	1112	26.57
2000	2558	10	0.26	1334	34.19
2001	2266	6	0.18	1122	33.06
2002	3348	6	0.15	656	16.36
2003	2683	14	0.34	1383	33.90
2004	2514	7	0.20	931	26.97
2005	2523	7	0.22	611	19.45
2006	2730	11	0.34	483	14.98
2007	2995	16	0.51	130	4.14
2008	3041	23	0.64	542	15.03
2009	3146	37	1.07	283	8.17
2010	3605	9	0.20	955	20.90
2011	3404	9	0.21	866	20.24
2012	3582	24	0.59	429	10.63

Economy:IRL

Year	Active	Defaults #	Defaults %	Others #	Others %
1992	31	0	0.00	4	11.43
1993	37	0	0.00	4	9.76
1994	37	0	0.00	5	11.90
1995	37	0	0.00	1	2.63
1996	43	0	0.00	0	0.00
1997	51	0	0.00	3	5.56
1998	50	0	0.00	5	9.09
1999	51	0	0.00	6	10.53
2000	59	0	0.00	5	7.81
2001	54	0	0.00	6	10.00
2002	48	0	0.00	6	11.11
2003	43	0	0.00	5	10.42
2004	42	0	0.00	3	6.67
2005	42	0	0.00	2	4.55
2006	47	0	0.00	2	4.08
2007	52	0	0.00	2	3.70
2008	49	0	0.00	3	5.77
2009	43	1	2.04	5	10.20
2010	40	0	0.00	4	9.09
2011	38	0	0.00	2	5.00
2012	33	0	0.00	5	13.16

Economy:ISL

Year	Active	Defaults #	Defaults %	Others #	Others %
1992	0	0	NaN	0	NaN
1993	0	0	NaN	0	NaN
1994	0	0	NaN	0	NaN
1995	0	0	NaN	0	NaN
1996	26	0	0.00	0	0.00
1997	33	0	0.00	3	8.33
1998	50	0	0.00	3	5.66
1999	59	0	0.00	9	13.24
2000	58	0	0.00	17	22.67
2001	64	0	0.00	12	15.79
2002	55	0	0.00	17	23.61
2003	40	0	0.00	22	35.48
2004	32	0	0.00	13	28.89
2005	25	0	0.00	11	30.56
2006	25	0	0.00	5	16.67
2007	26	0	0.00	5	16.13
2008	11	4	13.79	14	48.28
2009	10	1	6.67	4	26.67
2010	8	0	0.00	4	33.33
2011	9	0	0.00	4	30.77
2012	12	0	0.00	1	7.69

Economy:ISR

Year	Active	Defaults #	Defaults %	Others #	Others %
1992	0	0	NaN	0	NaN
1993	0	0	NaN	0	NaN
1994	9	0	0.00	0	0.00
1995	82	0	0.00	2	2.38
1996	627	0	0.00	7	1.10
1997	632	0	0.00	21	3.22
1998	610	0	0.00	45	6.87
1999	622	0	0.00	50	7.44
2000	594	0	0.00	84	12.39
2001	582	0	0.00	171	22.71
2002	541	2	0.28	176	24.48
2003	525	0	0.00	157	23.02
2004	510	2	0.34	85	14.24
2005	524	0	0.00	47	8.23
2006	552	0	0.00	39	6.60
2007	592	0	0.00	28	4.52
2008	565	0	0.00	46	7.53
2009	562	0	0.00	30	5.07
2010	553	1	0.17	43	7.20
2011	538	1	0.17	50	8.49
2012	485	0	0.00	77	13.70

(Continued)

Table A.11. *(Continued)*

Economy:ITA

Year	Active	Defaults #	Defaults %	Others #	Others %
1992	185	0	0.00	5	2.63
1993	181	0	0.00	8	4.23
1994	195	0	0.00	13	6.25
1995	209	0	0.00	14	6.28
1996	219	1	0.43	15	6.38
1997	218	0	0.00	28	11.38
1998	227	0	0.00	14	5.81
1999	252	0	0.00	7	2.70
2000	277	0	0.00	25	8.28
2001	280	0	0.00	17	5.72
2002	278	1	0.34	14	4.78
2003	258	6	2.09	23	8.01
2004	257	2	0.75	7	2.63
2005	264	0	0.00	15	5.38
2006	276	0	0.00	16	5.48
2007	296	0	0.00	13	4.21
2008	286	1	0.32	22	7.12
2009	278	4	1.32	20	6.62
2010	283	0	0.00	15	5.03
2011	277	0	0.00	26	8.58
2012	274	2	0.66	29	9.51

Economy:JOR

Year	Active	Defaults #	Defaults %	Others #	Others %
1992	0	0	NaN	0	NaN
1993	0	0	NaN	0	NaN
1994	0	0	NaN	0	NaN
1995	0	0	NaN	0	NaN
1996	0	0	NaN	0	NaN
1997	0	0	NaN	0	NaN
1998	0	0	NaN	0	NaN
1999	0	0	NaN	0	NaN
2000	0	0	NaN	0	NaN
2001	0	0	NaN	0	NaN
2002	0	0	NaN	0	NaN
2003	0	0	NaN	0	NaN
2004	0	0	NaN	0	NaN
2005	0	0	NaN	0	NaN
2006	0	0	NaN	0	NaN
2007	204	0	0.00	13	5.99
2008	217	0	0.00	17	7.26
2009	223	0	0.00	23	9.35
2010	215	0	0.00	29	11.89
2011	210	0	0.00	27	11.39
2012	208	0	0.00	31	12.97

Economy:JPN

Year	Active	Defaults #	Defaults %	Others #	Others %
1992	2535	2	0.08	21	0.82
1993	2616	3	0.11	24	0.91
1994	2762	0	0.00	17	0.61
1995	2943	1	0.03	17	0.57
1996	3096	4	0.13	21	0.67
1997	3215	6	0.18	31	0.95
1998	3269	12	0.36	37	1.12
1999	3332	6	0.18	47	1.39
2000	3474	12	0.34	59	1.66
2001	3581	16	0.44	64	1.75
2002	3605	29	0.78	93	2.50
2003	3636	20	0.53	98	2.61
2004	3739	11	0.29	85	2.22
2005	3824	9	0.23	89	2.27
2006	3953	2	0.05	85	2.10
2007	3982	6	0.15	104	2.54
2008	3907	35	0.86	107	2.64
2009	3779	28	0.71	136	3.45
2010	3682	9	0.24	129	3.38
2011	3627	5	0.13	100	2.68
2012	3584	6	0.16	101	2.74

Economy:KAZ

Year	Active	Defaults #	Defaults %	Others #	Others %
1992	0	0	NaN	0	NaN
1993	0	0	NaN	0	NaN
1994	0	0	NaN	0	NaN
1995	0	0	NaN	0	NaN
1996	0	0	NaN	0	NaN
1997	0	0	NaN	0	NaN
1998	0	0	NaN	0	NaN
1999	0	0	NaN	0	NaN
2000	0	0	NaN	0	NaN
2001	0	0	NaN	0	NaN
2002	7	0	0.00	6	46.15
2003	9	0	0.00	4	30.77
2004	12	0	0.00	13	52.00
2005	3	0	0.00	13	81.25
2006	2	0	0.00	4	66.67
2007	23	0	0.00	12	34.29
2008	21	0	0.00	15	41.67
2009	14	4	10.26	21	53.85
2010	11	0	0.00	17	60.71
2011	13	0	0.00	10	43.48
2012	15	0	0.00	10	40.00

(Continued)

Table A.11. *(Continued)*

Economy:KOR

Year	Active	Defaults #	Defaults %	Others #	Others %
1992	635	0	0.00	1	0.16
1993	643	0	0.00	0	0.00
1994	674	0	0.00	0	0.00
1995	701	0	0.00	2	0.28
1996	747	6	0.79	3	0.40
1997	1003	50	4.67	17	1.59
1998	915	78	7.08	109	9.89
1999	1012	22	2.05	39	3.63
2000	1156	12	0.99	44	3.63
2001	1302	18	1.34	26	1.93
2002	1450	14	0.94	32	2.14
2003	1494	13	0.85	31	2.02
2004	1510	7	0.45	55	3.50
2005	1560	8	0.49	52	3.21
2006	1634	2	0.12	12	0.73
2007	1706	0	0.00	16	0.93
2008	1734	8	0.45	34	1.91
2009	1724	7	0.38	90	4.94
2010	1745	8	0.43	95	5.14
2011	1750	3	0.16	89	4.83
2012	1723	7	0.39	75	4.16

Economy:KWT

Year	Active	Defaults #	Defaults %	Others #	Others %
1992	0	0	NaN	0	NaN
1993	0	0	NaN	0	NaN
1994	0	0	NaN	0	NaN
1995	0	0	NaN	0	NaN
1996	51	0	0.00	2	3.77
1997	66	0	0.00	1	1.49
1998	67	0	0.00	1	1.47
1999	72	0	0.00	7	8.86
2000	70	0	0.00	10	12.50
2001	73	0	0.00	0	0.00
2002	76	0	0.00	6	7.32
2003	94	0	0.00	0	0.00
2004	104	0	0.00	4	3.70
2005	139	0	0.00	4	2.80
2006	156	0	0.00	6	3.70
2007	176	0	0.00	13	6.88
2008	176	1	0.52	17	8.76
2009	182	1	0.47	31	14.49
2010	182	0	0.00	44	19.47
2011	164	1	0.44	62	27.31
2012	184	0	0.00	38	17.12

Economy:LKA

Year	Active	Defaults #	Defaults %	Others #	Others %
1992	0	0	NaN	0	NaN
1993	1	0	0.00	0	0.00
1994	0	0	0.00	1	100.00
1995	139	0	0.00	1	0.71
1996	132	0	0.00	42	24.14
1997	140	0	0.00	33	19.08
1998	153	0	0.00	30	16.39
1999	149	0	0.00	35	19.02
2000	149	0	0.00	35	19.02
2001	163	0	0.00	25	13.30
2002	172	0	0.00	24	12.24
2003	176	0	0.00	28	13.73
2004	191	0	0.00	10	4.98
2005	204	0	0.00	10	4.67
2006	210	0	0.00	12	5.41
2007	216	0	0.00	10	4.42
2008	215	0	0.00	13	5.70
2009	219	0	0.00	10	4.37
2010	239	0	0.00	0	0.00
2011	259	0	0.00	9	3.36
2012	276	0	0.00	4	1.43

Economy:LTU

Year	Active	Defaults #	Defaults %	Others #	Others %
1992	0	0	NaN	0	NaN
1993	0	0	NaN	0	NaN
1994	0	0	NaN	0	NaN
1995	0	0	NaN	0	NaN
1996	0	0	NaN	0	NaN
1997	0	0	NaN	0	NaN
1998	0	0	NaN	0	NaN
1999	0	0	NaN	0	NaN
2000	34	0	0.00	5	12.82
2001	32	0	0.00	12	27.27
2002	42	0	0.00	4	8.70
2003	39	0	0.00	7	15.22
2004	40	0	0.00	1	2.44
2005	40	0	0.00	0	0.00
2006	39	0	0.00	2	4.88
2007	37	0	0.00	3	7.50
2008	38	0	0.00	0	0.00
2009	36	0	0.00	3	7.69
2010	37	0	0.00	2	5.13
2011	32	1	2.63	5	13.16
2012	32	0	0.00	0	0.00

(Continued)

Table A.11. (*Continued*)

Economy:LUX

Year	Active	Defaults #	Defaults %	Others #	Others %
1992	2	0	0.00	1	33.33
1993	2	0	0.00	1	33.33
1994	2	0	0.00	0	0.00
1995	30	0	0.00	12	28.57
1996	28	0	0.00	15	34.88
1997	37	0	0.00	9	19.57
1998	34	0	0.00	13	27.66
1999	34	0	0.00	14	29.17
2000	32	0	0.00	13	28.89
2001	28	0	0.00	13	31.71
2002	27	0	0.00	10	27.03
2003	28	0	0.00	11	28.21
2004	36	0	0.00	7	16.28
2005	37	0	0.00	7	15.91
2006	36	0	0.00	16	30.77
2007	34	0	0.00	8	19.05
2008	26	0	0.00	14	35.00
2009	23	0	0.00	8	25.81
2010	18	1	3.45	10	34.48
2011	14	0	0.00	8	36.36
2012	14	0	0.00	5	26.32

Economy:LVA

Year	Active	Defaults #	Defaults %	Others #	Others %
1992	0	0	NaN	0	NaN
1993	0	0	NaN	0	NaN
1994	0	0	NaN	0	NaN
1995	0	0	NaN	0	NaN
1996	0	0	NaN	0	NaN
1997	0	0	NaN	0	NaN
1998	0	0	NaN	0	NaN
1999	0	0	NaN	0	NaN
2000	12	0	0.00	5	29.41
2001	33	0	0.00	6	15.38
2002	35	0	0.00	3	7.89
2003	26	0	0.00	11	29.73
2004	29	0	0.00	3	9.38
2005	33	0	0.00	3	8.33
2006	31	0	0.00	5	13.89
2007	32	0	0.00	6	15.79
2008	27	0	0.00	7	20.59
2009	28	0	0.00	9	24.32
2010	31	0	0.00	4	11.43
2011	28	1	2.78	7	19.44
2012	29	0	0.00	5	14.71

Economy:MAR

Year	Active	Defaults #	Defaults %	Others #	Others %
1992	0	0	NaN	0	NaN
1993	0	0	NaN	0	NaN
1994	0	0	NaN	0	NaN
1995	0	0	NaN	0	NaN
1996	16	0	0.00	0	0.00
1997	40	0	0.00	3	6.98
1998	48	0	0.00	1	2.04
1999	46	0	0.00	6	11.54
2000	51	0	0.00	1	1.92
2001	52	0	0.00	7	11.86
2002	52	0	0.00	7	11.86
2003	49	0	0.00	8	14.04
2004	48	0	0.00	7	12.73
2005	52	0	0.00	3	5.45
2006	59	0	0.00	5	7.81
2007	72	0	0.00	2	2.70
2008	77	0	0.00	1	1.28
2009	75	0	0.00	2	2.60
2010	73	0	0.00	4	5.19
2011	75	0	0.00	2	2.60
2012	76	0	0.00	0	0.00

Economy:MEX

Year	Active	Defaults #	Defaults %	Others #	Others %
1992	0	0	NaN	0	NaN
1993	0	0	NaN	0	NaN
1994	90	0	0.00	37	29.13
1995	97	0	0.00	22	18.49
1996	107	0	0.00	19	15.08
1997	117	0	0.00	23	16.43
1998	113	0	0.00	21	15.67
1999	112	1	0.74	23	16.91
2000	107	1	0.79	18	14.29
2001	110	1	0.77	19	14.62
2002	98	1	0.78	29	22.66
2003	103	2	1.65	16	13.22
2004	108	0	0.00	11	9.24
2005	101	0	0.00	23	18.55
2006	105	0	0.00	10	8.70
2007	103	0	0.00	18	14.88
2008	95	2	1.67	23	19.17
2009	102	3	2.61	10	8.70
2010	107	2	1.63	14	11.38
2011	104	0	0.00	23	18.11
2012	105	0	0.00	11	9.48

(*Continued*)

Table A.11. *(Continued)*

Economy:MKD

Year	Active	Defaults #	Defaults %	Others #	Others %
1992	0	0	NaN	0	NaN
1993	0	0	NaN	0	NaN
1994	0	0	NaN	0	NaN
1995	0	0	NaN	0	NaN
1996	0	0	NaN	0	NaN
1997	0	0	NaN	0	NaN
1998	0	0	NaN	0	NaN
1999	0	0	NaN	0	NaN
2000	0	0	NaN	0	NaN
2001	0	0	NaN	0	NaN
2002	0	0	NaN	0	NaN
2003	0	0	NaN	0	NaN
2004	13	0	0.00	0	0.00
2005	62	0	0.00	70	53.03
2006	84	0	0.00	69	45.10
2007	92	0	0.00	75	44.91
2008	73	0	0.00	76	51.01
2009	68	0	0.00	66	49.25
2010	66	0	0.00	61	48.03
2011	58	0	0.00	64	52.46
2012	51	1	0.85	65	55.56

Economy:MLT

Year	Active	Defaults #	Defaults %	Others #	Others %
1992	0	0	NaN	0	NaN
1993	0	0	NaN	0	NaN
1994	0	0	NaN	0	NaN
1995	0	0	NaN	0	NaN
1996	5	0	0.00	0	0.00
1997	6	0	0.00	0	0.00
1998	7	0	0.00	0	0.00
1999	7	0	0.00	1	12.50
2000	9	0	0.00	0	0.00
2001	9	0	0.00	2	18.18
2002	10	0	0.00	2	16.67
2003	10	0	0.00	3	23.08
2004	11	0	0.00	2	15.38
2005	11	0	0.00	2	15.38
2006	13	0	0.00	0	0.00
2007	14	0	0.00	3	17.65
2008	13	0	0.00	7	35.00
2009	12	0	0.00	3	20.00
2010	12	0	0.00	2	14.29
2011	14	0	0.00	2	12.50
2012	19	0	0.00	1	5.00

Economy:MYS

Year	Active	Defaults #	Defaults %	Others #	Others %
1992	356	0	0.00	10	2.73
1993	405	0	0.00	0	0.00
1994	466	0	0.00	7	1.48
1995	523	0	0.00	2	0.38
1996	615	0	0.00	0	0.00
1997	702	0	0.00	2	0.28
1998	696	14	1.92	21	2.87
1999	704	8	1.10	14	1.93
2000	735	8	1.06	12	1.59
2001	739	10	1.30	18	2.35
2002	767	7	0.87	30	3.73
2003	835	3	0.35	20	2.33
2004	911	3	0.32	17	1.83
2005	984	0	0.00	27	2.67
2006	994	5	0.48	36	3.48
2007	968	6	0.58	65	6.26
2008	927	17	1.68	66	6.53
2009	923	12	1.23	41	4.20
2010	922	16	1.64	36	3.70
2011	924	2	0.21	33	3.44
2012	907	4	0.42	39	4.11

Economy:NGA

Year	Active	Defaults #	Defaults %	Others #	Others %
1992	0	0	NaN	0	NaN
1993	0	0	NaN	0	NaN
1994	0	0	NaN	0	NaN
1995	0	0	NaN	0	NaN
1996	0	0	NaN	0	NaN
1997	0	0	NaN	0	NaN
1998	0	0	NaN	0	NaN
1999	0	0	NaN	0	NaN
2000	0	0	NaN	0	NaN
2001	0	0	NaN	0	NaN
2002	114	0	0.00	31	21.38
2003	77	0	0.00	58	42.96
2004	115	0	0.00	41	26.28
2005	127	0	0.00	27	17.53
2006	139	0	0.00	30	17.75
2007	171	0	0.00	25	12.76
2008	177	0	0.00	47	20.98
2009	190	0	0.00	22	10.38
2010	184	0	0.00	24	11.54
2011	160	0	0.00	38	19.19
2012	162	0	0.00	17	9.50

(Continued)

Table A.11. (*Continued*)

Economy:NLD

Year	Active	Defaults #	Defaults %	Others #	Others %
1992	161	0	0.00	6	3.59
1993	171	0	0.00	5	2.84
1994	174	0	0.00	5	2.79
1995	187	0	0.00	5	2.60
1996	196	1	0.50	4	1.99
1997	198	0	0.00	17	7.91
1998	210	0	0.00	10	4.55
1999	213	0	0.00	19	8.19
2000	201	1	0.45	21	9.42
2001	176	7	3.40	23	11.17
2002	158	10	5.43	16	8.70
2003	153	0	0.00	14	8.38
2004	145	0	0.00	11	7.05
2005	141	0	0.00	8	5.37
2006	137	1	0.68	8	5.48
2007	134	0	0.00	9	6.29
2008	126	1	0.72	11	7.97
2009	122	3	2.33	4	3.10
2010	120	0	0.00	5	4.00
2011	115	0	0.00	8	6.50
2012	111	0	0.00	9	7.50

Economy:NOR

Year	Active	Defaults #	Defaults %	Others #	Others %
1992	81	0	0.00	8	8.99
1993	101	0	0.00	2	1.94
1994	115	0	0.00	3	2.54
1995	137	0	0.00	2	1.44
1996	159	0	0.00	4	2.45
1997	201	0	0.00	12	5.63
1998	216	0	0.00	19	8.09
1999	201	0	0.00	28	12.23
2000	195	1	0.44	33	14.41
2001	213	3	1.21	32	12.90
2002	206	4	1.63	35	14.29
2003	184	3	1.31	42	18.34
2004	198	0	0.00	18	8.33
2005	235	0	0.00	23	8.91
2006	262	0	0.00	37	12.37
2007	270	0	0.00	47	14.83
2008	243	4	1.38	42	14.53
2009	225	6	2.23	38	14.13
2010	224	1	0.40	24	9.64
2011	221	1	0.43	13	5.53
2012	213	1	0.44	14	6.14

Economy:NZL

Year	Active	Defaults #	Defaults %	Others #	Others %
1992	29	0	0.00	1	3.33
1993	33	0	0.00	0	0.00
1994	41	0	0.00	0	0.00
1995	42	0	0.00	2	4.55
1996	46	0	0.00	2	4.17
1997	49	0	0.00	0	0.00
1998	50	0	0.00	1	1.96
1999	56	0	0.00	0	0.00
2000	63	0	0.00	1	1.56
2001	72	0	0.00	0	0.00
2002	77	0	0.00	0	0.00
2003	89	0	0.00	0	0.00
2004	103	0	0.00	1	0.96
2005	108	0	0.00	0	0.00
2006	114	0	0.00	0	0.00
2007	124	0	0.00	1	0.80
2008	114	0	0.00	14	10.94
2009	122	0	0.00	9	6.87
2010	121	0	0.00	15	11.03
2011	122	0	0.00	12	8.96
2012	121	0	0.00	18	12.95

Economy:PAK

Year	Active	Defaults #	Defaults %	Others #	Others %
1992	0	0	NaN	0	NaN
1993	0	0	NaN	0	NaN
1994	0	0	NaN	0	NaN
1995	0	0	NaN	0	NaN
1996	0	0	NaN	0	NaN
1997	0	0	NaN	0	NaN
1998	248	0	0.00	132	34.74
1999	371	0	0.00	112	23.19
2000	381	0	0.00	157	29.18
2001	326	0	0.00	180	35.57
2002	431	0	0.00	97	18.37
2003	469	0	0.00	61	11.51
2004	503	0	0.00	48	8.71
2005	491	0	0.00	89	15.34
2006	472	0	0.00	97	17.05
2007	492	0	0.00	77	13.53
2008	304	0	0.00	296	49.33
2009	518	0	0.00	68	11.60
2010	491	0	0.00	53	9.74
2011	503	0	0.00	105	17.27
2012	454	0	0.00	87	16.08

(*Continued*)

Table A.11 *(Continued)*

Economy:PER

Year	Active	Defaults #	Defaults %	Others #	Others %
1992	1	0	0.00	0	0.00
1993	1	0	0.00	0	0.00
1994	63	0	0.00	2	3.08
1995	97	0	0.00	22	18.49
1996	94	0	0.00	46	32.86
1997	118	0	0.00	40	25.32
1998	107	0	0.00	59	35.54
1999	92	0	0.00	67	42.14
2000	74	0	0.00	74	50.00
2001	64	0	0.00	54	45.76
2002	75	0	0.00	50	40.00
2003	66	0	0.00	46	41.07
2004	75	0	0.00	40	34.78
2005	78	0	0.00	42	35.00
2006	78	0	0.00	40	33.90
2007	90	0	0.00	26	22.41
2008	79	0	0.00	50	38.76
2009	94	0	0.00	33	25.98
2010	89	0	0.00	31	25.83
2011	78	0	0.00	39	33.33
2012	82	0	0.00	37	31.09

Economy:PHL

Year	Active	Defaults #	Defaults %	Others #	Others %
1992	80	0	0.00	24	23.08
1993	108	1	0.80	16	12.80
1994	129	0	0.00	26	16.77
1995	158	0	0.00	15	8.67
1996	178	0	0.00	14	7.29
1997	186	0	0.00	22	10.58
1998	179	1	0.48	28	13.46
1999	186	4	1.98	12	5.94
2000	173	1	0.48	36	17.14
2001	170	3	1.42	39	18.40
2002	152	6	2.82	55	25.82
2003	173	4	1.90	33	15.71
2004	177	7	3.04	46	20.00
2005	181	3	1.35	38	17.12
2006	188	2	0.92	28	12.84
2007	193	2	0.90	27	12.16
2008	183	1	0.46	34	15.60
2009	203	2	0.90	18	8.07
2010	207	0	0.00	18	8.00
2011	220	0	0.00	14	5.98
2012	215	0	0.00	22	9.28

Economy:POL

Year	Active	Defaults #	Defaults %	Others #	Others %
1992	0	0	NaN	0	NaN
1993	0	0	NaN	0	NaN
1994	31	0	0.00	19	38.00
1995	59	0	0.00	0	0.00
1996	77	0	0.00	0	0.00
1997	137	0	0.00	3	2.14
1998	191	0	0.00	3	1.55
1999	212	0	0.00	3	1.40
2000	218	1	0.44	6	2.67
2001	220	1	0.44	5	2.21
2002	203	2	0.88	22	9.69
2003	191	3	1.44	14	6.73
2004	212	0	0.00	8	3.64
2005	233	1	0.41	9	3.70
2006	252	0	0.00	9	3.45
2007	327	0	0.00	10	2.97
2008	425	0	0.00	5	1.16
2009	453	0	0.00	11	2.37
2010	548	0	0.00	8	1.44
2011	732	0	0.00	14	1.88
2012	814	8	0.94	31	3.63

Economy:PRT

Year	Active	Defaults #	Defaults %	Others #	Others %
1992	1	0	0.00	0	0.00
1993	69	0	0.00	13	15.85
1994	79	0	0.00	12	13.19
1995	92	0	0.00	18	16.36
1996	96	0	0.00	21	17.95
1997	93	0	0.00	29	23.77
1998	84	0	0.00	34	28.81
1999	88	0	0.00	24	21.43
2000	84	0	0.00	17	16.83
2001	69	0	0.00	20	22.47
2002	62	0	0.00	19	23.46
2003	65	0	0.00	6	8.45
2004	67	0	0.00	7	9.46
2005	64	0	0.00	7	9.86
2006	62	0	0.00	11	15.07
2007	58	0	0.00	9	13.43
2008	57	0	0.00	8	12.31
2009	56	0	0.00	9	13.85
2010	56	0	0.00	7	11.11
2011	54	2	3.23	6	9.68
2012	54	0	0.00	5	8.47

(Continued)

Table A.11. *(Continued)*

Economy:ROM

Year	Active	Defaults #	Defaults %	Others #	Others %
1992	0	0	NaN	0	NaN
1993	0	0	NaN	0	NaN
1994	0	0	NaN	0	NaN
1995	0	0	NaN	0	NaN
1996	0	0	NaN	0	NaN
1997	0	0	NaN	0	NaN
1998	78	0	0.00	1	1.27
1999	340	0	0.00	30	8.11
2000	355	0	0.00	100	21.98
2001	333	0	0.00	177	34.71
2002	279	0	0.00	197	41.39
2003	275	0	0.00	165	37.50
2004	311	0	0.00	113	26.65
2005	305	1	0.20	198	39.29
2006	514	0	0.00	160	23.74
2007	719	0	0.00	698	49.26
2008	557	0	0.00	444	44.36
2009	445	0	0.00	445	50.00
2010	509	0	0.00	371	42.16
2011	444	1	0.11	438	49.60
2012	347	0	0.00	349	50.14

Economy:RUS

Year	Active	Defaults #	Defaults %	Others #	Others %
1992	0	0	NaN	0	NaN
1993	0	0	NaN	0	NaN
1994	0	0	NaN	0	NaN
1995	0	0	NaN	0	NaN
1996	0	0	NaN	0	NaN
1997	74	0	0.00	28	27.45
1998	35	1	0.76	96	72.73
1999	38	0	0.00	42	52.50
2000	53	0	0.00	70	56.91
2001	84	0	0.00	63	42.86
2002	55	0	0.00	111	66.87
2003	78	0	0.00	64	45.07
2004	105	4	2.33	63	36.63
2005	169	0	0.00	83	32.94
2006	226	1	0.25	176	43.67
2007	317	0	0.00	177	35.83
2008	273	1	0.19	253	48.01
2009	298	8	1.92	110	26.44
2010	306	1	0.23	131	29.91
2011	271	2	0.43	195	41.67
2012	482	1	0.16	144	22.97

Economy:SAU

Year	Active	Defaults #	Defaults %	Others #	Others %
1992	0	0	NaN	0	NaN
1993	0	0	NaN	0	NaN
1994	0	0	NaN	0	NaN
1995	0	0	NaN	0	NaN
1996	0	0	NaN	0	NaN
1997	0	0	NaN	0	NaN
1998	0	0	NaN	0	NaN
1999	0	0	NaN	0	NaN
2000	62	0	0.00	4	6.06
2001	63	0	0.00	4	5.97
2002	66	0	0.00	3	4.35
2003	69	0	0.00	2	2.82
2004	72	0	0.00	0	0.00
2005	76	0	0.00	0	0.00
2006	86	0	0.00	0	0.00
2007	109	0	0.00	2	1.80
2008	126	0	0.00	1	0.79
2009	134	0	0.00	1	0.74
2010	145	0	0.00	0	0.00
2011	148	0	0.00	1	0.67
2012	156	0	0.00	1	0.64

Economy:SGP

Year	Active	Defaults #	Defaults %	Others #	Others %
1992	177	0	0.00	11	5.85
1993	203	0	0.00	3	1.46
1994	233	0	0.00	4	1.69
1995	250	1	0.39	6	2.33
1996	272	1	0.36	8	2.85
1997	299	1	0.31	18	5.66
1998	318	4	1.19	14	4.17
1999	358	4	1.06	15	3.98
2000	428	0	0.00	18	4.04
2001	437	2	0.43	31	6.60
2002	450	2	0.41	34	7.00
2003	500	1	0.19	15	2.91
2004	576	2	0.34	9	1.53
2005	623	4	0.62	17	2.64
2006	667	1	0.14	25	3.61
2007	711	0	0.00	19	2.60
2008	703	4	0.53	41	5.48
2009	717	14	1.84	31	4.07
2010	721	0	0.00	36	4.76
2011	704	0	0.00	53	7.00
2012	700	0	0.00	40	5.41

(Continued)

Table A.11. *(Continued)*

Economy:SVK

Year	Active	Defaults #	Defaults %	Others #	Others %
1992	0	0	NaN	0	NaN
1993	0	0	NaN	0	NaN
1994	0	0	NaN	0	NaN
1995	0	0	NaN	0	NaN
1996	0	0	NaN	0	NaN
1997	0	0	NaN	0	NaN
1998	7	0	0.00	13	65.00
1999	8	0	0.00	24	75.00
2000	12	0	0.00	11	47.83
2001	15	0	0.00	14	48.28
2002	23	0	0.00	15	39.47
2003	40	0	0.00	26	39.39
2004	44	0	0.00	31	41.33
2005	41	0	0.00	26	38.81
2006	48	0	0.00	42	46.67
2007	24	0	0.00	47	66.20
2008	34	0	0.00	26	43.33
2009	38	0	0.00	31	44.93
2010	55	0	0.00	21	27.63
2011	53	0	0.00	42	44.21
2012	47	0	0.00	31	39.74

Economy:SVN

Year	Active	Defaults #	Defaults %	Others #	Others %
1992	0	0	NaN	0	NaN
1993	0	0	NaN	0	NaN
1994	0	0	NaN	0	NaN
1995	0	0	NaN	0	NaN
1996	0	0	NaN	0	NaN
1997	0	0	NaN	0	NaN
1998	75	0	0.00	8	9.64
1999	98	0	0.00	9	8.41
2000	94	0	0.00	34	26.56
2001	112	0	0.00	29	20.57
2002	103	0	0.00	36	25.90
2003	104	0	0.00	19	15.45
2004	108	0	0.00	22	16.92
2005	87	0	0.00	34	28.10
2006	77	0	0.00	28	26.67
2007	65	0	0.00	22	25.29
2008	67	0	0.00	15	18.29
2009	60	2	2.30	25	28.74
2010	69	0	0.00	11	13.75
2011	59	1	1.33	15	20.00
2012	56	1	1.67	3	5.00

Economy:SWE

Year	Active	Defaults #	Defaults %	Others #	Others %
1992	121	0	0.00	2	1.63
1993	144	0	0.00	2	1.37
1994	171	0	0.00	2	1.16
1995	184	0	0.00	0	0.00
1996	223	0	0.00	15	6.30
1997	270	0	0.00	28	9.40
1998	299	1	0.31	19	5.96
1999	338	1	0.27	27	7.38
2000	370	1	0.25	35	8.62
2001	362	4	1.01	31	7.81
2002	350	7	1.81	29	7.51
2003	338	3	0.82	26	7.08
2004	353	1	0.27	22	5.85
2005	389	2	0.50	12	2.98
2006	433	0	0.00	22	4.84
2007	502	1	0.19	14	2.71
2008	510	2	0.37	30	5.54
2009	497	4	0.75	32	6.00
2010	501	2	0.38	29	5.45
2011	495	3	0.56	34	6.39
2012	474	0	0.00	47	9.02

Economy:THA

Year	Active	Defaults #	Defaults %	Others #	Others %
1992	280	0	0.00	1	0.36
1993	331	0	0.00	1	0.30
1994	378	0	0.00	1	0.26
1995	402	1	0.24	9	2.18
1996	420	7	1.56	21	4.69
1997	370	21	4.59	67	14.63
1998	346	16	3.87	51	12.35
1999	322	15	4.04	34	9.16
2000	303	18	5.19	26	7.49
2001	304	8	2.42	19	5.74
2002	322	4	1.17	17	4.96
2003	352	3	0.83	8	2.20
2004	392	1	0.24	21	5.07
2005	428	3	0.66	22	4.86
2006	443	0	0.00	12	2.64
2007	443	2	0.43	19	4.09
2008	441	0	0.00	24	5.16
2009	455	7	1.49	8	1.70
2010	458	4	0.85	9	1.91
2011	463	1	0.21	10	2.11
2012	478	0	0.00	7	1.44

(Continued)

Table A.11. (*Continued*)

Economy:TUR

Year	Active	Defaults		Others	
		#	%	#	%
1992	8	0	0.00	0	0.00
1993	15	0	0.00	0	0.00
1994	33	0	0.00	1	2.94
1995	200	0	0.00	3	1.48
1996	220	0	0.00	3	1.35
1997	256	0	0.00	8	3.03
1998	275	0	0.00	3	1.08
1999	273	0	0.00	13	4.55
2000	294	2	0.64	16	5.13
2001	282	0	0.00	17	5.69
2002	285	0	0.00	7	2.40
2003	283	0	0.00	6	2.08
2004	295	0	0.00	0	0.00
2005	302	0	0.00	3	0.98
2006	313	0	0.00	6	1.88
2007	317	0	0.00	5	1.55
2008	314	0	0.00	5	1.57
2009	314	0	0.00	4	1.26
2010	336	0	0.00	0	0.00
2011	361	0	0.00	3	0.82
2012	391	0	0.00	9	2.25

Economy:TWN

Year	Active	Defaults		Others	
		#	%	#	%
1992	236	0	0.00	2	0.84
1993	259	0	0.00	1	0.38
1994	291	0	0.00	1	0.34
1995	371	0	0.00	0	0.00
1996	442	0	0.00	1	0.23
1997	496	0	0.00	3	0.60
1998	572	4	0.68	12	2.04
1999	695	7	0.99	8	1.13
2000	794	8	0.98	17	2.08
2001	886	9	0.98	23	2.51
2002	996	7	0.67	38	3.65
2003	1082	2	0.18	21	1.90
2004	1350	6	0.43	28	2.02
2005	1363	8	0.56	67	4.66
2006	1389	3	0.21	41	2.86
2007	1444	3	0.20	35	2.36
2008	1446	9	0.60	49	3.26
2009	1503	4	0.26	22	1.44
2010	1601	2	0.12	24	1.48
2011	1666	1	0.06	40	2.34
2012	1722	2	0.11	48	2.71

Economy:UKR

Year	Active	Defaults		Others	
		#	%	#	%
1992	0	0	NaN	0	NaN
1993	0	0	NaN	0	NaN
1994	0	0	NaN	0	NaN
1995	0	0	NaN	0	NaN
1996	0	0	NaN	0	NaN
1997	0	0	NaN	0	NaN
1998	20	0	0.00	31	60.78
1999	38	0	0.00	37	49.33
2000	58	0	0.00	30	34.09
2001	25	0	0.00	75	75.00
2002	12	0	0.00	35	74.47
2003	16	0	0.00	18	52.94
2004	33	0	0.00	24	42.11
2005	56	0	0.00	29	34.12
2006	120	0	0.00	44	26.83
2007	157	0	0.00	78	33.19
2008	103	0	0.00	129	55.60
2009	76	1	0.48	131	62.98
2010	53	0	0.00	73	57.94
2011	61	0	0.00	33	35.11
2012	58	0	0.00	42	42.00

Economy:USA

Year	Active	Defaults		Others	
		#	%	#	%
1992	5321	18	0.33	107	1.96
1993	6006	25	0.40	172	2.77
1994	6666	18	0.26	279	4.01
1995	7031	20	0.27	389	5.23
1996	7582	19	0.24	404	5.05
1997	7769	54	0.64	564	6.72
1998	7405	85	1.02	872	10.43
1999	7058	89	1.10	929	11.50
2000	6769	133	1.73	786	10.22
2001	6064	199	2.85	716	10.26
2002	5616	137	2.19	506	8.08
2003	5276	91	1.56	462	7.93
2004	5247	34	0.60	378	6.68
2005	5211	39	0.69	380	6.75
2006	5171	21	0.38	379	6.80
2007	5115	29	0.52	447	7.99
2008	4817	77	1.46	367	6.98
2009	4561	96	1.93	313	6.30
2010	4484	35	0.73	308	6.38
2011	4327	38	0.81	312	6.67
2012	4251	37	0.81	263	5.78

(*Continued*)

Table A.11. *(Continued)*

Economy:VEN					
		Defaults		Others	
Year	Active	#	%	#	%
1992	0	0	NaN	0	NaN
1993	7	0	0.00	0	0.00
1994	12	0	0.00	1	7.69
1995	15	0	0.00	3	16.67
1996	15	0	0.00	2	11.76
1997	47	0	0.00	17	26.56
1998	40	0	0.00	25	38.46
1999	39	0	0.00	18	31.58
2000	37	0	0.00	12	24.49
2001	30	1	2.33	12	27.91
2002	20	0	0.00	19	48.72
2003	25	0	0.00	10	28.57
2004	27	0	0.00	9	25.00
2005	29	0	0.00	7	19.44
2006	27	0	0.00	7	20.59
2007	24	0	0.00	8	25.00
2008	24	0	0.00	32	57.14
2009	26	0	0.00	21	44.68
2010	23	0	0.00	14	37.84
2011	30	0	0.00	16	34.78
2012	15	0	0.00	18	54.55

Economy:VNM					
		Defaults		Others	
Year	Active	#	%	#	%
1992	0	0	NaN	0	NaN
1993	0	0	NaN	0	NaN
1994	0	0	NaN	0	NaN
1995	0	0	NaN	0	NaN
1996	0	0	NaN	0	NaN
1997	0	0	NaN	0	NaN
1998	0	0	NaN	0	NaN
1999	0	0	NaN	0	NaN
2000	5	0	0.00	0	0.00
2001	10	0	0.00	0	0.00
2002	20	0	0.00	0	0.00
2003	22	0	0.00	0	0.00
2004	25	0	0.00	0	0.00
2005	31	0	0.00	0	0.00
2006	91	0	0.00	0	0.00
2007	222	0	0.00	3	1.33
2008	296	0	0.00	2	0.67
2009	397	0	0.00	29	6.81
2010	675	0	0.00	26	3.71
2011	739	1	0.13	52	6.57
2012	739	0	0.00	86	10.42

Economy:ZAF					
		Defaults		Others	
Year	Active	#	%	#	%
1992	395	0	0.00	0	0.00
1993	394	0	0.00	39	9.01
1994	420	0	0.00	22	4.98
1995	467	0	0.00	25	5.08
1996	492	0	0.00	13	2.57
1997	537	0	0.00	23	4.11
1998	573	2	0.31	60	9.45
1999	593	3	0.47	48	7.45
2000	534	6	0.99	66	10.89
2001	460	9	1.59	98	17.28
2002	346	8	1.71	113	24.20
2003	327	1	0.27	49	13.00
2004	289	2	0.59	48	14.16
2005	293	2	0.60	36	10.88
2006	310	0	0.00	23	6.91
2007	335	0	0.00	40	10.67
2008	336	0	0.00	26	7.18
2009	320	1	0.28	31	8.81
2010	312	2	0.60	22	6.55
2011	310	1	0.30	21	6.33
2012	294	5	1.56	22	6.85

APPENDIX B: PERFORMANCE ANALYSIS

Table B.1. Accuracy Ratios (AR) and Area Under Receiver Operating Characteristic (AUROC) for different economies.

	AR				AUROC			
Economy	**1 mth**	**1 yr**	**2 yr**	**5 yr**	**1 mth**	**1 yr**	**2 yr**	**5 yr**
AUS	0.809	0.641	0.513	0.359	0.905	0.821	0.758	0.684
CHN	0.582	0.515	0.435	0.308	0.791	0.760	0.724	0.673
HKG	0.691	0.417	0.318	0.205	0.846	0.709	0.660	0.606
IND	0.701	0.617	0.523	0.441	0.850	0.809	0.762	0.722
IDN	0.771	0.688	0.576	0.435	0.886	0.845	0.790	0.725
JPN	0.910	0.824	0.765	0.635	0.955	0.912	0.883	0.819
MYS	0.842	0.734	0.644	0.406	0.921	0.867	0.823	0.708
PHL	0.661	0.597	0.558	0.434	0.831	0.799	0.781	0.725
SGP	0.765	0.627	0.439	0.270	0.882	0.814	0.721	0.639
KOR	0.882	0.719	0.646	0.616	0.941	0.860	0.825	0.813
TWN	0.875	0.729	0.666	0.500	0.938	0.865	0.834	0.753
THA	0.838	0.753	0.702	0.563	0.919	0.877	0.853	0.789
USA	0.938	0.815	0.702	0.514	0.969	0.908	0.853	0.762
CAN	0.928	0.785	0.654	0.475	0.964	0.893	0.828	0.742
DNK	0.880	0.797	0.630	0.459	0.940	0.899	0.816	0.733
FRA	0.868	0.678	0.613	0.522	0.934	0.840	0.807	0.763
DEU	0.885	0.724	0.597	0.499	0.943	0.863	0.800	0.755
NLD	0.809	0.752	0.640	0.525	0.905	0.877	0.822	0.767
NOR	0.962	0.809	0.624	0.311	0.981	0.905	0.813	0.659
GBR	0.899	0.722	0.563	0.382	0.949	0.861	0.782	0.694
AsiaDev	0.860	0.721	0.639	0.533	0.930	0.861	0.821	0.769
EMR	0.826	0.740	0.670	0.508	0.913	0.871	0.836	0.758
EU	0.876	0.722	0.588	0.421	0.938	0.861	0.795	0.713

Notes: The calibration groups, Developed Asia, Emerging Markets and Europe, are indicated by AsiaDev, EMR and EU. Only economies with more than 20 defaults are listed.

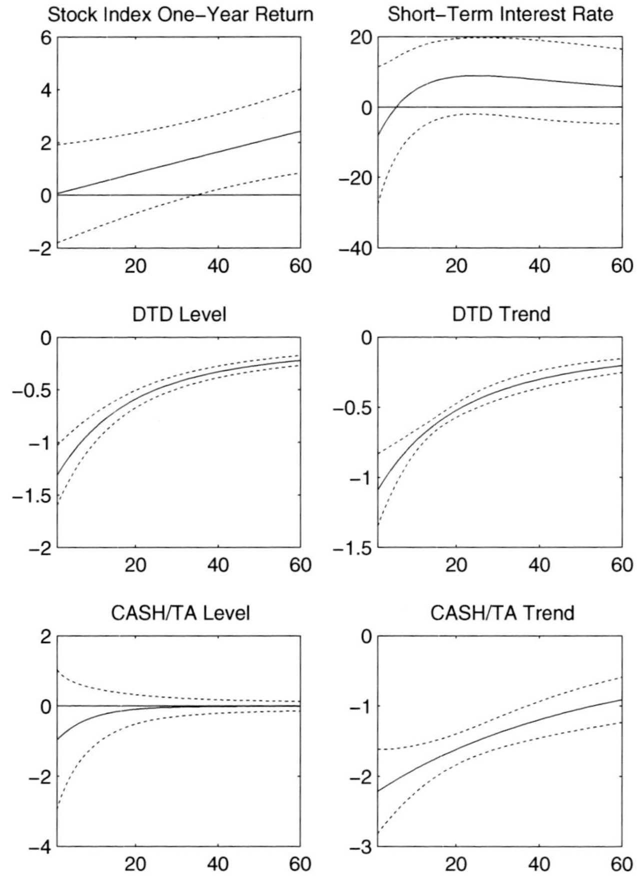

Figure B.1. Plots of US default parameters across all horizons for the Stock index one-year return, Short-term interest rate, DTD Level, DTD Trend, CASH/TA Level and CASH/TA Trend.

Notes: Solid lines are the parameter estimates and dashed lines are the 90% confidence level. The horizontal axis is the horizon in months.

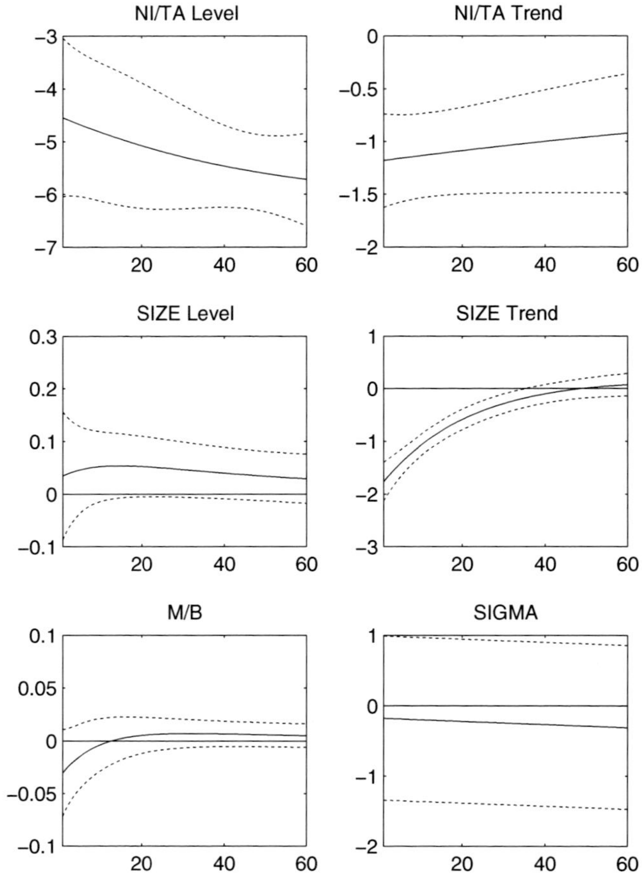

Figure B.2. Plots of US default parameters across all horizons for the NI/TA Level, NI/TA Trend, SIZE Level, SIZE Trend, M/B and SIGMA.

Notes: Solid lines are the parameter estimates and dashed lines are the 90% confidence level. The horizontal axis is the horizon in months.

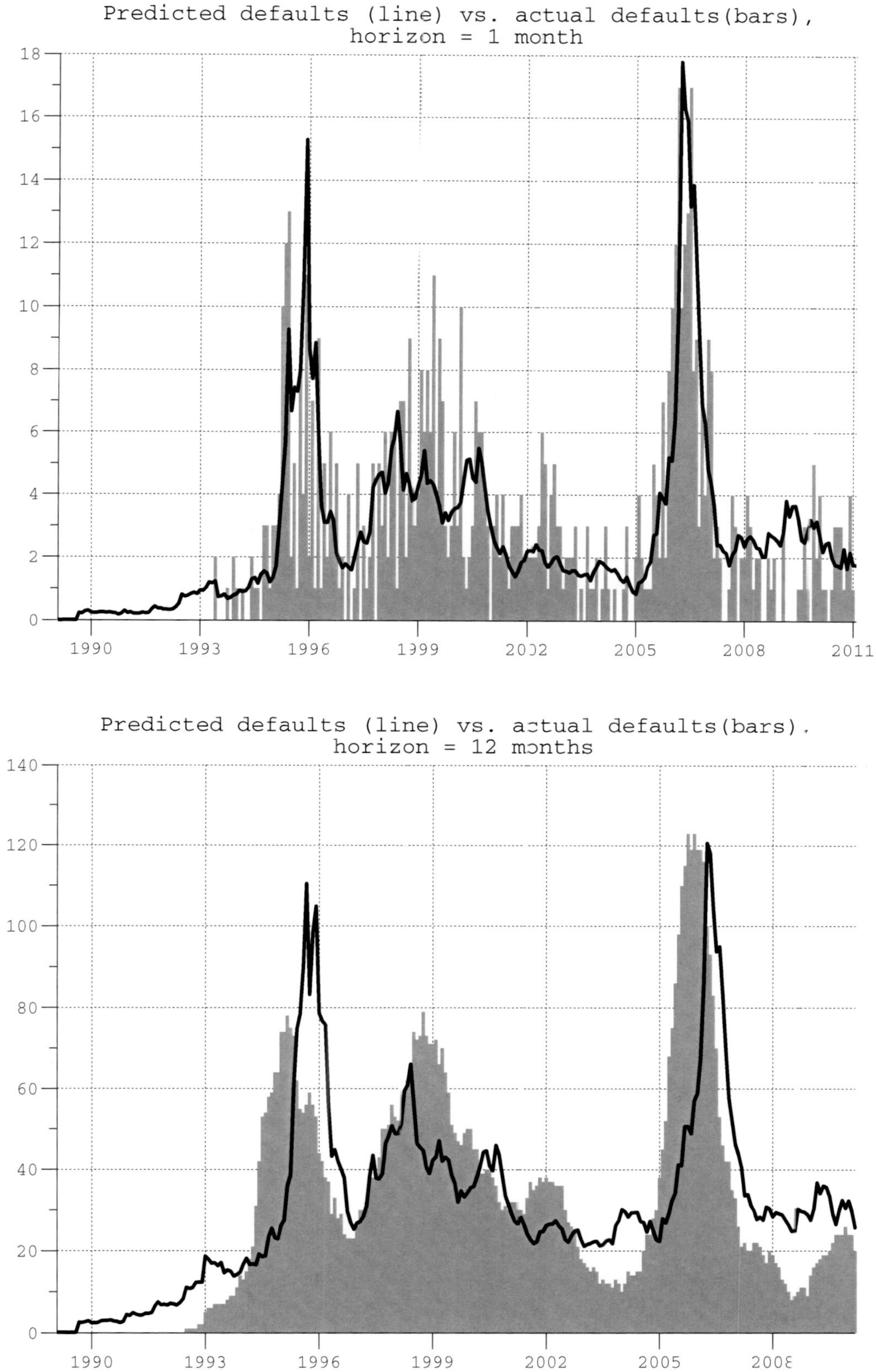

Figure B.3. Performance test for Developed Asia, in sample.

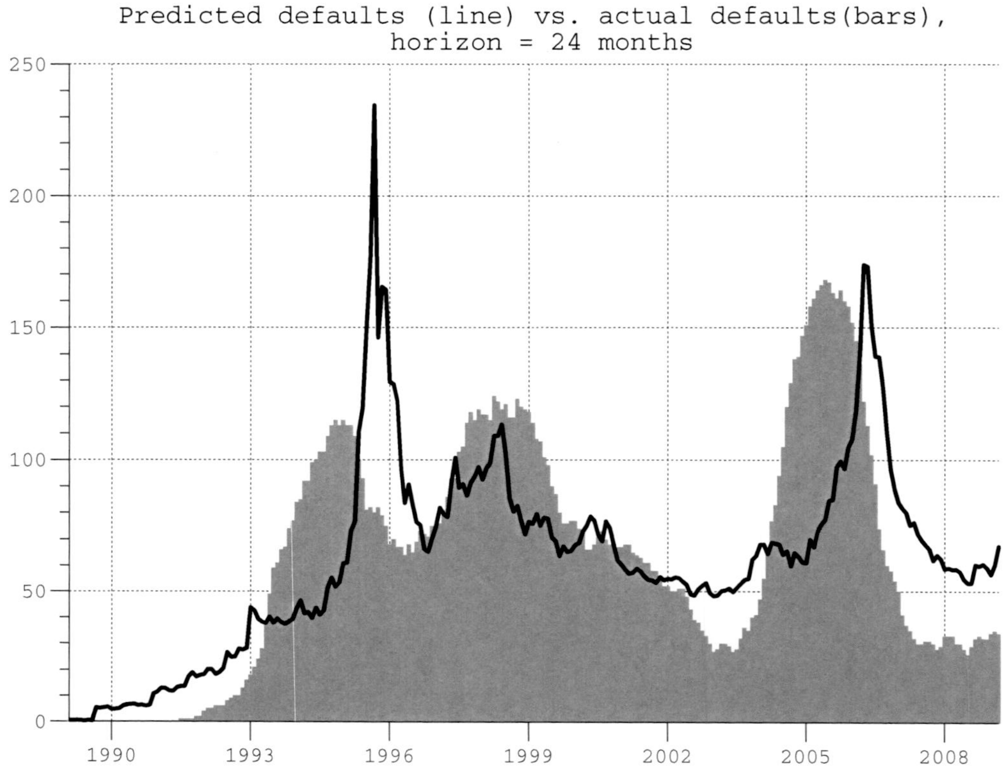

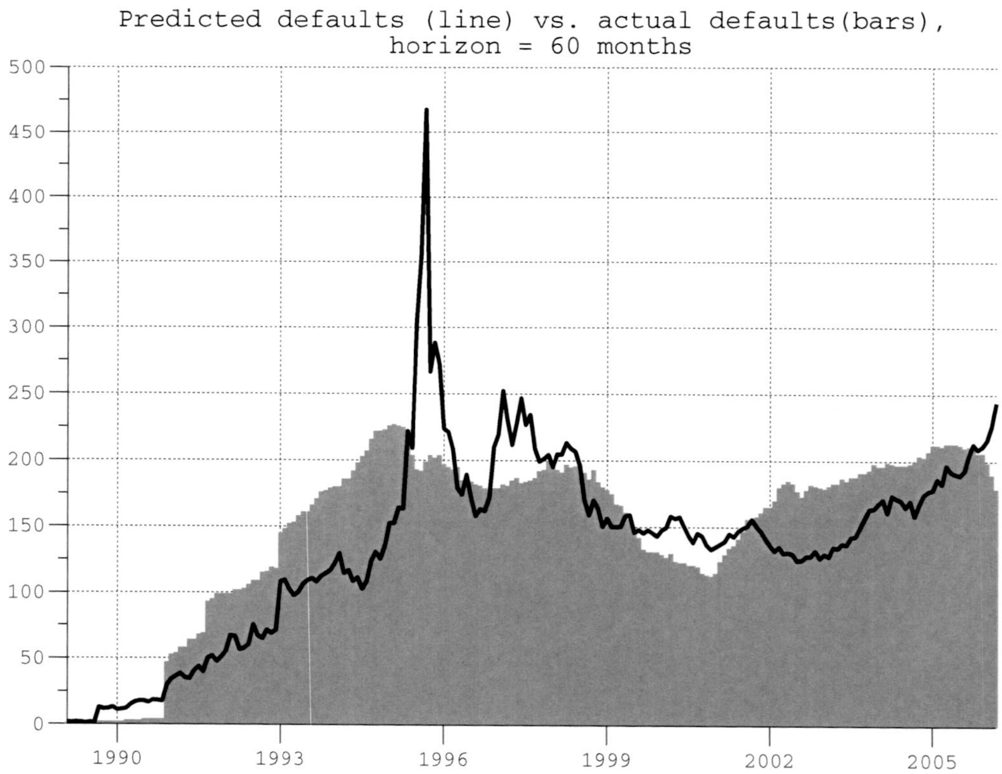

Figure B.3. (*Continued*)

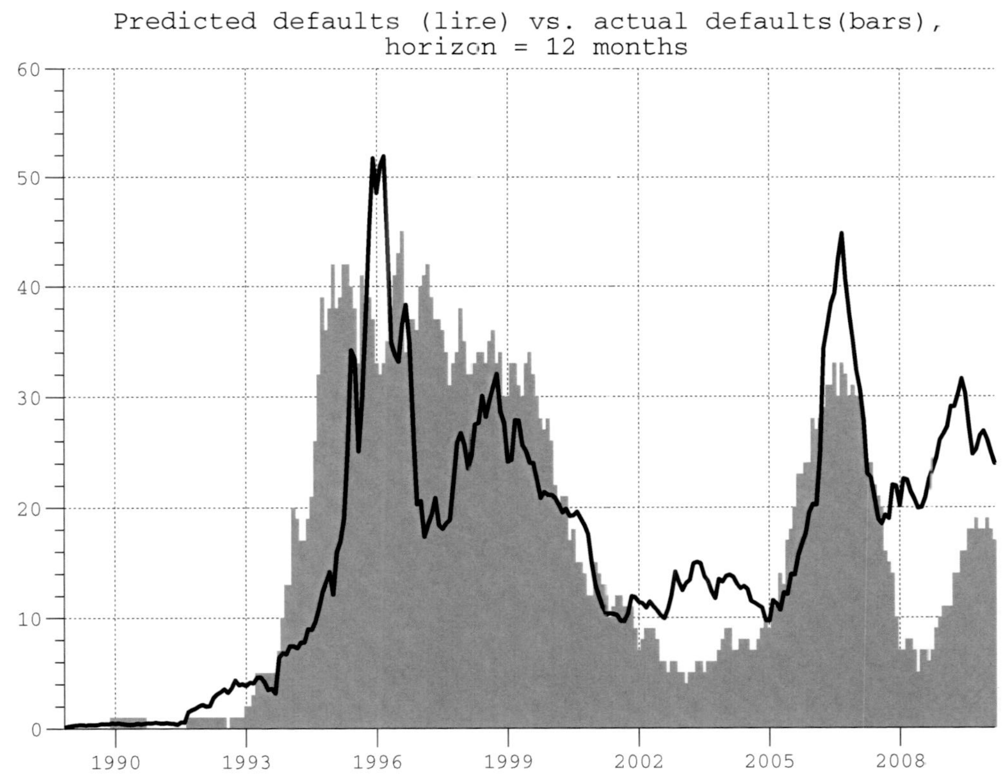

Figure B.4. Performance test for the Emerging Markets group, in sample.

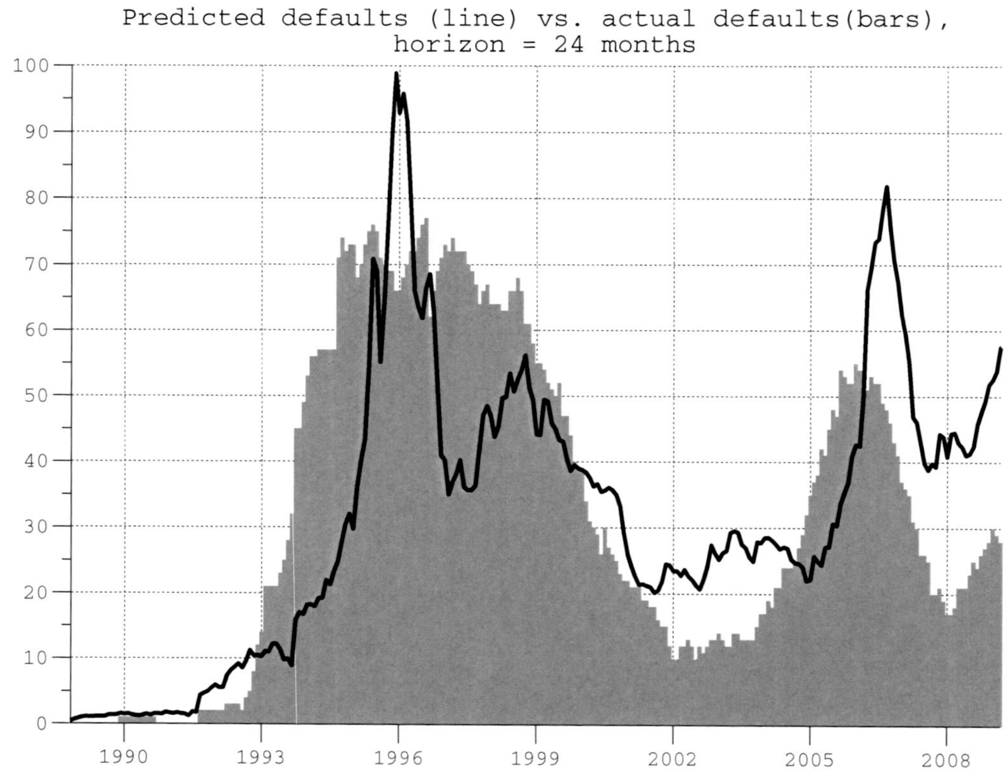

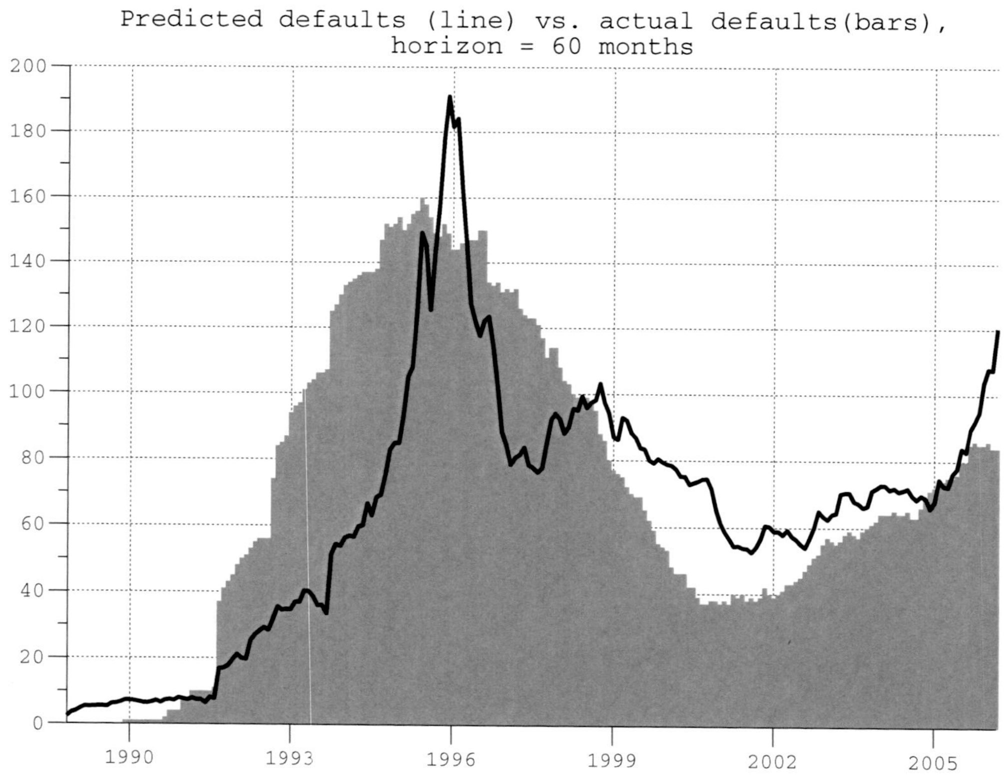

Figure B.4. *(Continued)*

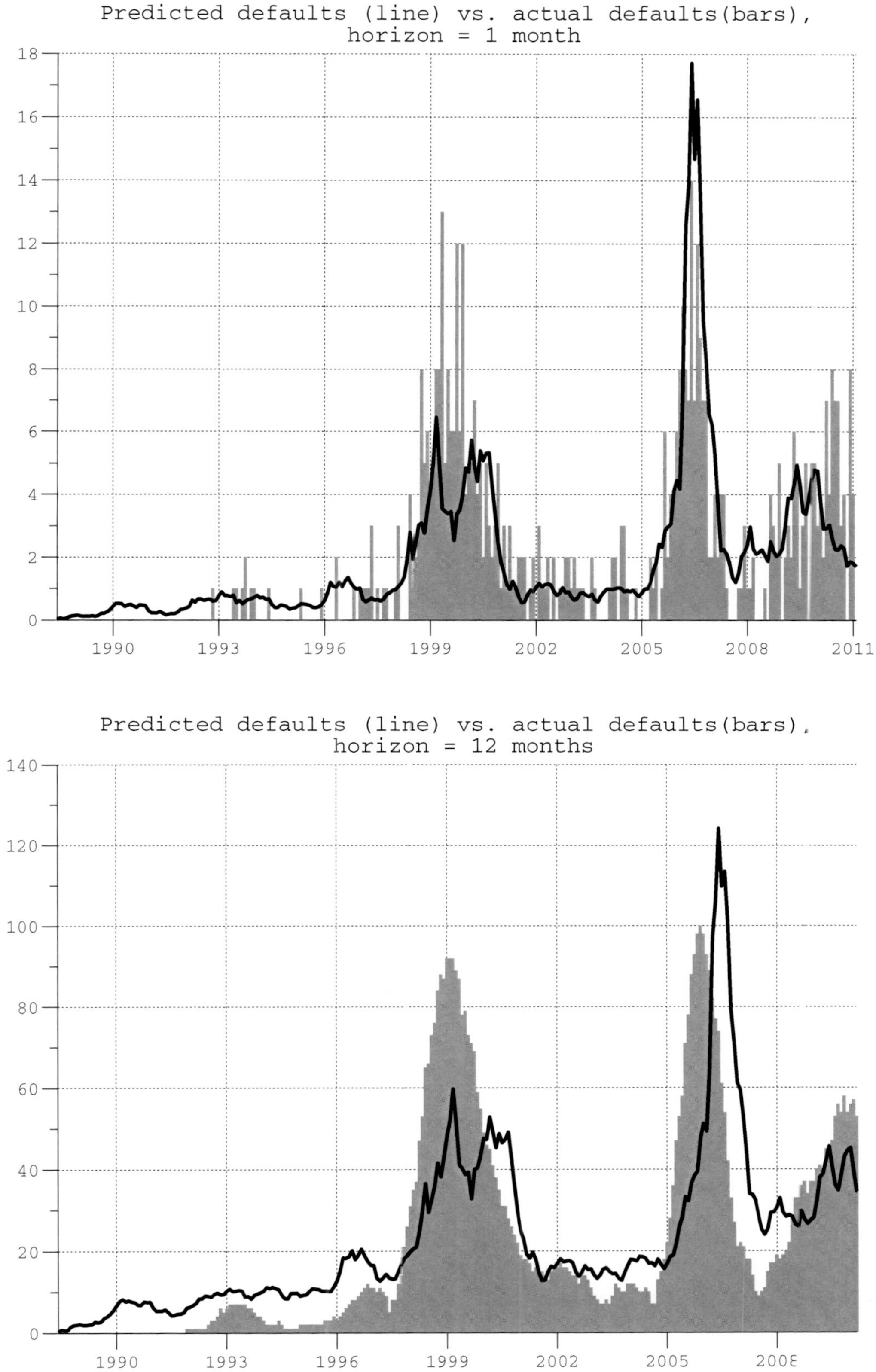

Figure B.5. Performance test for the Europe group, in sample.

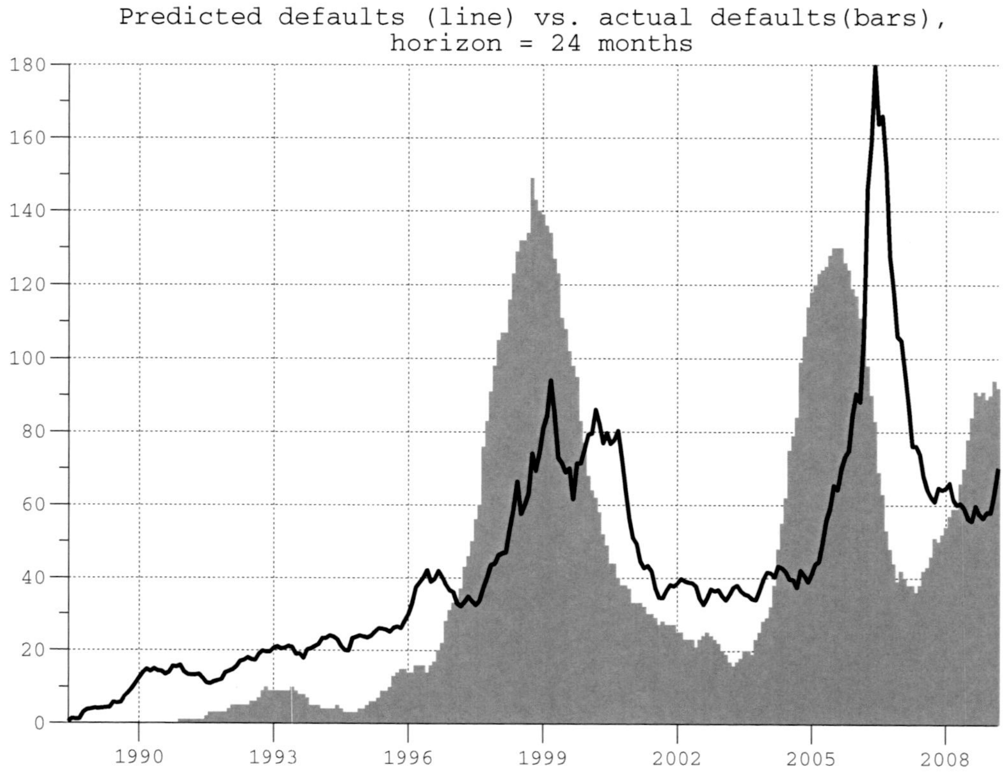

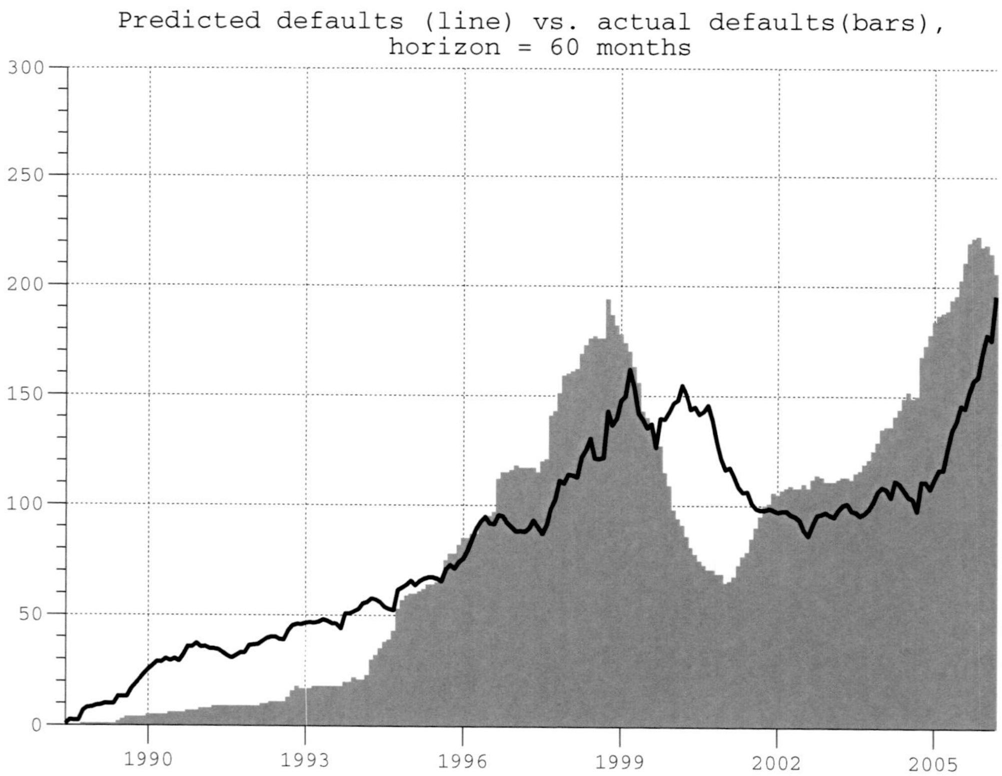

Figure B.5. *(Continued)*

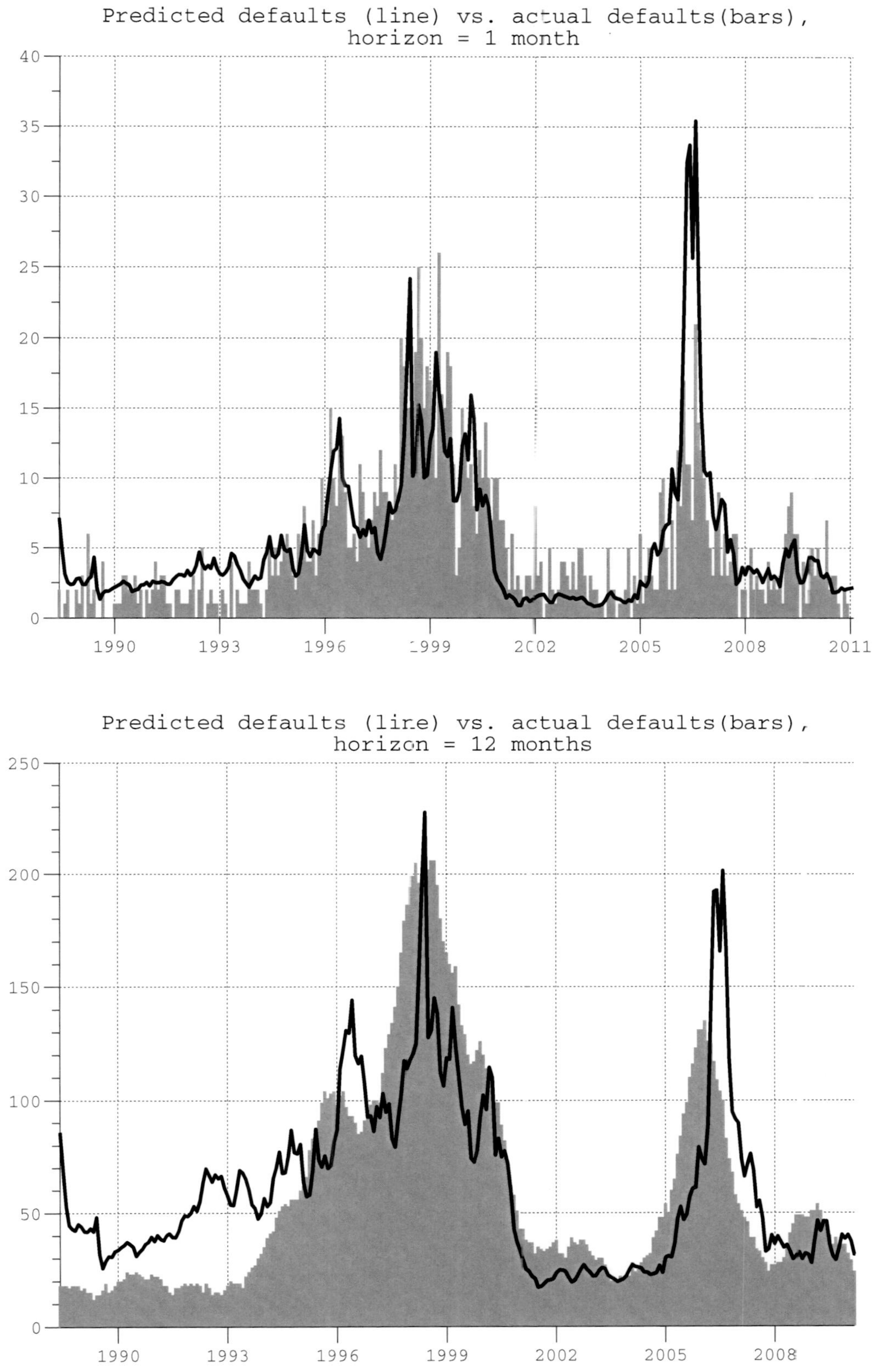

Figure B.6. Performance test for the North America group, in sample.

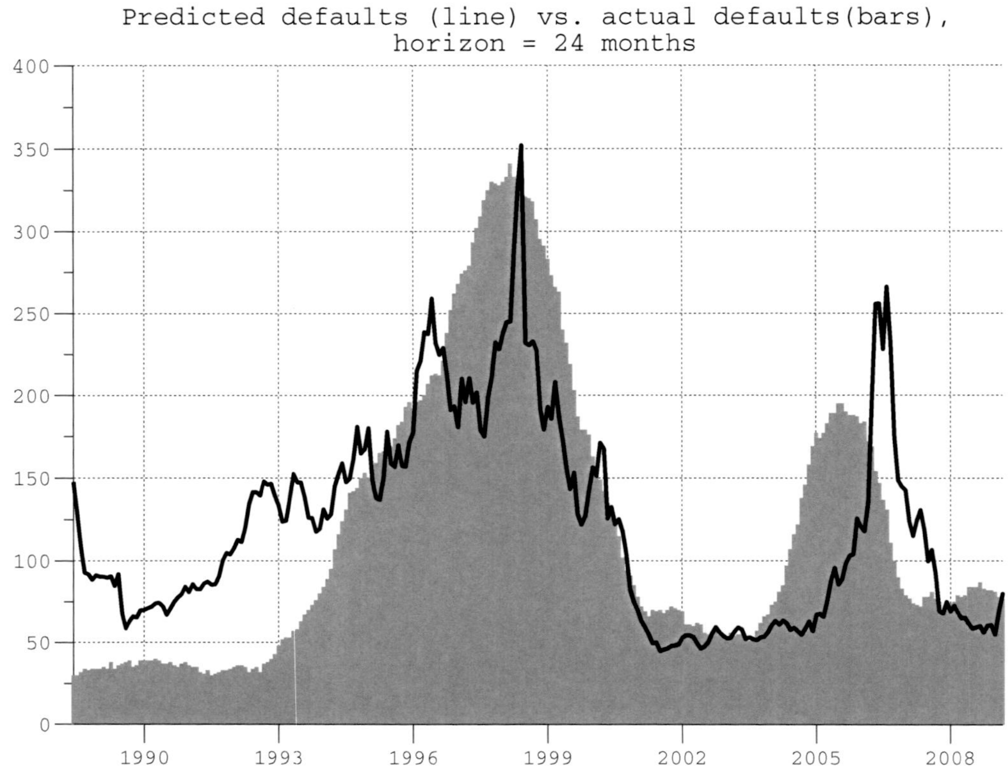

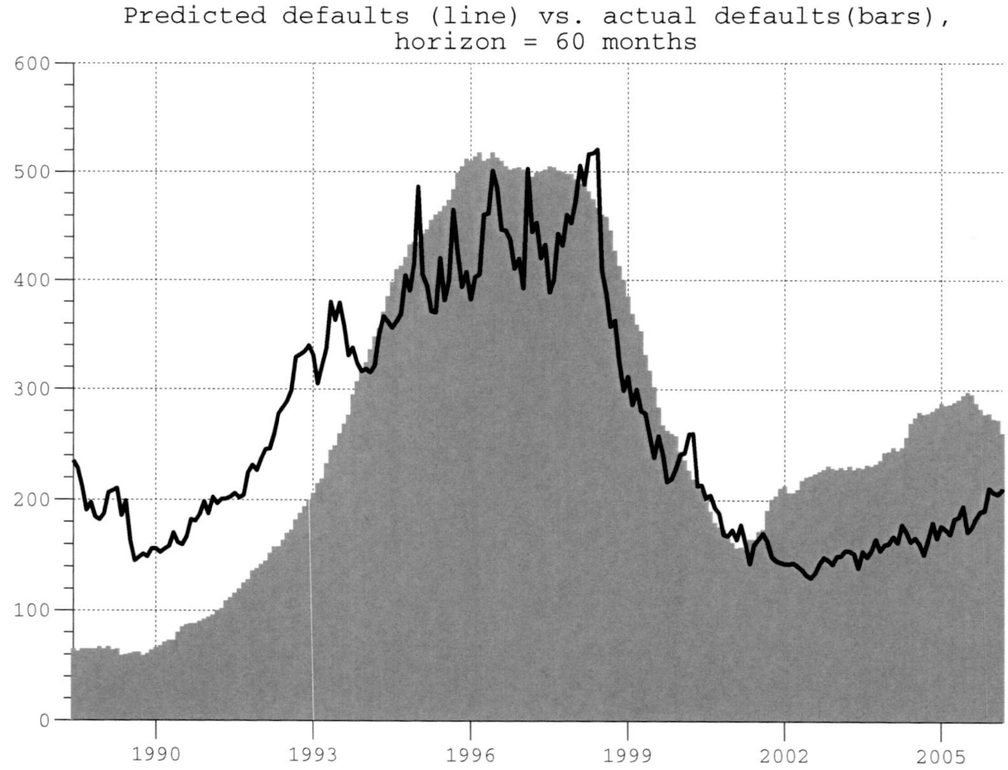

Figure B.6. *(Continued)*

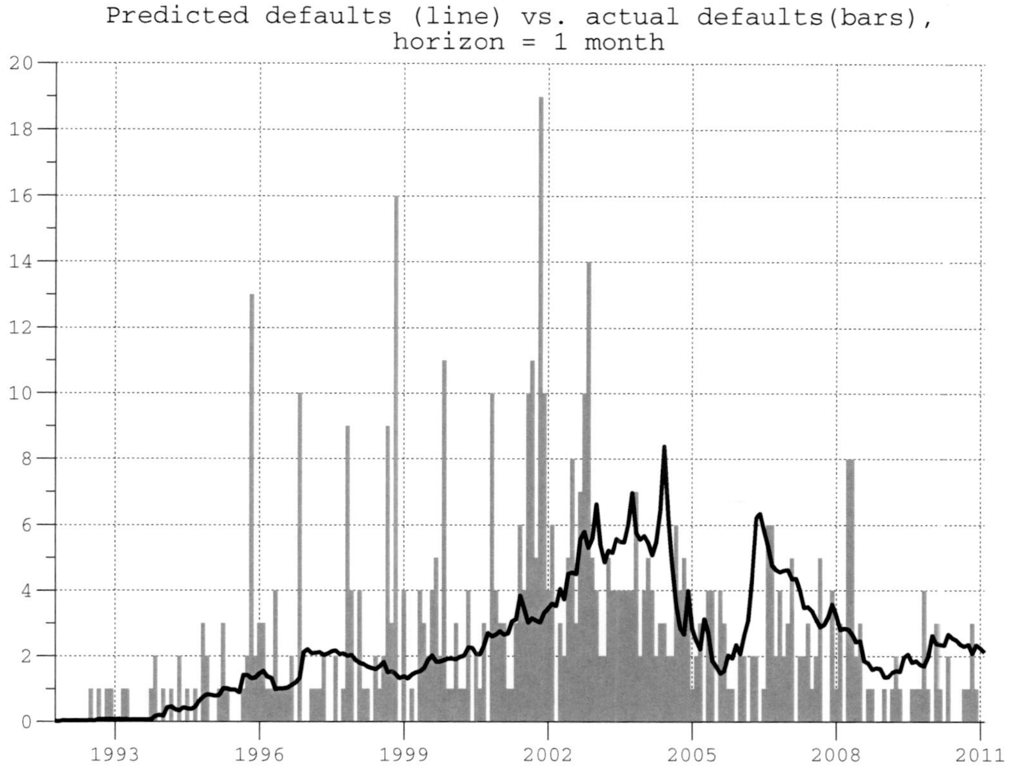

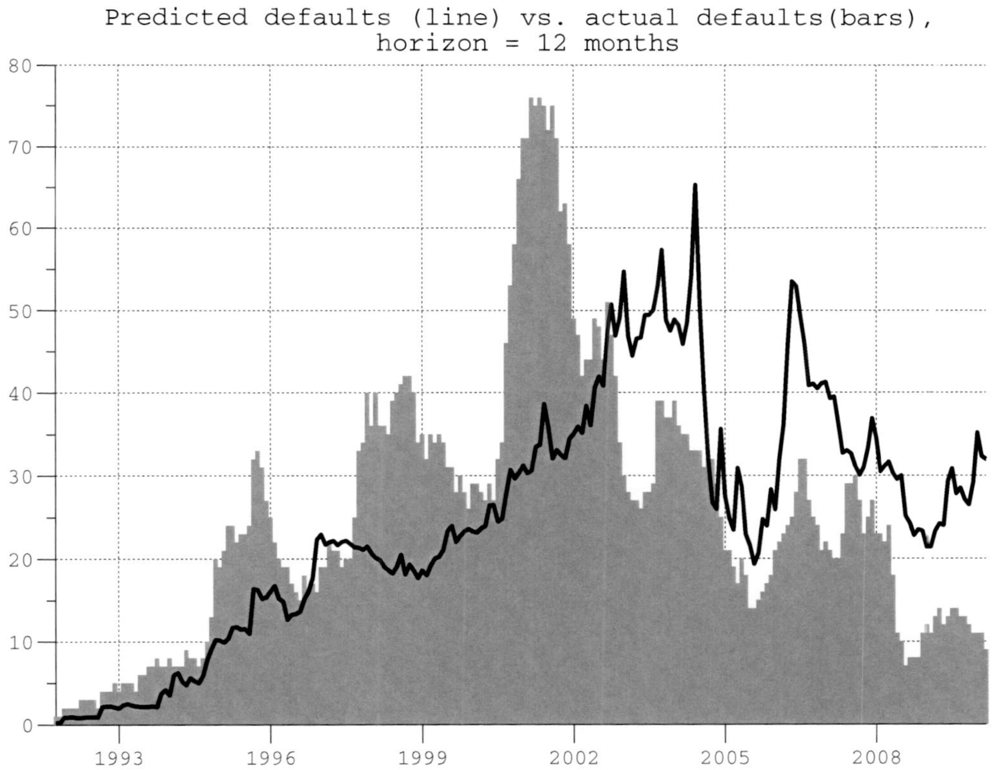

Figure B.7. Performance test for China, in sample.

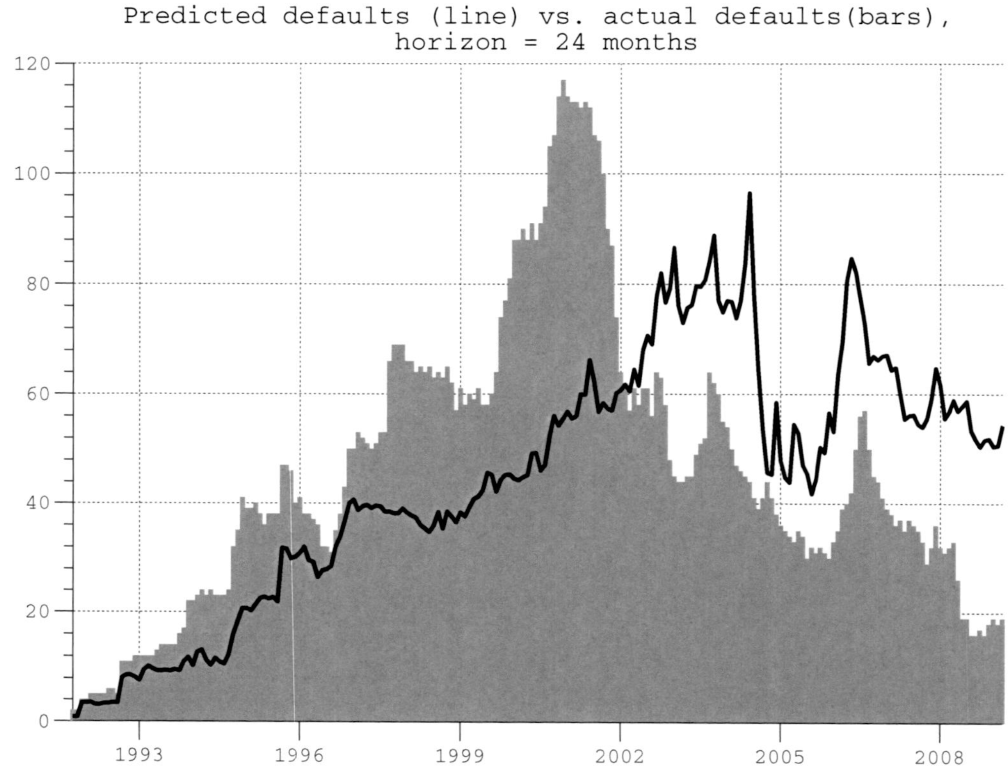

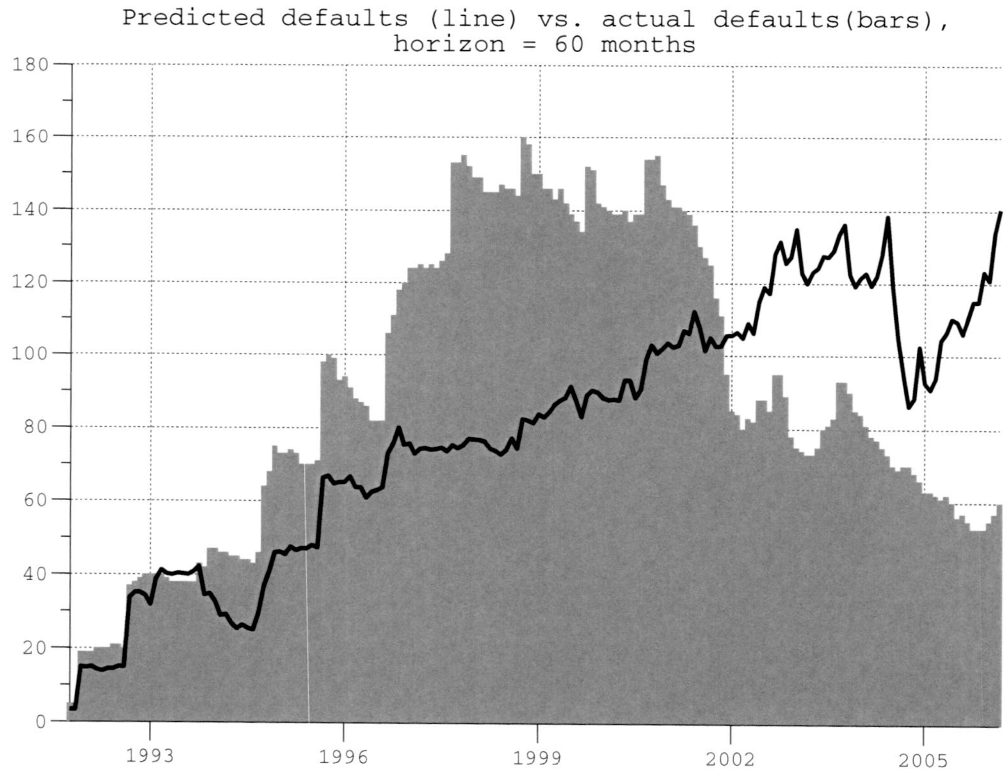

Figure B.7. *(Continued)*

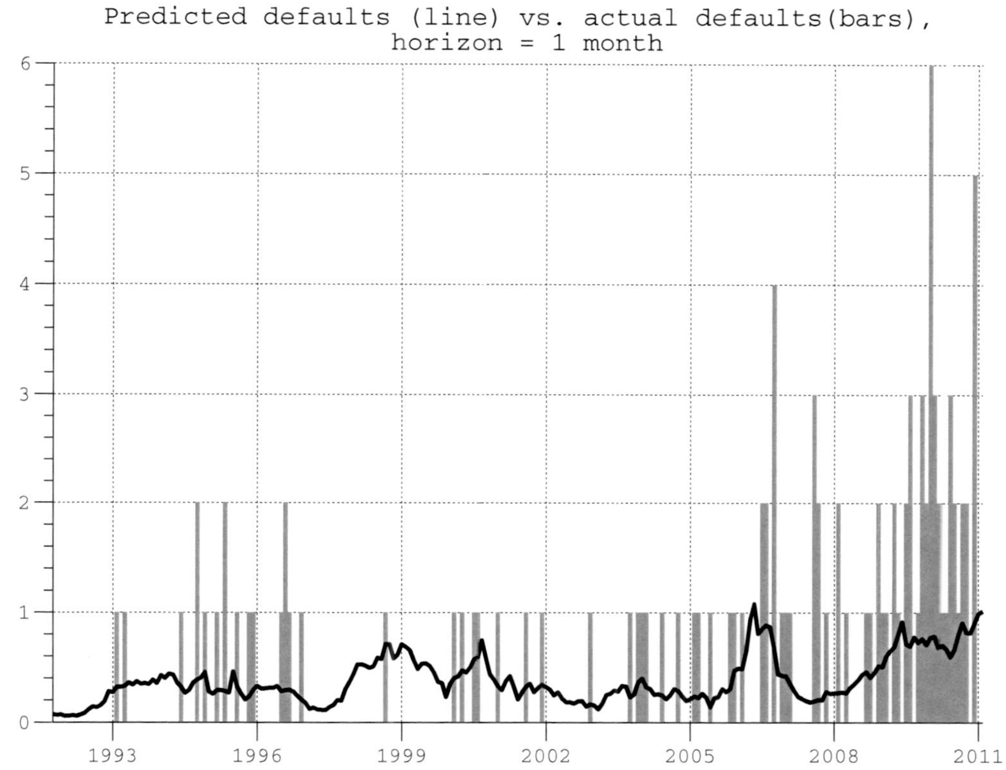

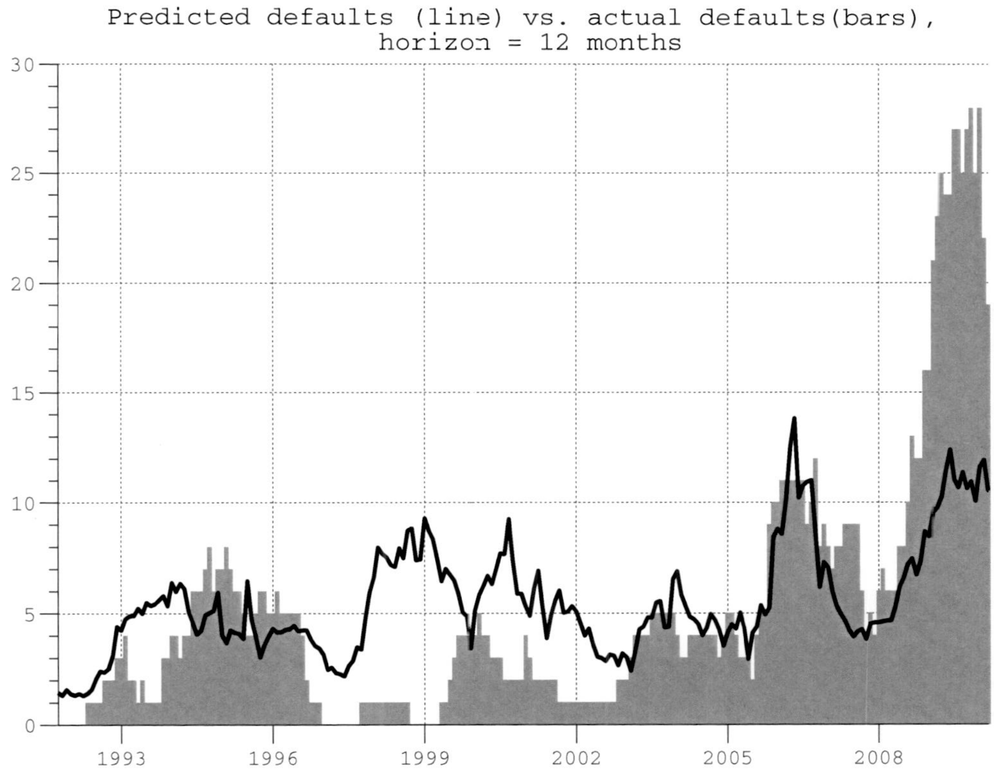

Figure B.8. Performance test for India, in sample.

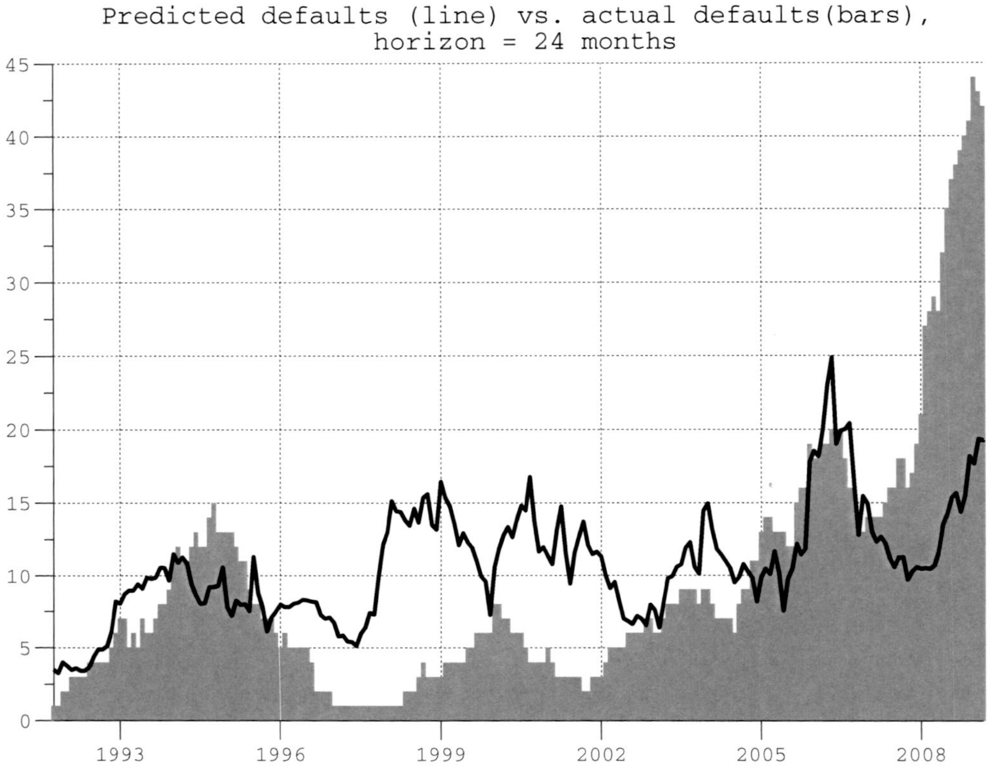

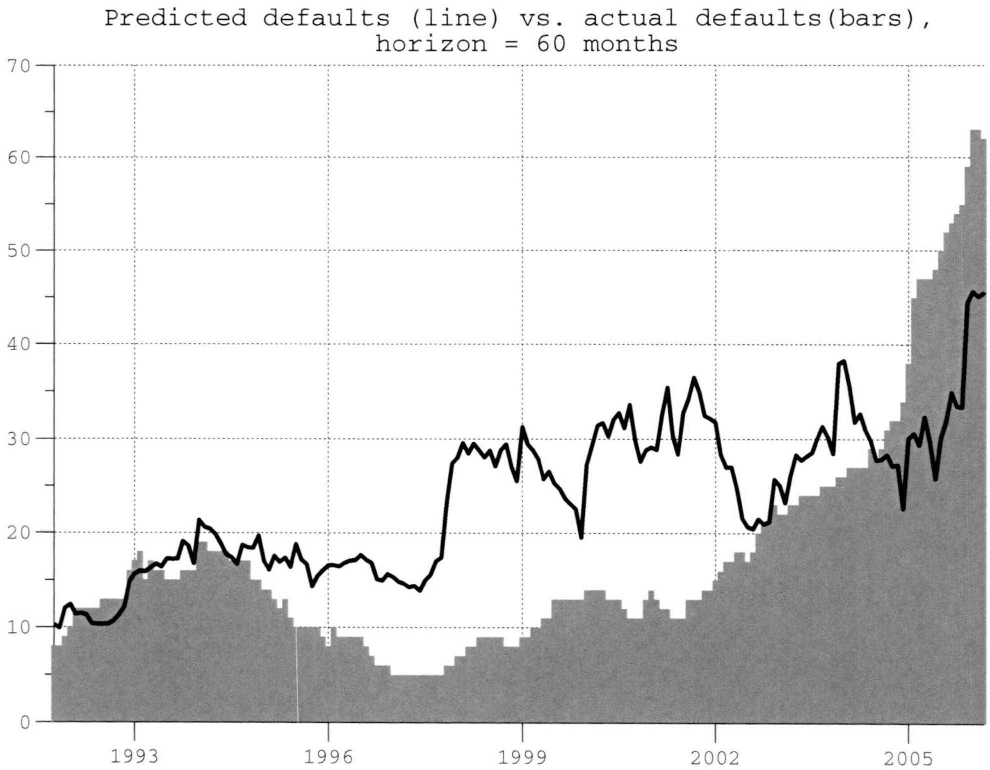

Figure B.8. *(Continued)*